Further Papers on
DANTE

DOROTHY L. SAYERS

Further Papers on
DANTE

LONDON
METHUEN & CO LTD
BARNES & NOBLE BOOKS
NEW YORK

First published in 1957
This edition reprinted 1973 by
Methuen & Co Ltd
11 New Fetter Lane
London EC4P 4EE
and Barnes & Noble Books New York
10 East 53rd Street
New York NY 10022
(a division of Harper & Row Publishers Inc.)
Printed in Great Britain by
Whitstable Litho, Straker Brothers Ltd

Methuen SBN 416 18840 0
Barnes & Noble SBN 06 476137 1

AUTHOR'S PREFACE

WITH one exception, these papers, like those in the preceding volume,[1] were originally delivered viva voce on various occasions—some to the members of the Summer Schools arranged by the Society for Italian Studies, others to audiences with a less specialised interest in Dante. They bear the marks of their origin, both in the characteristic rhythm of the spoken word, and in the occasional overlapping of subject-matter between one paper and another. To efface these vestiges, it would have been necessary to re-write the papers completely; and it has seemed better on the whole to offer them to the reader as they stand, adding in footnotes such amplifications as seemed desirable of points which had to be passed briefly over in the time allotted for a public address.

The former series presented a more or less closely connected study of the theological and ethical aspects of the *Commedia*. The present series is more heterogeneous in subject-matter, and pays, by and large, more attention to the literary and poetic aspects of Dante's work—so far as that may be done when addressing audiences of whom not all are acquainted with the Italian original. Here and there, an attempt has been made to rescue Dante from the exalted isolation in which reverential awe has placed him, and to compare him with other poets writing on similar themes. It seems to me that, in the vast and intensively-cultivated field of Dante studies, too little has as yet been done along these lines—as though, when immediate "sources" and "influences" had been discussed, the poet's achievement could be left enthroned in a vacuum. But it is not so. Every poet that ever wore the bays is a perpetual competitor in the Olympian games, on an equal footing with his heirs and his ancestors. Poets do not merely pass on the torch in a relay race; they toss the ball to one another, to and fro, across the centuries. Dante would have been different if Virgil had never been, but if Dante had never been we should know Virgil differently; across both their heads Ezekiel calls to Blake, and Milton to Homer. To label any poet *hors concours* is in a manner to excommunicate him: it has happened, inevitably, to the poets of the Bible; it might well have happened to Shakespeare, had not the commerce of

---

[1] *Introductory Papers on Dante* (Methuen, 1954).

the theatre kept him perforce in constant battle with his peers; it has very nearly happened to Dante.

The only paper which was originally written to be read by the eye is the first: ". . . *And Telling you a Story.*" It is earlier in date than any other paper in either volume, and has perhaps a certain interest as representing a spontaneous and almost unconsidered reaction to the work of a major poet, encountered for the first time in middle life and, as far as may be, with no preconceptions at all. My immediate impressions were jotted down as I read, in a series of letters to Charles Williams, who was entertained by these comments and had intended to make some use of them in one of his critical works. His death prevented the carrying-out of this project, and eventually, in order that his intention might not be altogether lost, the general substance of the letters, tidied into a form more decorous than one uses in writing to a friend, took shape in this essay, which was published in the memorial volume entitled *Essays Presented to Charles Williams.*[1] What Williams valued in the letters was, I think, their witness to the excitement that Dante could produce, on a first reading, in a mind left naked to his assault.[2] That excitement, like the Beatrician rapture, must of necessity become overlaid in the course of minute and prolonged study; but it is never lost, and may be recalled at will:

> *credo ch'io vidi, perchè più di largo,*
> *dicendo questo, mi sento ch'io godo*—[3]

and, re-reading my first fine careless rapture, I have nothing to recant and very little to modify. If only *Hamlet* and *Lear* could rush upon one with the same unmuffled impact! It is arguable that all very great works should be strictly protected from young persons; they should at any rate be spared the indignity of having their teeth and claws blunted for the satisfaction of examiners. It is the first shock that matters. Once that has been experienced, no amount of later familiarity

---

[1] Edited by C. S. Lewis (O.U.P., 1947).

[2] On my paper on *The Comedy of the Comedy* in the First Series I quoted a couple of paragraphs from these letters in their original unpruned state, greatly scandalising thereby certain reviewers (Tennyson had a word for them) who, skipping the context and ignoring the inverted commas, took them to be representative of my habitual lecturing style, and so missed the point altogether. I have accordingly taken this opportunity to make it again.

[3] Yes, I believe I saw, because I feel
Even as I speak, fresh springs of rapture rise.
Para. xxxiii. 92.

will breed contempt; but to become familiar with a thing before one is able to experience it only too often means that one can never experience it at all. This much at least is certain; it is not age that hardens the arteries of the mind; one can experience the same exaltation of first love at fifty as at fifteen—only it will need a greater work to excite it. There is, in fact, an optimum age for encountering every work of art; did we but know, in each man's case, what it was, we might plan our educational schemes accordingly. Since our way of life makes this impossible, we can only pray to be saved from murdering delight before it is born.

Though first impressions, like natural love, may be exempt from error,[1] the same cannot be said of all the critical judgements which one throws out by the way, and I must hasten to retract a quite indefensible statement which I made in my previous paper on *The Meaning of Purgatory*.[2] There I said in my haste that nobody had "succeeded in discovering what prompted Dante to transfer the venue [of Purgatory] to the Antipodes". This was quite ridiculous of me, for I knew the answer very well, if only I had stopped to think. Purgatory went to the Antipodes—or at any rate into the Southern Hemisphere—in attendance on the Earthly Paradise, which was already there. Parallel with the tradition which located it in Mesopotamia, there ran another, which Thomas Burnet notes in his *Telluris Theoria Sacra*: "The ancients supposed generally that paradise was in the other hemisphere . . . and yet they believed that Tygris, Euphrates, Nile, and Ganges, were the rivers of paradise, or came out of it; and these two opinions they could not reconcile . . . but by supposing that these four rivers had their fountain-heads in the other hemisphere, and by some wonderful trajection broke out again here." [3] This citation had been staring me in the face for years from the familiar pages of John Livingston Lowes' *The Road to Xanadu*, which also adduces the following, quoted by Athanasius Kircher from Moses bar-Cepha: "This also we assert, that Paradise lies in a much higher region than this land, and so it happens that the rivers, impelled by so mighty a force, descend thence through huge chasms and subterranean channels, and, thus confined, are hurried away beneath the bottom of the sea, and boil up in this our orb." This, clearly, is the tradition that Dante is following; and perhaps he wishes us to understand that when, at first sight, he took

[1] *Purg.* xvii. 94.
[2] *Introductory Papers*, p. 89.
[3] *Op. cit*, (Constable, revised ed. 1930), pp. 388–390.

the twin fountainhead of Lethe and Eunoë to be that of Tigris and Euphrates,[1] he was not altogether wrong. For he shows us one of these streams,[2] duly descending through "chasms and subterranean channels" and by-passing Lucifer and the Centre,[3] to emerge—where, but on "our side"? True, Dante's stream is a gentle one; he has not, like bar-Cepha, faced the hydraulic problem of forcing water past the centre of gravity with such vigour as to make it "boil up" at the point of exit; but we cannot have everything. He was a poet, and his poem called here for a gentle declivity and a devious course; he did not wish to turn our attention northward.

Having thus made my retractation, it only remains for me to say what I ought to have said in my previous volume, namely that the English translations of passages from the *Commedia* in all these papers are taken from the version which I am making for the "Penguin Classics", and that I am indebted to Messrs. Allen Lane for permitting me to quote them.

DOROTHY L. SAYERS
1956

[1] *Purg.* xxxiii. 112–114.

[2] Usually identified with Lethe, on the strength of *Inf.* xiv. 131, and the fact that Lethe is "a river of Hell"; but the *ruscelletto* of *Inf.* xxxiv. 127–132 does not appear to flow into Hell (see note following).

[3] Luogo e laggiù *da Belzebù remoto*
    tanto, quanto la tomba si distende,
    che non per vista, ma per suono è noto

d'un ruscelletto, che quivi discende
    per la buca d'un sasso, ch'egli a roso
    col corso ch'egli avvolge e poco pende.

There is a place low down there underground,
    As far from Belzebub as his tomb's deep,
    Not known to sight, but only by the sound

Of a small stream which trickles down the steep,
    Hollowing its channel, where with gentle fall
    And devious course its wandering waters creep.
                    Inf. xxxiv. 127–132.

CONTENTS

". . . AND TELLING YOU A STORY"

"IT isn't at all what I expected," said the friend whom I had persuaded into having a go at *The Divine Comedy*; "I thought it would be all grand and solemn—you know—'Of Man's First Disobedience and the Fruit of that Forbidden Tree . . . Sing, Heavenly Muse', that sort of thing. But it's like someone sitting there in an arm-chair and telling you a story."

My friend meant no disparagement to Milton, for whom she has an especial reverence. She meant only that since, somehow or other, nobody had ever taken the trouble to tell her what kind of poet Dante was, she had dimly supposed him to have written his great religious poem in the Miltonic, or the classical, or at any rate the "epic" manner, and was astonished to find it start off with no more fuss than *The Pilgrim's Progress*, and so continue. My own experience was exactly the same as hers.

While I still knew Dante chiefly by his repute, *The Figure of Beatrice* was published, and I read it—not because it was about Dante, but because it was by Charles Williams. It became immediately evident that here was an Image, and here an Image-maker, with whom one had to reckon, and that the world had been right to call Dante a Great Poet—perhaps the greatest. But it was still some time before I made up my mind to tackle Dante in person; after all, fourteen thousand lines are fourteen thousand lines, especially if they are full of Guelfs and Ghibellines and Thomas Aquinas. A friendly critic can often give the impression that a poem is more colourful and exciting than it really is by picking out the jolly bits and passing over the rest, and I knew well enough the rambling and disjointed habits of the average mediaeval writer. Besides, the world always hinted that Dante, besides being great, grim, religious, and intellectual, was also "obscure". It was only a sense of shame and a series of accidents that made me at last blow off the dust from the three volumes of the Temple *Divine Comedy* which had originally belonged, I think, to my grandmother, and sit down to *Inferno, Canto* I, resolute, but inwardly convinced that I should read perhaps ten cantos with conscientious and self-conscious interest and attention, and then—in the way these things happen— one day forget to go on.

It did not happen that way. Coming to him as I did, for the first time, rather late in life, the impact of Dante upon my unprepared mind was not in the least what I had expected, and I can remember nothing like it since I first read *The Three Musketeers* at the age of thirteen. Neither the world, nor the theologians, nor even Charles Williams had told me the one great, obvious, glaring fact about Dante Alighieri of Florence—that he was simply the most incomparable story-teller who ever set pen to paper. However foolish it may sound, the plain fact is that I bolted my meals, neglected my sleep, work, and correspondence, drove my friends crazy, and paid only a distracted attention to the doodle-bugs which happened to be infesting the neighbourhood at the time, until I had panted my way through the Three Realms of the Dead from top to bottom and from bottom to top; and that, having finished, I found the rest of the world's literature so lacking in pep and incident that I pushed it all peevishly aside and started out from the Dark Wood all over again. In the course of these feverish wanderings I discovered three other things about Dante; first, that his diction was not, as I had imagined, uniformly in the grand manner, but homely, lucid, and fluent; secondly, that he himself was not, as tradition painted him, grim and austere, but sweet and companionable, and, if an arch-angel in stature, a very "affable archangel"; thirdly, that he was a very great comic writer—which was quite the last thing one would ever have inferred from the things people say in their books.

When I say that Dante is a miraculous story-teller, I mean that he enthralled me with his story-telling; I have not bothered to find out who taught him to tell stories or where he got his stories from. He says Virgil taught him—and I can see for myself that he has, for example, taken a number of ideas from the sixth book of the *Aeneid* and distributed them judiciously in the places where they would do most good. I am aware that he read Ovid and Statius, and a mixed collection of philosophers from Aristotle to Aquinas, and that he knew the Vulgate inside out. But all that is of secondary importance; many people are steeped in Virgil, sodden with Aristotle, or Bible-ridden to the verge of mania, who yet cannot tell an after-dinner story without mislaying the point and making their audience "yawn as though over-come by fever or sleep". Nor am I equipped to offer any theories about the Veltro, or to expound the numerology of the DXV, and the date of the *De Vulgari Eloquentia*, or to argue about texts; very likely I shall come to that kind of thing in time, but not now. At the moment I am only concerned with the little gentleman, suitably (but not expensively) dressed, rather stooping in the shoulders and tired about the eyes, who is at present sitting in that arm-chair "and telling you a story".

"It consists", says J. W. Mackail of Thomson's unfortunate poem on *Liberty*, "of between three and four thousand lines of blank verse, in the mixture of history, philosophy, politics and preaching on which poets always make shipwreck when they fail to fuse disparate and impracticable material by the heat of poetical genius." The *Divine Comedy* is all those things (except, of course, that it is 14,000 lines long and in rhyme); it is also a satire, a love-romance, a spiritual auto-biography, and a story of adventure. Because it is the last of these things it can afford to be all the others. It has, to be sure, the heat of poetical genius, without which "all other words are but as dead cinders", but though Dante rated his own genius at least as high as his most fervent admirer has ever done, he had too good a sense of reality to think he could do without the story. He had tried already to improve people's minds by condescending to expound his Odes to them, expatiating on the pleasures of philosophy and, incidentally, upon his own impeccable behaviour which had, he complained, been much misunderstood. But he abandoned the attempt—possibly because his readers did not seem to be responding, possibly because he realised that some of the Odes were such that no ingenuity could represent them as Hymns to Philosophy and get away with it—but chiefly, I think, because during that period he had himself been down to Hell and come up again, to be faced with himself at the top of Mount Purgatory. It seems to me useless to ask what sin "exactly" it was which led to those sharp reproaches and those miserable tears—whether it was a *pargoletta* or a theological error or a loss of faith. One has only to compare the Dante of the *Convivio* with the Dante of the *Vita* and the *Commedia* to see what it was that had happened to him and then unhappened. The Dante of the *Convivio* has everything that the other Dante has—the great intellect, the great curiosity, the great poetry, the great piety, even—but without humility and without charity. The sin is not primarily girls or anybody's system of philosophy; it is simply the thing known as hardness of heart; and to recognise it there is no need to take a magnifying glass to the text to hunt out heresies, nor yet to pore over contemporary scandal to identify the lady of the Pietra poems. It is there, writ large—not "a" sin, but simply sin. It was beginning to undermine his integrity when he "came to himself" and found he was in the Dark Wood. And eventually he got out, or

was led out (that is the story he is going to tell) and the frost in his
heart broke up:

> Io gel che m' era intorno al cor ristretto,
> spirito ed acqua fessi.[1]

He stopped justifying himself and admitted that he was a fool and a
miserable sinner. He took down the defensive barrier with which he
had shut the "blessed and glorious Beatrice" out of the *Convivio*. He
stopped telling people how much older and more mature he was than
the Dante of the *Vita*, and accepted that dreaming, enthusiastic, gawky,
and slightly absurd young man as his inalienable self. And he stopped
lecturing people; and, throwing to the winds all his theories about
noble diction and the elegant construction of Odes, he sat down, using
any language that came handy—dialect forms, baby-language, Latin
tags, nonsense-words, and even (if absolutely necessary) inferior lines
of no more than ten syllables—and with colossal humility, colossal
self-confidence, and a very practical charity he started telling them a
story.

Not, of course, that the mere fact of telling a story was such proof
of humility as it would have been had he lived 600 years later. He did,
after all, call Virgil "his master and author"; and nobody had taught
him the strange theory of the early twentieth-century novelists, that
one is a better story-teller for having no story to tell. He had not been,
however, altogether free from the notion that talking over people's
heads was a sign of superiority:

> Canzone, i' credo che saranno radi
>   Color che tua ragione intendan bene,
>   Tanto la parti faticosa e forte . . . [2]

and all the rest of it; and his manner towards his readers in the *Convivio*,
though doubtless meant for their good, is often of the kind that would
be "intolerable from almighty God to a blackbeetle". In the *Comedy*
there is a change of relationship: the reader is his familiar friend,
entering into the story and entering sympathetically into his worst and
weakest moments—"*pensa, lettor, se io mi sconfortai*"—"just think,

---

[1] The icy bonds which held my heart compressed
   Melted to breath and water.
               Purg. xxx. 97–98.

[2] Song, I think they will be few indeed that shall rightly understand thy
meaning, so dark and intricate is thy utterance . . .
               Canz: *Voi che intendendo.*

reader, what a shock this gave me"; he is not trying to be obscure—those with sane intellects will divine the doctrine beneath the "strange verses", or pierce the thin veil of the allegory; he is trying to be clear, and if his *"penna abborra"*—if his pen runs astray—he begs to be excused—the subject is new and strange, or so lofty that he and every artist must fail. True, light-minded readers are advised not to follow him into the uncharted spaces of deep Heaven lest they should lose him and destroy themselves, but those who have fed on the Bread of Angels are welcome companions; and if, while our "little skiffs" are trailing after him—as all the gondolas will collect in Venice behind a barge on which someone is singing, winding like a charmed serpent through canal after canal by moonlight—if, I say, he has suddenly the assurance to look round over his shoulder and catch us with our ears wagging and our eyes standing out like organ-stops:

> *Pensa, lettor, se quel che qui s'inizia*
> *non procedesse, come tu avresti*
> *di più sapere angosciosa carizia,*[1]

the grin is a friendly one, and dash it! he is perfectly right.

With a colossal humility, then, but with a colossal self-confidence all the same. Nobody who did not know beforehand what the *Comedy* was all about would guess from its opening the audacity of its scope and aim. Mr. C. S. Lewis has well pointed out the reason for the "ritualistic or incantatory" style of the Virgilian and Miltonic epic: The invocation, the formal opening, the "grand manner" are all there "to give us the sensation that some great thing is now to begin", "to compensate for—to counteract—the privacy and informality of silent reading in a man's own study". That is true, and the *solempne* way is one great and right way with a great subject. Dante's way is not necessarily greater or more right; it is simply quite different. If Boccaccio is telling the truth he did at one time intend to lose himself in an *O Altitudo*, and start off in the Latin tongue and the formal style.

> *Ultima regna canam, fluido contermina mundo—*[2]

---

[1] Think, reader, if this tale I have begun
   Broke off abruptly here, how thou wouldst fret,
   Wondering and wondering how it should go on.
                    Para. v. 109–111.
[2] I sing the farthest realms, conterminous with the flowing Universe. . . .
            cit Boccaccio, *Vita:* Perchè la commedia sia stata scritta
                    in Italiano.

but all that unhappened with the rest of the great unhappening. By the time he has humbled himself to write in the vulgar tongue, *"in qua et mulierculae communicant"*,[1] he is so certain of his vocation and his skill that he abandons, or at least postpones, all ritual aids. He does not assume his singing robes; he merely assumes that he has them on, and he moves as freely in them as a practised actor in a period costume. He does not attempt to prepare the reader's mind; he merely walks casually into it and makes himself at home there. He does not try to counteract the informality of private reading; he takes advantage of it. Oddly enough, almost the first epithet which comes into one's mind for the style of the *Comedy* is "unpretentious". The poem does not start off like an epic, but with the disarming simplicity of a ballad or a romance or a fairy-tale:

> It fell about the Martinmas
>   When the wind blows shrill and cold . . .

> King Arthur was at Caerlleon upon Usk; and
>   one day he sat in his chamber . . .

> Childe Rowland and his brothers twain
>   Were playing at the ball . . .

> *Nel mezzo del cammin di nostra vita*
> *mi ritrovai per una selva oscura,*
> *che la diritta via era smarrita.*[2]

Dante has acknowledged his debt to his classical masters; but there must be, I think, also an unacknowledged debt to the romance-writers of the northern tradition, whom, after all, he had read. They are apt to begin with this kind of abruptness; and what, indeed, is he telling but a *roman courtois* of the achievement of a lady by means of one of those other-world journeys in which the *matière de Bretagne* abounds? Only that where they are moving farther and farther from their supernatural origins into favour and prettiness, or sensation, or at the best a rather tentative morality and psychology, he is moving back to the origins and taking all the rest with him. And also (which is more to my immediate purpose) that where they are rambling and diffuse, he is pregnant, articulated, and architectural.

---

[1] in which even simple women converse.
[2] Midway this way of life we're bound upon,
    I woke to find myself in a dark wood,
      Where the right road was wholly lost and gone.
                                    Inf. i. 1–3.

The structure of the thing is in every way astonishing. Assuming that a story-teller is going to attempt this remarkable mixture of "history, philosophy, politics, and preaching", satire, romance, auto-biography, and adventure, what kind of form would one expect him, nowadays, to give it? The obvious answer is, the most elastic form possible, capable of the utmost variety, so as to accommodate all this "disparate and impracticable material"; "film technique"—or, at the very least, the elbow-room afforded by the chronicle-novel or the *roman picaresque*; a broad treatment, without too much finicking detail, and, above all, freedom from any suggestion of sameness or monotony.

What Dante in fact does is to take the whole thing and cramp it, as though into a steel corset, into three sets of concentric and similar rings—forty-four rings in all—and to lead us remorselessly, never missing a turn or a step, down four-and-twenty rings one after the other, in which people are suffering various forms of trouble and pain; then up ten rings one after another, in nine of which people are suffering various forms of trouble and pain; and finally up ten more rings, in which (for a change) people are enjoying slightly varied forms of an unvarying bliss. It sounds like the surest recipe for an almost screaming boredom. He need not have done it like that; the ten circular Heavens may have been imposed on him by Ptolemaic astronomy; the twenty-four circles of Hell and the ten ascents of Purgatory he went out of his way to invent. He liked it like that; he deliberately chose for his material the most rigid form conceivable, because he was a superb story-teller and knew, first, that you can hold disparate material much better together if you box it in so that it can't fall out; secondly, that you can hold people's attention more closely to the matter in hand if you focus it resolutely on some un-deviating purpose (which is one reason why detective stories are popular and why everybody is so much more virtuous and industrious in war than in peace); finally, that if you want the reader not only to follow but to accept and believe a tale of marvels, you can do it best by the accumulation of precise and even prosaic detail.

He started well equipped. He had a tidy mind, that loved order and symmetry for their own sake, or perhaps fell in love with them at the same time that he fell in love with scholastic theology. And the years that led him into the Dark Wood had not been wholly wasted by any means. Just as beneath the lovely fluency of the *terza rima*, which with a heart-breaking simplicity will do anything he wants—pray, sing, weep, thunder, grit its teeth, clinch an epigram, or report easy conversation in the high-comedy style—there lies the long apprenticeship to the fixed forms: ballata, sonnet, sestina, canzone; so the almost maddening schematisation of the *Convivio*, with its parallelisms, divisions and sub-divisions, orderly digressions and orderly returns to the main path, throwing editors into a frenzy of analytical diagrams and marginal alphabets, underlies the massive coherence of the *Comedy*; in which nothing is displaced, or forgotten, or disconnected, or allowed to ramble out of proportion; and in which "*ogni parte ad ogni parte splende*—each part reflects the light to every other", so that the whole scheme, as outlined in *Inferno*, i, is carried out unfalteringly to *Paradiso*, xxxiii; so that a question first raised in Hell may be answered in Purgatory, or a brilliant effect in the Heaven of the Fixed Stars plotted and prepared in the Eighth Chasm of Malebolge. In ten years of writing and fourteen thousand lines of verse there are few improvisations and scarcely an inconsistency; there is no disproportion.

Exactness and proportion by themselves will not, of course, make a story. The mere facts that the poem consists of precisely one hundred cantos, divided with as much symmetry as the nature of that number permits into books of thirty-four, thirty-three, and thirty-three cantos respectively; that between the longest and the shortest canto there is a difference of no more than forty lines; that each of the three Kingdoms of the Dead contains ten main divisions; that in the *Inferno* (which is the most complicated) the passage from Upper to Nether Hell comes almost exactly a quarter-way through the book, the passage from Violence to Fraud precisely half-way through, and the famous burlesque relief of the Ciampolo episode precisely half-way down Malebolge—these things may entertain the curious technician, but do not afford pleasure to the reader on first acquaintance, especially since they are so neatly managed that he probably will not notice them. But they do afford proof to people who require proof of such things, that shapes do not sculpture themselves, that oases of variety and refreshment do not grow of their own accord in the arid soil of Hell, but are put there, deliberately, at the points where they are calculated to be most useful. It is just because order is so accurately observed that episodes and descriptions and similes and fragments of Florentine politics and prophecies and prayers and humours and grotesques can flourish so abundantly at every turn without developing into jungly growths, obscuring the lines of the structure, and holding up the pace of the narrative.

The sheer pace is, in fact, extraordinary. We start without preliminary, and the first three lines inform us: that the story is to describe
the poet's own experience; it is to be told in the first person; he is
thirty-five years old; it is a story about a journey, and has an allegorical
meaning connected with "the Way"—the *cammin di nostra vita*; the
traveller has come to himself after some sort of aberration and has
found that he is in a Dark Wood, and has lost his way. At the thirteenth
line we come to the Mountain, and are thus linked immediately to the
subject of the second book; at line thirty-one the Leopard arrives,
followed within twenty minutes by the Lion and the She-Wolf, thus
preparing us for the three main divisions of Hell. After another dozen
lines Virgil appears, and there is a pause while he establishes himself
and Dante gives us a rapid sketch of his own poetic derivation. Then
come nine lines of prophecy about the Veltro, hinting at an eschato-
logical significance, and at the same time laying stress on the whole
allegory of "the City"; after that the entire scope and subject of the
three books is mapped out, and the journey is begun. One could
scarcely get more work out of a hundred and thirty-five lines. And
indeed, lest the pace should become so quick as to appear casual,
Canto II checks it abruptly. (Here an invocation at last makes its
appearance. It is addressed to the Muse, Genius and Memory, and
occupies exactly three lines.) Dante baulks—as we shall see him do a
good many times, up to that last, pathetic, poignant, and most
piercingly comic baulk of all on the Cornice of Fire—and produces a
whole set of highly cogent and perfectly ridiculous reasons for not
going on. The reasons are ridiculous, because he has, in fact, no choice
but either to go on or remain for ever in the Dark Wood which is
more terrible than death, but our heart warms to his absurdity; his
excuses are so like the excuses we make for ourselves. Virgil's reply
introduces Beatrice, sums up in a line or two everything which the
reader needs to know (if he has not previously read the *Vita*) about
the previous Dante–Beatrice connection, and lays down the lines on
which the *Paradiso* is to develop. Incidentally we get to know a good
deal more about Virgil himself: the three chief figures of the *Comedy*
are established. The action has paused, but the story has advanced. The
two poets—surely the most charming couple that ever walked side by
side through a story—set off again; and then, suddenly, at the opening of the Third Canto, we are really there. For the first time the
authentic Grand Manner makes its appearance, and the verse rings
like iron:

Per me si va nella città dolente;
per me si va . . .[1]

and through the gate we go, abandoning everything. Nothing could now keep us from the adventure.

It is a story of adventure. And it is written as all the best adventure stories are written. From century to century the trick is rediscovered —by Defoe, by Bunyan, by Jules Verne, by Conan Doyle, by H. G. Wells—and new generations thrill with astonished delight. The titles of three of Jules Verne's tales might well serve as sub-titles for the three books of the *Comedy*: *Voyage au Centre de la Terre*; *L'Île Mystérieuse*; *De la Terre à la Lune*—except that the last is not quite adventurous enough. And the trick is always the same trick: it is the trick—and to some minds the scandal—of particularity. Some very great poets have preferred to tell their stories without it, and done well; some great story-tellers who were not poets at all have used it and have also done well. When it is used by a story-teller who is also a poet of Dante's calibre the effect is extraordinary. Two kinds of excitement are blended together to make an excitement less heady than the excitement of either poetry or story-telling by itself, but more thirst-quenching than either. What the trick of particularity adds to the poetry is, I think, best described as a vivid conviction of fact— the sort of conviction that used to lead people to address letters to "Sherlock Holmes Esq., 221 Baker Street", begging him to investigate their problems. We believe in Dante's Three Kingdoms; not as we believe in the magic landscapes of Spenser or Keats, or even of Milton (though he had a touch of the trick too)—that is, by a willing surrender of the judgement to the spell-binding power of beautiful or terrible words. We believe in the Inferno as we believe in Robinson Crusoe's island—because we have trudged on our own two feet from end to end of it. We are convinced that it is *there*, independently of the poet; if necessary, we could find our way through it without him. We know the landmarks and should recognise them, just as we should recognise Crusoe's cave, or his arbour, or the place where the miraculous crop of wheat came up, or the current that threatened to carry him and his boat out to sea. It is not merely that, as Macaulay has pointed out,[2] Dante, having claimed to be the eye-witness and ear-witness of that which he relates, is obliged to substantiate his claim by minute particulars. "The reader would throw aside such a tale in incredulous disgust,

---

[1] Through me the road to the city of desolation,
     Through me . . .
[2] *Essay on Milton.*

unless it were told with the strongest air of veracity, with a sobriety even in its horrors, with the greatest precision and multiplicity in its details." That is true; it is true also that "he is the very man who has heard the tormented spirits crying out for the second death, who has read the dusky characters on the portal within which there is no hope, who has hidden his face from the terrors of the Gorgon, who has fled from the hooks and the seething pitch of Barbariccia and Draghignazzo." But that is not all; the important thing is that *we* have been there, and can indeed scarcely free ourselves from a dreadful conviction that one day we might even *go* there. The road is more clearly mapped even than that other road, "straight as a rule can make it", that runs from the Wicket Gate to the Celestial City; we know every outline by sight and every variation in the murky light: the serene illumination of the Elysian Fields, the red glow of the iron walls of Dis, the fiery rain, the moving flames "like fireflies" in the Eighth Bolgia, the pale glimmer of the ice at the bottom of the Pit. If we were led through Hell blindfold, the familiar sounds would tell us where we were: the sighs and wailings, and the wuthering of the *bufera infernal*, the howls of Cerberus, the yells of the hoarders and spendthrifts, the splashing and bubbling of the streams, the shrieks of the Furies, the sibilant voices of the Suicides "sizzling like green wood on the fire", the thunder of the cataract, the snuffling and blowing of the Flatterers, the quarrels and shouts of the Malebranche, the confused roar of the speaking flames, the teeth of the Traitors chattering like storks—all the hideous, intolerable clamour of Hell. And if we were both deaf and blind, we could almost smell our way through from stink to stink.

Coming to the Baedeker-like precision of Dante from the rich texture and vague vast suggestiveness of later poets, we may be inclined to feel that he lacks "poetry". It is true that he has no sustained passages of grandiose and sensuous description in which the mind can, as it were, plunge and lose itself; you could not, for example, pick out a hundred lines or so of terrible grandeur to set beside Milton's picture of the journey through Chaos. Such descriptive matter as there is is brief and austere to starkness:

> *Non fronde verdi, ma di color fosco;*
> *non rami schietti, ma nodosi e involti;*
> *non pomi v'eran, ma stecchi con tosco . . .* [1]

---

[1] No green here, but discoloured leaves and dark,
No tender shoots, but writhen and gnarled and tough,
No fruit, but poison-galls on the withered bark.
Inf. xiii. 4–6.

Sopra tutto il sabbion d'un cader lento
piovean di foco dilatate falde,
come di neve in alpe senza vento . . . [1]

A whole landscape of Perugino-like loveliness may be evoked and dismissed in a line or two:

Dolce color d'oriental zaffiro
che s'accoglieva nel sereno aspetto
dell' aer puro infino al primo giro . . . [2]

. . . di lontano
conobbi il tremolar della marina . . . [3]

But what is "poetry"? By some it is taken to mean the removal of concepts to a plane on which they become acceptable to the emotions just because, at that level, they neither demand the assent of the intellect nor challenge any issue in conduct. Thus we may accept Hell (or the Incarnation of God, or the brotherhood of Man or what not) "in a poetic sense" without feeling the need to do anything about it. To Dante this kind of poetry would have seemed (if nothing worse)

a barren noise
Though it blows legend-laden through the trees.[4]

He conceives that "his whole business is to show us Hell", and that is precisely what he shows us—not "the poetry of Hell", but simply Hell. Although he may, and I think does, make it acceptable to the intellect, to the complacent emotions, Dante's Hell is not acceptable, nor does he mean it to be. He desires that his Hell should evoke an emotional repulsion, issuing in a vigorous rejection by the will, just as he desires that his Purgatory and Paradise should be embraced, with equal vigour, by the undivided personality. If by "poetry" we mean

[1] And slowly, slowly dropping over all
The sand, there drifted down huge flakes of fire,
As Alpine snows in windless weather fall.
Inf. xiv. 28–30.
[2] Colour unclouded, orient-sapphirine,
Softly suffusing from meridian height
Down the still sky to the horizon-line.
Purg. i. 13–15.
[3]   and far off
I recognised the shimmering of the sea.
Purg. i. 116–117.
[4] Keats, *Fall of Hyperion.*

some sort of "backward mutters of dissevering power" which can disjoin the imagination from the will, then Dante is the least poetical of poets.

But if poetry has anything to do with compelling the imagination itself, then Dante's grand art does not fail him. We may think that he works by statement rather than by suggestion; yet in the end we find that he has suggested more than the content of his statements. Their effect is cumulative. As we are led down, relentlessly, from circle to circle of Hell, the steady piling-up of dry detail—the noise, stench, and squalor, the grit and greyness, the sterility, stuffiness, and heat, the narrowing circles, the weight and pressure of tier upon tier of rock, the sense of everything shelving down and closing in, ends by producing an oppression of spirits and an increasing claustrophobia compared with which a trip through Milton's Hell is as refreshing as an open-air picnic. Even in damnation, Milton's devils can *do* something —dig for metals, build a palace, make a causeway over Chaos; but here there is only an incessant restlessness without change, a monotonous miserable activity to no purpose, the fixation of choice, the endless self-devouring of the will turned in upon itself. The place is evil, with an evil stripped of its last shred of glitter; and the deeper we go the more suffocating does the atmosphere become, and the meaner grows the aspect of the evil selfhood thus stripped naked. "It is extraordinary," said the friend I have already quoted, on arriving at the bottom of the Tenth Bolgia; "when you look back from here, the upper part of Hell seems almost gay by comparison, with its rivers and cities and picturesque monsters." The disappearance of ornament has much to do with this, by negative suggestion; and so also has the mere looking back—the looking *up* the four thousand miles of that colossal shaft. From the ice of Cocytus Dante looks up, as in the *Paradiso* he will look down over the seven spheres and see the earth:

tal ch'io sorrisi del suo vil sembiante— [1]

"Look down", says Beatrice, "and see how great a universe I have put under thy feet." So, in the *Inferno*, a world is piled over his head. Its enormity is measured by the measure of our relief when we emerge "to look once more upon the stars"—the stars from which we shall presently see that same enormity dwindled to a pin's-head insignificance.

[1] Such that I smiled, it seemed so poor a thing.
Para. xxii. 135.

Continually, indeed, Dante's poetry suggests more than its statements contain. Once, having spoken enthusiastically of the exquisite
colour in which the Ante-Purgatorio was bathed, I referred to the text
for corroboration, and in all eight cantos could discover only a dozen
lines which mentioned colour at all—the rest was pure suggestion and
the poet's magic. However, the poetry of Dante is not our business
at the moment. What concerns us is that the spell-binding which we
choose to call "the poetry" as distinct from the poem is always so
controlled that it cannot hypnotise us into losing contact with story
and meaning.

This, for a long narrative poem, is of enormous importance. Our
inability to resist being carried unobservantly away on long rollers of
sensuous rhythm is the reason why Swinburne's *Tristram* fails to hold
us as a narrative. And I think that a kind of spell-bound submission to
the sheer dignity of the Miltonic line accounts largely for our tendency
to accept Milton's Satan at his own valuation. For a moment the ugly
"squat like a toad" shocks us into noticing what it is that we are so
ready to admire. But when it comes to Hell, then however often we
meet with words denoting pain and horror and degradation, the style
itself is too much for us; "the grand, infernal peers" remain—we
cannot help it—grand. Even the horrible allegory of Sin and Death
nowhere touches the squalid depth of grotesque and impotent misery
that affronts us in:

> *con sei occhi piangeva, e per tre menti*
> *gocciava il pianto e sanguinosa bava.*[1]

I know no poet who can compare with Dante in the "art of sinking"—
and rising again—"in poetry". Not even Shakespeare can do it so
swiftly and surely. The miracle of the style is its fluidity—it moves like
water, taking on every contour of the great rock-sculptured mass over
which it flows. Look, for instance, at the delicious, almost drawing-
room-comedy lightness of the little dialogue on the Fifth Cornice
where the two poets meet Statius, and Dante, by an inopportune smile,
gives away Virgil's identity. Statius's mild indignation at what looks
like bad manners, Virgil's humorous resignation, and Dante's schoolboy confusion are sketched with the delicate accuracy of the novel of

---

[1]   and he wept
From his six eyes, and down his triple chin
Runnels of tears and bloody slaver dripped.
Inf. xxxiv. 52–54.

manners—the trifling social *gaffe* might almost be occurring to Miss Catherine Morland in the Pump Room at Bath; and then, in a turn, in a twinkling, and without the slightest jerk in the line, we are pulled back to the tremendous scene and the cosmic realities: this is Mount Purgatory, these are Statius and Virgil, and they are great and dead:

> *Già si chinava ad abbracciar li piedi*
> *al mio dottor; ma egli disse: "Frate,*
> *non far, chè tu se' ombra, ed ombra vedi."* [1]

The story moves, and the style with it. Never, whether by over-lightness or over-loading, by any "inappropriate splendour", or by the *lussuria* of a too-prolonged lusciousness, does the obedient "poetry" betray its proper function.

Structure, speed, particularity, style—what next? Why, to be sure, that quality without which a tale may indeed take captive the imagination but can never root itself in the affections—the power to create a whole universe of breathing characters. It is often a fatal weakness in allegory to be populated by droves of frigid abstractions and perambulating labels; it is on his ability to endow these figures with the breath of life that the allegorist depends for his enduring persuasiveness. In this art Bunyan is, I suppose, acknowledged master, and it would be a bold man who should maintain that even Dante equalled or surpassed him. What one can say is that Dante, by an inspired tact in choosing his subject, side-stepped this besetting difficulty of allegory. His fable is such that he can fill his poem with real people who do not cease to be their earthly selves because they also typify everybody's sins and virtues. Dante is guided through Hell and Purgatory, not by Conscience, or Wisdom, or Counsel, or Good-wit, or what-not, but by Virgil—a Virgil who is not merely utterly charming and human, after the manner of Faithful or Mr. Ready-to-Halt, but is also so personally Virgil that he cannot resist telling the story of the founding of Mantua, and that in quoting (and indeed misquoting) his own poem he observes negligently to Dante: "My high Tragedy sings him somewhere or other—you'll remember, since you have the whole poem by heart." "*Non uomo, uomo già fui*"—he is not, but he was once a man—that

---

[1] Already stooping to my lord, he made
To kiss his feet, but: "Brother, do not so,
For shade thou art and look'st upon a shade."
Purg. xxi. 130-132.

is why his nostalgia can catch so terribly at one's heart:

> *Vespero è già colà, dov' è sepolto*
> *lo corpo, dentro al quale io facea ombra:*
> *Napoli l' ha, e da Brandizio è tolto.*[1]

That is why Sordello's anxious question is almost intolerably poignant:

> *O pregio eterno del loco ond' io fui,*
>
> *qual merito o qual grazia mi ti mostra?*
> *S'io son d'udir le tue parole degno,*
> *dimmi se vien d'inferno, e di qual chiostra.*[2]

Immortal courtesy gives him what reassurance it can; immortal courtesy receives it without comment; the fact of immortal sundering and immortal loss stands desolately between them.

So too with the other souls: blessed or damned, they remain eternally themselves. Cacciaguida is not just Ancestry or Derivation— he is that sturdy old Florentine gentleman, steeped in the archives— one might almost say the gossip—of the city. Belacqua, purging his laziness on the lower slopes of Purgatory, is lazy Belacqua still, curled sleepily with his face between his knees, and bestirring himself, to twit Dante, with the smallest possible expenditure of energy:

> *Allor si volse a noi, e pose mente,*
> *movendo il viso pur su per la coscia.*[3]

As the damned become more and more dehumanised in the fixed quality of their corruption the closer they lie to the bottom of the Pit, so the survival of their essential personality becomes more and more shocking to us. The human pathos and the rippling beauty of

---

[1] 'Tis vesper-tide already where the tomb
    Yet holds the body wherein I once cast shade;
    Naples received it from Brundisium.
                                Purg. iii. 25–27.
[2]   O deathless fame of the land where I was bred,

    What merit or grace has let me see thee here?
    If of thy words I am but worthy, say
    Art thou from Hell, and from what cloister there?
                                Purg. vii. 18–21.
[3] Then he gave heed, and turning just a little
    Only his face upon his thigh, he grunted . . .
                                Purg. iv. 112–173.

Master Adam's agonising vision of unattainable waᵗer:

> *Li ruscelletti, che dei verdi colli*
> *del Casentin discendon giuso in Arno,*
> *facendo i lor canali freddi e molli,*

> *sempre mi stanno innanzi, e non indarno . . .* [1]

make still more hideous its resolution into an inhuman bestiality of vindictiveness:

> *Ma s'io vedessi qui l'anima trista*
> *di Guido o d'Alessandro o di lor frate,*
> *per fonte Branda non darei la vista.* [2]

Even the mythical monsters and "greedy organisms of hell" are not *just* embodied attributes. They were once something that had to do with human life and poetry; Chiron is a person, and indeed a sympathetic person—he and his centaurs gallop round the shore of Phlegethon:

> *come solean nel mondo andare a caccia.* [3]

Cerberus is not simply a projection of gluttonous desire; he is a dog, a classic dog, and an old acquaintance, existing apart from his allegorical function.

Charles Williams has memorably established for us the reality of the figure of Beatrice herself;[4] and Dean Church has summed up the matter in a pregnant sentence: "We may infer from the *Convito* that the eyes of Beatrice stand definitely for the *demonstrations*, and her smiles for the *persuasions* of wisdom; but the poetry of the *Paradiso* is not about demonstrations and persuasions, but about looks and smiles." [5] It is not sufficient to allow that Beatrice is *a* real woman; she is *that* real

---

[1] The little brooks that ripple from the hills
    Of the green Casentin to Arno river,
    Suppling their channels with their cooling rills

  Are in my eyes and in my ears for ever;
    And not for naught.   *Inf.* xxx. 64–68.
[2] But might I here see Guido or Alexander
    Damned, or their brother, I would not miss that sight
    For all the water in the fount of Branda.
                  Inf. xxx. 76–78.
[3] As when through the woods of the world they went a-chasing.
                  Inf. xii. 37.
[4] *The Figure of Beatrice*, from which I have quoted various phrases *passim*.
[5] *Essay on Dante*.

woman: the same Florentine girl who once made fun of Dante at a party, who once cut him in the street, whose mere presence in the same city with him filled him with inexplicable anguish and ecstasy. In the *Purgatorio* the refusal of her salutation is more shattering; in the *Paradiso* her laughter is a thing that he learns, rapturously, to bear. The young man's unforgettable experience is taken up—repeated and resolved upon a higher level. Strangely enough, he has not told us in the *Vita* how, or even whether, the Florentine Beatrice forgave him and restored the blessing of her *salute*; we shall now never know whether the reconciliation with the celestial Beatrice is the image of something that did happen or only of something that might and ought to have happened. Either way, the thing bears the stamp of authenticity: two real lovers are estranged; they meet, quarrel, and are reconciled; a new relationship is established. The story is more than that, but it is at least that.

The greatness of the story-teller is seen in the handling of the story. If Dante needed any model for his love-romance outside his own experience he might—and indeed he may—have found it in Chrestien de Troyes' *Charrette*. Here, too, the lover, after a long and perilous series of adventures, wins through to the presence of his lady. She receives him coldly and repudiates him. The King pleads for Lancelot, rather as the attendant Graces plead for Dante: "Lady, why do you shame him so?" At this point in the French romance there intervenes a debauch of sentimentalities: Lancelot leaves the court, is captured and reported killed; Guinevere becomes ill with remorse, and *she* is reported dead; Lancelot hears the rumour and tries to commit suicide; Guinevere again hears that he is dead and again falls into a transport of grief. Eventually these misunderstandings are cleared up and the lovers once more brought face to face; Guinevere reproaches Lancelot for having failed in that utter devotion exacted by the code of courtly love; tears of penitence are shed (in this case on both sides) and thereafter they are reconciled and Lancelot becomes Guinevere's lover within the meaning of the act.

Disregarding the comparative vulgarity of Chrestien's intrigue, the resemblance in structural outline between these two "turning-point" episodes is sufficient to show at once the *Comedy's* debt to the *roman courtois* and the distance it has travelled beyond it. The Beatrician element in the *Comedy* is simply the transvaluation of "courtly love" to a plane on which it makes profound spiritual sense instead of social chaos. But setting all this aside, what leaps to the eye is the enormous advance in technique by which Dante has made the characters their own destiny, and their actual confrontation in itself both the crisis and the resolution. Chrestien—an excellent story-teller of his kind—dissipates his situation in repeated efforts to pile up the agony, so that in the end the reconciliation, separated by so much time, space, and bustle from the repudiation-scene, falls curiously flat. Even so, the reconciliation is not itself the crisis: it merely prepares the real crisis of the poem. Dante, coming to his task a hundred years later, an incomparably greater poet with an incomparably greater story to tell, reveals in addition an incomparably greater power of sheer narration. He has the essential dramatic gift—an unerring sense of the *scène à faire*, and upon that scene he single-mindedly concentrates, dissipating no energy, welding action and character together with an intense economical compactness of passion and irony, until he has wrung the resolution of the situation out of the situation itself. It is the technique of the psychological novel, centuries in advance of its time, and it bears no marks of immaturity or fumbling. But the mind of Dante is so adult that it is always difficult to remember that he died twenty years before Chaucer was born, and forged his own language as he wrote it.

Which brings us to the figure of Dante himself. There have been many schools of thought about Beatrice, but nobody (so far) has attempted to disprove the actual existence of Dante. Like so many writers of adventure-stories, he has told his tale in the first person, and it is usually conceded that the adventure described is substantially his own, whether there is any element of "vision" in it or whether it is merely an imaginative record of interior experience. The autobiographical method has two enormous advantages for this kind of storytelling: it surrounds the most startling occurrences with a powerful illusion of verisimilitude, and it prevents the narrative from becoming disjointed and flying apart in all directions. Its danger is that the adventuring ego will become either a self-glorifying bore or else a characterless mirror for the reception of fleeting impressions. Dante avoids both these pitfalls by a brilliant technical expedient for which he has never (I think) been given sufficient credit. Except for those clearly indicated passages in which he allows his prophetic function, and not himself, to speak by his mouth, he has conceived his own character from start to finish in a consistent spirit of comedy. Seldom has an autobiographer presented the world with a less heroic picture of himself, or presented his own absurdities so lovably. Whether he is mumbling excuses for himself in the Dark Wood, or turning green in the face before the Gates of Dis, or lingering like a reluctant child at Farinata's tomb while his escort is calling him to come on, or being "less intelligent than usual" about the *Ethics*, or pottering "bemused" along rocky terraces in imminent peril of falling off, or likening himself to a little goat, or a baby stork, or to a man walking along the street in blissful unconsciousness of something funny stuck in his hat, or asking inappropriate questions which make Beatrice look at him "as a mother looks on her delirious child", or trotting forward to answer St. Peter's *viva voce* "like a Baccalaureate, equipping himself with every argument" and anxious to do credit to himself and his teachers, his self-portrait is saturated with a delicate and disarming awareness of himself as a comic figure. I do not think this is just a craftsman's device—I think it is, on the contrary, a sincere and touching humility. The fact remains that no other treatment of himself could have served his artistic ends so well. It enables him to dissect himself with an almost alarming acuteness and candour; it imparts a singular balance and truthfulness to his relationship with Virgil; it turns the plunge into the fire of the Seventh Cornice from the conventional heroic gesture it might so easily have been into the kind of exhibition which leaves us uncertain whether to laugh or cry; it sharpens the edge of that crucial humiliation on the banks of Lethe, and at the same time makes it just tolerable—we feel it embarrassing and almost indecent to see any human creature stripped so naked, and yet we accept it, since humiliation, one way and another, is the lot of every comic character.

His own is not, of course, the only comic character in Dante. There are the ugly, rollicking, Ingoldsby-Legend burlesques of the Fifth Bolgia, conceived in a mood of savage satire and tearing high spirits. There are sly satiric portraits like that of Belacqua. There are the preposterous Nimrod and the vain Antaeus; there is Pope Nicholas, grotesquely wedged upside-down and "lamenting with his shanks" while Dante adds to the discomforts of Hell by chanting a solemn denunciation at him:

forte spingava con ambo le piote [1]

no wonder! There are those charming shades in the Ante-Purgatorio who, having died excommunicate, wander out their waiting-time like shepherdless sheep:

[1] He writhed and jerked his feet with all his power.
Inf. xix. 120.

e ciò che fa la prima, e l'altre fanno,
  addossandosi a lei s'ella s'arresta,
  semplici e quete, e lo 'mperchè non sanno.[1]

There are, at every turn, lines and similes through which irrepressible little chuckles bubble up—images of squatting and darting frogs, sleepy ostlers, or sculptured corbels which give the beholder a crick in the back to look at them; shrewd little comments on human nature; polite ironies and friendly legpulls—together with turns of phrase so equivocal and delivered with such a poker-faced gravity that it is hard to be certain whether mockery is intended or not. Once there is the faintest flicker of a smile at Virgil—him, even—when he has allowed himself to be taken in by the Malebranche and is drily mocked for his credulity by Fra Catalano:

Appresso il duca a gran passi sen gì
  turbato un poco d'ira nel sembiante.[2]

"*A gran passi*"; there is pique in every line of that striding form. Dante the pilgrim hastens on, distressed, "following the prints of the beloved feet"; but as Dante the poet looks after them his mouth twitches, just perceptibly, at the corners.

But the comedy of the *Comedy* is matter for a small treatise in itself. I will only reaffirm my (possibly revolutionary) opinion that Dante Alighieri is a very great comic artist indeed, with a range extending from Swift on the one hand to Jane Austen on the other; and that his comic spirit is an enormous asset to his story-telling.

But the comic spirit, delighting as it does in disproportion and incongruity, is itself the best safeguard against these errors, and it is precisely this genius for comedy that endows Dante with the all-important gift of tact. I do not mean that he never gives offence to anybody; few writers have given so much to so many people, and no writer worth his salt gives none. I am thinking of the special brand of tact displayed by the ingenious traveller in Saki's tale appropriately

---

[1] And what the first one does, the others do,
  Bumping against her if she stops, and wait
  Silly and meek, though why they do not know.
                    Purg. iii. 82–84.
[2] My guide with raking steps strode off in haste,
  Troubled in his looks, and showing some small heat
  Of anger.
                    Inf. xxiii. 145–147.

entitled *The Story-Teller*. It consists largely in the avoidance of unnecessary difficulties and imprudently-placed explanations. It is a trick of narration which prevents the children from interrupting with questions at the wrong moment. I have mentioned Dante's choice of real people for the images of his allegory as an instance of this tact; he is thus enabled to make them exhibit a multiplicity of human traits and interests which would be unsuitable in *merely* allegorical figures— "accidents in a substance" and no more. "Why" (one would begin to ask) "should a simple personification of Dante's own evil passions pester him with inquiries about the present state of Romagna, or an emblematic figure of Repentance go out of its way to instruct him in embryology?" But given the right choice of fable to start with, there are still a number of things which have to be explained—it is indeed a great part of the intention of the poem that they should be explained; and the tactful placing of these explanations provides an absolute model of sheer narrative skill.

There has to be, for example, some sort of verbal map to explain the very complicated divisions and sub-divisions of Hell. But it would never do for Virgil, or the author, to hold us up at the beginning of the adventure with a lengthy disquisition on the *Ethics*. If he did, Dante might still have courage to embark on the journey, but the reader quite certainly would not. So we are led at a brisk pace through the Vestibule and the first five Circles with little more than the necessary Cook's-Tour commentary: "On your left, Westminster Abbey; on your right, the Houses of Parliament; the statues in the square are those of distinguished statesmen; observe the pigeons; there is Westminster Bridge, made famous in Wordsworth's sonnet; this is the Thames Embankment." Then follow two cantos of alarms and excursions—the passage of Styx, the burning walls of Dis, opposition by devils, the dread of losing Virgil, the slammed gates, Furies, Gorgons, the tremendous apparition of the Angel and the triumphant entry. Then, a little calmer in mind but still excited, we interview Farinata in his burning tomb. So far so good, and the story has carried us along by sheer impetus. But the time has arrived when we really must know where we are going and what it is all about, or we shall become puzzled and fretful and keep on wondering why this and why that, when we ought to be attending to the images. So a pause is made —the poet can afford it, for we could no more get away from him now than from the Ancient Mariner; and we are really glad of it, for the pace has made us breathless, and we are quite content to sit down behind the tomb of Anastasius and have a little lesson in infernal geography and the various kinds of sins. The timing is perfect: earlier, we should not have listened; later, we should have had too much difficulty in remembering the ground we have gone over. But now it can be done, all in one go, and finished with, and not intruded upon us in places where it would only distract us by interrupting the story.

There are, however, other questions, of a specifically awkward sort, which are bound to crop up eventually in any tale which has to handle a mixture of spiritual and physical bodies. It is, I think, pretty safe to say that nobody, reading the *Inferno* for the first time with his mind on the story, was ever seriously worried by any query about weights and measures, any more than he would be in reading a fairy-tale. Dante is there in his physical body; the shades are not—so much is insisted on and we accept it. The innumerable anomalies with which the story is packed do not trouble us. Hell is, apparently, a great funnel stretching down to the centre of the physical globe, "on which all weights down-weigh", yet Dante in his physical body can cover the 4,000 miles or so of the descent in thirty-six hours without food or sleep. Very well, he can; in this nightmare place anything can happen. The shades are *vanità*, yet Dante can twist the hair of Bocca's head, and Virgil, "weightless" as he is, has yet solidity enough to pick Dante up and carry him, as the spectral boat of Phlegyas can carry him. The boat's gunwale sinks deep under the unaccustomed load; Virgil is exhausted by the scramble down and up the flanks of Dis; well and good—there is classic precedent for that kind of thing. Dante can cross the rivulet which moats the Elysian castle "as though upon dry ground", but he cannot so cross Phlegethon, nor can Virgil carry him; they have to enlist the aid of a Centaur. Dante tells us these things and we do not question them because he takes it for granted that we shall not.

But the time is coming when such questions cannot be avoided, if only for the reason that it is part of Dante's intention to tell us about the nature of these spiritual—or rather, of these interim—bodies, which at the Resurrection will be replaced by the true spiritual bodies, the "glorious and holy flesh" in its final glory and sanctity. And being faced by this necessity, Dante grapples with it in the proper crafts-man's way—he turns it to glorious gain. We have ended our nightmare groping through Hell; we are on the fresh and open shores at the foot of Mount Purgatory; the ship of blessed souls has touched land; the sun is rising and our spirits are rising with it. It is at this moment that Dante is dealt two sharp shocks in swift succession: he finds that the form of Casella has no substance and the form of Virgil casts no shadow. He is suddenly reminded of the otherness of those beloved souls. The moment of panic when he sees his own shadow thrown solitary upon the hillside recalls that earlier terror before the gates of Dis; it anticipates and prepares us for that silent final separation in the Earthly Paradise, for which "all that our First Mother lost" can hardly console either Dante or us. But now look how skilfully the rising curiosity is diverted, half-satisfied, quelled, and transmuted into a wholly different emotion. "Why do you distrust? Do you not believe that I am with you and guide you? The body in which I used to cast a shadow is the world's width away—as for this:

> *A sofferir tormenti e caldi e gieli*
> *simili corpi la virtù dispone,*
> *che, come fa, non vuol che a noi si sveli."* [1]

Reason cannot compass the infinite mysteries of the Godhead—if it could

> *"mestier non era partorir Maria;*
>
> *e disiar vedeste senza frutto*
> *tai, che sarebbe lor disio quetato,*
> *ch'eternalmente è dato lor per lutto.*
>
> *Io dico d'Aristotele e di Plato*
> *e di molti altri." E qui chinò la fronte;*
> *e più non disse, e rimase turbato.* [2]

"And of many others." Distress for Virgil's sake drives all other feelings from our minds; inquisitiveness seems here an impertinence, and it is not till we have pulled ourselves together that we realise that

[1] Bodies like mine, to bear pain, cold, and heat,
    That power ordains, whose will forever spreads
    A veil between its working and our wit.
                        Purg. iii. 31–33.

[2] " No need had been for Mary to conceive;

    And you have seen such great souls thirst in vain
        As else had stilled that thirst in quietness
        Which now is given them for eternal pain;

    I speak of Plato, Aristotle—yes,
        And many others." Here he bent his head
        And moved on, silent, with a troubled face.
                        Purg. iii. 39–45.

our question has in fact been answered. The bodies "disposed" to the souls are sufficient for what is required of them; they "exist for the sake of their function and not their function for them". If, in the Divine intention, it is necessary that the dead Virgil should be able to carry the living Dante, the strength is supplied; if it is undesirable that Dante should embrace Casella, the substance is withdrawn. Subsequently, the mechanism (so to call it) of the airy body is explained by Statius, high up on the Sixth Cornice, objectively, and in connection with spirits for whom it is possible to feel a more detached and less emotional interest.

The skill and delicacy with which all this is done can best be appreciated by observing how the same problem is handled by Milton. Great and high and delicate poet as he is, Milton is just lacking in Dante's faultless tact. Adam, courteously welcoming Raphael to his bower, begs him to taste human hospitality:

> "... unsavourie food perhaps
> To spiritual Natures; only this I know,
> That one Celestial Father gives to all."
> To whom the Angel: "Therefore what he gives
> (Whose praise be ever sung) to man in part
> Spiritual, may of purest Spirits be found
> No ingrateful food."

All this is very proper. But the Angel then proceeds to volunteer the information that not only is the food not "unsavourie", but also that celestial organisms like his own can

> smell, touch, taste,
> Tasting concoct, digest, assimilate,
> And corporeal to incorporeal turn.

This, being presented as so intimately personal a matter, is a trifle embarrassing. However, it may pass, since Raphael, with what Beatrice would call his "infallible advisement", may know that Adam is bursting with curiosity on a subject to which he is too polite to refer. He concludes by answering the question Adam did ask:

> "... and to taste
> Think not I shall be nice." So down they sat,
> And to their viands fell.

And there it would have been well to leave it. But Milton, having a bone to pick with the theologians, cannot leave the thing alone, and repeats that Raphael's eating was not done "seemingly or in mist"

> but with keen dispatch
> Of real hunger, and concoctive heate
> To transubstantiate: what redounds, transpires
> Through Spirits with ease . . .

But there the reader's good manners rise up in protest. We resent being compelled to inspect a gentleman's interior plumbing while he is at lunch. Earlier, later, or elsewhere, we should be deeply interested, but not at table.

Milton has often been derided for the unconscious humour of this passage, which is variously attributed to his pompous euphemism, or his over-materialistic angelology, or to other sins which he has not committed. As a matter of fact there is nothing whatever wrong with the passage except faulty timing and placing; and from that, indeed, a livelier sense of comedy would have saved him.

Much the same thing happens in another pair of parallel passages. Some laughter and some rebuke have been aimed at Milton for his wounded angels whose "ethereal substance closed, not long divisible"; yet Dante has used the same device and, so far as I know, got away with it unreproved. But Dante has kept this piece of grotesque futility for the Circle of the Schismatics, where it is highly relevant, and extremely suitable to the vain repetitions and meaningless monotony of Hell. Milton has introduced us to it in Heaven, and, what is worse, thrust it into the middle of a battle, where it holds up the action—as though Dante had delayed the mad rush over the cliff of the Sixth Bolgia to explain how Virgil was able to lift him. And once again Milton might have carried the thing off triumphantly if he had not harped upon it; nothing could be more splendid than:

> then Satan first knew pain,
> And writh'd him to and fro convolv'd; so sore
> The griding sword with discontinuous wound
> Pass'd through him . . .

But he cannot leave it alone, and starts again a dozen lines further down:

> for Spirits that live throughout
> Vital in every part . . .

It is too much; we must have *either* a battle *or* an explanation—we cannot with propriety have both at once. If only the explanation could have been worked in at some earlier point, then the mention of the griding sword and discontinuous wound would have sufficed superbly for the combat. Dante's fable called for no celestial wars, therefore he was able to place the non-divisibility of ethereal substance in Hell and leave it there. In his adult and intellectual Heaven such things have no place; he is even careful explicitly to exclude from it all weights and measures, including his own:

> *S'io era sol di me quel che creasti*
> *novellamente, Amor che il ciel governi,*
> *tu il sai, che col tuo lume mi levasti.*[1]

---

[1] If I was naught, O Love that rul'st the Height,
    Save that of me which Thou didst last create
    Thou know'st, that didst uplift me with Thy light.
                    Para. i. 73–75.

Similarly, by removing even the appearance of human form from all the blissful souls between the Second Heaven and the Empyrean, Dante's tact avoids the unfortunate implications suggested by Raphael's

> smile that glowed
> Celestial rosie red, Love's proper hue,

on being asked whether heavenly spirits expressed their love

> . . . by looks onely, or do they mix
> Irradiance, virtual or immediate touch?

I doubt whether Milton intended this to be a "blush" in our rather simpering sense of the word. He probably meant to express something more like

> *L'altra letizia, che m'era già nota*
> *preclara cosa, mi si fece in vista*
> *qual fin balascio in che lo sol percota*
>
> *Per letiziar lassù folgor s'acquista,*
> *Sì come riso qui . . .*

(The other [spirit of] joy, already apparent to me as a thing outshining, became to my eyes like a fine ruby smitten by the sun; joy up there declares itself by greater brightness, as here by a smile . . .—*Para.* ix. 67–71.)

But the human shape, the previous insistence on the material concoction and evacuation, and the stress laid in the present passage on the materiality of angelic forms, compel the imagination, no matter how carefully the hypothesis of total interpenetrability is worded. What we cannot help *seeing* is a human figure going self-consciously red in the face. It is noteworthy that when the human form disappears from the *Paradiso* it does so, quietly and without comment, precisely in the sphere of Venus. Not even to annoy rival theologians or to rub in the glorious sanctity of the flesh was Dante going to take any chances with the commonness of the common reader; the Florentine exile was a man of the world.

And having thus got Dante, with or without his body, into Heaven, I find myself faced with analysing a piece of narrative craftsmanship which almost defies analysis. It is the manner in which the very technique of the telling mirrors in itself the actual content of the poem.

Of the examples which came readily to my hand to illustrate the processes of Dante's craftsmanship the *Inferno* offered the greatest number, the *Purgatorio* the next greatest, and the *Paradiso* the fewest. That is not because the poet's skill grew less as he went on. Far from it. But in the *Inferno* the "tricks of the trade" (if one may call them so in no disparaging sense) find their most obvious and concrete expressions. The poet has presented himself with a richly romantic landscape full of picturesque inventions, and has used this material to the full. There is, rightly, a grossness in Hell, and, corresponding to it, there is a certain crowded and close-grained quality in the workmanship. But as the soul ascends Mount Purgatory, it strips off grossness; the poetry effects this purging in two ways simultaneously. Directly, of course, it effects it by an immediate change of atmosphere and colour. If the interior of Hell is like a painting by Michael Angelo, the wind- and sea-swept exterior of Mount Purgatory is like a painting by Perugino. The loveliness of the sky, passing from the "*dolce color d'oriental zaffiro*" to the shifting hues of dawn, the dew-drenched grass and swaying reeds, the faint shimmering of the sea, the boat, seen through the mist like Mars setting, and gradually revealing the white wings of the heavenly pilot, the eager souls singing as they come and gladly leaping to the shore—the whole picture is of a translucent and tender and unearthly beauty so utterly unlike anything in the *Inferno* that the sense of relief and escape is almost physical. Equally lovely, though touched in with slightly stronger tints, is the Valley of the Rulers, with its enamelled flowers, green-robed angels, and the sliding glitter of the snake. The landscape, as well as the poetry and the "feel" of the first eight cantos of the *Purgatorio*, is of a quality so rare and strange that criticism has invented no suitable language to describe it. That is the *direct* mirroring of the process of purgation. But from the moment that we ascend the three steps and pass the actual gate of Purgatory, the second, indirect, mirroring begins. It may perhaps be best expressed by saying that the poetic technique itself begins to strip off its adventitious aids.

Dante's narrative power of excitement, his speed, precision, humour and so on, do not depend upon the piling up of Gothic landscapes or the multiplication of agitating incidents. Between the mysterious and lovely shore at the Mountain's foot and the mysterious and lovely wood at its summit there is nothing one can really call landscape—unless one counts the sculptures on the First Cornice, a couple of trees on the Sixth, and one or two beautiful night-sky effects. Nor, except for the earthquake and the meeting with Statius, is there any agitating incident until the plunge through the fire; at most we share Virgil's mild uncertainty whether he is going round the Mountain the right way and his passing anxiety that Dante shall not inadvertently fall over the edge of the cliff. Yet we know the Terraces and Cornices as intimately and accurately as the Infernal Circles. So, too, we know the characters: yet our attention is less, as it were, distracted by them: attention is beginning to sharpen and focus itself towards the crisis of separation and reunion. Virgil—so soon to be withdrawn—is closer to Dante and to us; in Hell he was usually "*il duca*", "*il mio dottore*", "*il maestro*", and was only once or twice called by his name, and that towards the end of the descent; now the verse rings like a chime of bells with: "*Virgilio ... Virgilio*". And the expectation of Beatrice, no longer remote but imminent, begins to modify the relationship: "If my words have put you in a perplexity which I cannot resolve for you, do not be content till you have had it all explained by her

> *che lume fia tra il vero e l'intelletto.*
> *Non so se intendi: io dico di Beatrice*," [1]

> *Quanto ragion qui vede*
> *dirti poss' io; da indi in là t'aspetta*
> *pure a Beatrice, ch'opera è di fede.*[2]

> *Lo dolce padre mio, per confortarmi,*
> *pur di Beatrice ragionando andava.*[3]

---

[1]   who is
Set as a light 'twixt truth and intellect—
I know not if thou understandest this:
I mean Beatrice.
        Purg. vi. 44–47.
[2] "So much as reason here distinguisheth
I can unfold," said he: "thereafter, sound
Beatrice's mind alone, for that needs faith."
        Purg. xviii. 46–48.
[3] My gentle father talked to cheer me, 'twas
Beatrice all the way.
        Purg. xxvii. 52–53.

The comedy has lost its harsher and deeper notes, but is no less comedy for that; just as the *Egoist* or *Pride and Prejudice* is no less filled with the comic spirit than *Tom Jones* or *Don Juan*, though remaining consistently on one high, sweet, subtle, and civilised level. Laughter is able, at the poet's will, to maintain itself out of its own resources, without special apparatus of grotesques and comic turns. The narrator's art *si raccoglie*. Growing as a tree grows, organically, into self-contained shapeliness, it dispenses with exterior props, and the poem, like the pilgrim, is crowned and mitred over itself.

In the *Paradiso* the liberation is completed. In so far as it is possible for a narrative style to be "transhumanised", the thing is done. Landscape vanishes: there is nothing that could be called so, except the vertiginous visual plunge from Gemini over the Seven Spheres to the tiny threshing-floor which is the Earth. The River of Life—the last of Dante's great rivers—is not "landscape" except as it recalls those other rivers of Hell and the Earthly Paradise; it is visioned Time, as the Rose into which it transmutes itself is visioned Eternity. The whole outward aspect of things is resolved into light and motion; "landscape" becomes a dance of geometrical patterns, touched in from a palette of pure light. From the nacreous sheen of Luna, past the triple coronal of the Sun, and the Cross of Mars, and the Eagle of Jupiter, up to that infinitesimal point from which

depende il ciclo e tutta la natura,[1]

we have traversed these lucidities, and know them as intimately as we knew the granite cliffs of Malebolge; precision and particularity are still there; the romantic method remains, but instead of working through the customary pictorial paraphernalia it is directed to the primary forms.

The human outline vanishes, its place taken by the living lights which "nestle in their own brightness". Of Beatrice herself we are shown only the eyes and the smile and, once, the wave of a wafting hand. The other characters are known to us no longer by look and gesture, but by voice and word—by intellectual being; as God is One with His Word, so they, in their degree, are what they speak.

Incident vanishes; in the *Paradiso* no *event*, in the ordinary sense of

---

[1] Heaven and all nature hangs.
Para. xxviii. 42.

the word, takes place. There is only the soaring flight into Heaven after Heaven—all of which (it is explained to us) are in fact one and the same Heaven; a continuous pressing closer to the heart of reality. The excitement, once maintained by encounters with monsters, by perils and escapes, by peripeteia and "strange surprising adventures", is now transmuted into a steadily increasing exhilaration, a piling-up of that *stupor* which, as a younger Dante had pointed out, comes over us in the presence of great and wonderful things. It was surprising to crane over the Great Barrier and see Geryon come slowly swimming up through the thick air: it is surprising also to gaze up at the Eagle of Jupiter and see the pagan soul of just Rhipeus flashing in this Christian Paradise; but the surprise is of another kind. It is a joy and a wonder to emerge from the din and squalor of the Pit into the stillness and starlight of Purgatory; but it belongs to a different frame of discourse from the joy and wonder of that astonishing moment when the singing and circling *trionfo* of the Hierarchies is "little by little quenched from sight", leaving Dante with Beatrice alone in an empty Heaven. The story is still one of adventure, but it has become purely and simply an adventure of the passionate intellect. "As lightning bursts from the cloud, dilating itself till it can no longer be contained,

> *la mente mia così, tra quelle dape*
> *fatta più grande, di sè stessa uscìo,*
> *e, che si fesse, rimembrar non sape ...*" [1]

It excites him, and his excitement is infectious.

Excitement about *getting* to Heaven is not rare in works of literature; excitement about *being* in Heaven is a much rarer thing. Few poets venture to linger very long after the first trumpet-blast that heralds the opening of the gates. To devote three-and-thirty cantos to the mere exploration of Paradise, without assistance from celestial conflicts, terrestrial judgements, or Olympian fun and games, is a cracking test of the poet's confidence both in his skill and in his theme. But the thing is done: the possibility of enduring delight is grasped and presented in a way that the adult intellect can accept. And now we can at last understand why Dante's beloved master had to be

---

[1] My mind, grown heavy with high festival,
    Gushed and o'erbrimmed itself; and what strange style
    It then assumed remembers not at all.
                    Para. xxiii. 43–45.

excluded from this Paradise, and what is meant by the sentence:

> *Io son Virgilio; e per null' altro rio*
> *lo ciel perdei, che per non aver fè.*[1]

Faith is imagination actualised by the will; what was lacking to Virgil's faith was precisely the imagination. To the great heathen Dante has allotted just that beautitude which they were able to imagine for themselves. On the "enamelled green" within that "goodly castle" about which

> *plurimus Eridani per silvam volvitur amnis* [2]

the heroes and sages of Antiquity dwell in a serene, unearthly light, just as Virgil had said:

> *largior hic campos aether et lumine vestit*
> *purpureo, solemque suum, sua sidera norunt.*[3]

And here, doubtless, though Dante does not expressly mention it:

> *pars in gramineis exercent membra palestris,*
> *contendunt ludo et fulva luctantur harena;*
> *pars pedibus plaudunt choreas et carmina dicunt . . .*
> *stant terra defixae hastae, passimque soluti*
> *per campam pascuntur equi.*[4]

Such was their best imagination; and now from the height of the Empyrean we look down with Dante and recognise it for what it is. Beautiful and peaceful, pathetic and fatigued, "all passion spent", it is only the upper circle of an immense despair. The *ben dell' intelletto* is here not lost, but it is arrested in an interminable adolescence. The endless games, the shining phantom horses, the odes and the choric measures are touched with the eternal futility, the eternal melancholy

---

[1] Virgil am I, and I came short of Heaven
   For no default, save that I had not faith.
                    Purg. vii. 7–8.
[2] The full flood that Eridanus athwart the wood doth pour.
                    Aen. vi. 659 (trans. W. Morris).
[3] Therein a more abundant heaven clothes all the meadows' face
   With purple light, and their own sun and their own stars they have.
                    Aen. vi. 640–641.
[4] Here some in games upon the grass their bodies breathing gave;
   Or on the yellow face of sand they strive and play the play;
   Some beat the earth with dancing foot, and some, the song they say . .
   . . . stand the spears in earth, unyoked the horses are,
   And graze the meadows all about.   *Aen.* vi. 642–644; 651–653.

of Hell. "With how many teeth does this love bite you?" asks St. John of Dante. In the *inania regna* love and all other raptures have had their teeth drawn. There is no pressure, no driving-power, and, significantly, there is no laughter.[1]

Laughter, indeed, does not vanish in the *Paradiso*: it is intensified. The spheres and the hierarchy whirl, dizzy with delight, "like a mill-wheel"; angels and rejoicing souls spin and weave their fantastic dance; it is, one feels, only by a supreme act of blessed courtesy that they momentarily suspend their celestial merriment to answer Dante's questions, so eager do they seem to be off again, hands across and down the middle. Yet to stand or to go is equally their bliss; they poise, they hover quivering, they glow, they laugh a little at the simplicity of the living man, they speak "joyously", and then

> *li santi cerchi mostrar nuova gioia*
> *nel tornear e nella mira nota.*[2]

Beatrice, gently mocking, delicately teasing her *fidele*, draws him even deeper into the wonder of her smile. "Look at me." Indeed he asks nothing better, and remains entranced. She rounds on him with enchanting inconsistency:

> *Perchè la faccia mia sì t'innamora,*
> *che tu non ti rivolgi al bel giardino*
> *che sotto i raggi di Cristo s'infiora?* [3]

She has used hard words to him, she has called him childish-foolish; but that is only love's way. With a delighted pride, as of a fond mother,

---

[1] Dante, as Charles Williams pointed out, could not have let Virgil and the other great pagans into the Christian heaven without making nonsense of their work: "We have more tenderness for them, but Dante had more honour." One last service, however, he did perform for his "master and author". By a touching and beautiful act of piety he has taken Virgil's simile of the bees visiting the flowers and transplanted it from the Elysian Fields to the Empyrean itself (*Aen.* vi. 707–709; *Para.* xxxi. 7–12). So long as poetry endures, one image of Virgil is established in that place where Beatrice, according to her promise, many a time speaks Virgil's praises to her Saviour.

[2] Renewed delight did those blest circles show
In wondrous song and swift revolving reel.
Para. xiv. 23–24.

[3] Why art thou so enamoured of my face
Thou wilt not turn thee to the garden bright
Shone on by Christ, and flowering in His rays?
Para. xxiii. 70–72.

or a heavenly schoolmistress with a really exceptional pupil, she presents him to the examiners: "*Tenta costui*", she says to St. Peter; and to St. James:

> *La Chiesa militante alcun figliuolo*
> *non ha con più speranza . . .*
>
> *Gli altri due punti . . .*
> *a lui lasc' io; chè non gli saran forti,*
> *nè di iattanza; ed egli a ciò risponda.*[1]

Humanity is not lost, and so even comedy is not lost, as the mirth kindles into a more mysterious ecstasy of glory and all Heaven rejoices

> *sì che m'inebbriava il dolce canto.*
>
> *Ciò ch'io vedeva, mi sembiava un riso*
> *dell' universo; per che mia ebbrezza*
> *entrava per l'udire e per lo viso.*[2]

This, then, was what he really wanted—sour Dante, grim Dante of the uncompromising profile—this is what he thought reality was like, when you got to the *eterna fontana* at the centre of it: this laughter, this inebriation, this riot of charity and hilarity. Possibly, in the flesh, he did not smile very much upon the universe; certainly, during his twenty years of exile, it had not smiled much on him. But he claimed, rightly, that he had never lost faith in it, nor hope nor love either. He had never thought to blame God for his misfortunes, nor "blasphemously to inveigh against the creation", and wherever he is now, he is not sprawled upon the burning sand with Capaneus. Out of some inexhaustible spring in his fierce heart this great fountain of happiness comes bursting and bubbling. The *stupor* that we share with Dante, thus "from glory unto glory advancing", is accompanied by a minor, yet not unworthy, *stupor* at "the achieve, the mastery of the

---

[1] No son of the Church Militant has more hope than he . . . the other two points I leave to him, for he will not find them hard, nor will he try to show off; so let him answer to this.

> *Para.* xxv. 52–53; 58, 61–62.

[2]   . . . till I grew
    Drunk with the sweetness of the singing host;

And everywhere I looked I seemed to view
    One smile of all creation, ear and eye
    Drinking alike the inebriate rapture through.
                    Para. xxvii. 3–6.

thing". It is a marvel to watch mere poetry, mere words, thus go up and up, and to feel such inner certainty that we can trust the poet to take them all the way, the song growing shriller and sweeter the higher it soars:

> quale allodetta che in aere si spazia
> prima cantando, e poi tace contenta
> dell' ultima dolcezza che la sazia.[1]

With Dante it is for once not true that to travel hopefully is better than to arrive. We arrive, and the arrival is satisfactory. The adventure of the passionate intellect is achieved, and it is so because Dante's passions really are seated in his intellect, and not, as with so many of us, marooned in his heart and liver, without means of access to the brain. On whatever rarefied flights the story-teller sets out, he can take his whole equipment with him.

This accounts for a phenomenon which shocks some readers as much as it transports others. Throughout the entire *Comedy* one thing remains constant: the quality of the similes. They are all brief and all directly functional,[2] and from first to last they are earthy, homely, and concrete. Driven at close intervals into the fabric of the poem, they stud the surface like strong holding-pins, pegging it immovably to daily experience, and superimposing on its flowing pattern an all-over diaper of their own. Considered in themselves they are astonishingly varied, ranging from the coarsest to the most delicate, and from the ridiculous to the sublime; but this variety does not coincide with the progressive variation of the poetic treatment. We do not find all the gross similes in the gross bits and all the noble similes in the noble bits; and the images are neither dehumanised in Hell nor trans-humanised in Heaven. Almost anything may be likened to almost anything, provided that it is like, and that we shall follow the story

---

[1] Like to the lark, which soars into the sky
Singing at first, and then, with utter bliss
Filled to the full, falls silent by and by.
Para. xx. 73–75.

[2] That is, they all directly illuminate the story by supplying a real likeness for the object or action described. They are never "fudged in" for the *sole* purpose of creating a mood or an atmosphere, although they frequently do this as well. Compare, for example, the handling of the phoenix-simile which trails a whiff of incense across the squalors of the Seventh Bolgia (*Inf.* xxiv. 106–111) with that of the fish-stink parallel which performs an equal and opposite office in *Paradise Lost,* iv. 166–171.

better for seeing the likeness. The lovely similes of the fireflies, and the chariot of Elijah—"*la fiamma sola, sì come nuvoletta*"[1]—occur in the Eighth Bolgia; in the Eighth Heaven the form of our great First Father, hidden in the light that veils it (as those other spirits are shrouded in the fire of their own torment) makes itself guessed—how? like something one might see in any market town:

> *Tal volta un animal coperto broglia*
> *sì che l'affetto convien che si paia*
> *per lo seguir che face a lui l'invoglia.*[2]

It was like that, says Dante, anxious that we should get this rather difficult picture clear, and caring nothing for the outraged suscepti-bilities of Mr. John Addington Symonds. In the Heaven of Mars, the noble Maccabaeus flashes and spins, "*e letizia era ferza del paleo*—and joy was the whip to the top". On Mount Purgatory the souls impor-tune Dante for his prayers, like the hangers-on who cluster round a successful gambler. In Hell the lost lovers wheel like starlings and drop like doves; and deep in the filthy circle of disease and madness two leprous horrors sit propped together domestically, "like a couple of pans set to warm by the fire". Fish, frogs, insects, beasts, and birds of every description flit and gambol through all the circles of the Three Kingdoms; cooks, tailors, blacksmiths, shepherds, and seamen ply their trades indiscriminately in deep Hell or high Heaven, and flowers spring up in the most unexpected places.

But this unity-in-diversity of the incidental imagery is only made appropriate or possible by the massive unity of the poem itself; and this is something which we cannot perceive unless we read the thing properly, from start to finish, as a story should be read. An anthology of the "beauties of Dante" would exclude the architectural beauty which is the poem's chief glory, and would successfully prevent the full appreciation even of such beauties as it did include. Even artisti-cally the powerful substructure of the *Inferno* appears objectless until we see the great leaping shafts and pinnacles it was built to carry; consequently, those who spend their whole time grubbing about the vaults of the *Comedy* rather naturally carry away with them little

---

[1] just a flame, like a little cloud.
[2] Sometimes an animal, concealed from view
　　Inside a sack, wriggles, and so we see
　　Its every movement as the sack moves too.
                    Para. xxvi. 97–99.

impression of Dante except a grimness of heavy stone and a savour of decay. But it would be equally disastrous if a fashion for "spirituality" and a reluctance to believe in judgement should swing us to the opposite extreme, and cause the *Inferno* to be boycotted in its turn; for, even artistically, it is impossible to appreciate the narrative method of the *Paradiso* unless we see just what it is that has been thus trans-humanised and transmuted into air and fire. "Begin at the beginning", said the King of Hearts, very properly, "and go on till you come to the end; then stop." Having done this once, we can, of course, go back and linger over the bits we like best, or begin all over again; but a story is a story and our first acquaintance with it should not be made higgledy-piggledy or back to front. That is not the author's intention; if it had been he would have written something else—a bunch of lyrics or a Manual of Devotions, or a Handy Guide to Trecento Politics, or a series of Pen-portraits of Mediaeval Celebrities. The *Comedy* is none of these things: it is a story. It is called a "comedy", says Dante, because "if we have respect to its content, at the beginning it is horrible and fetid, for it is Hell; and in the end it is prosperous, desirable and gracious, for it is Paradise". And, having by singular good fortune contrived to make its acquaintance in the order, and under the aspect, intended by its creator, I find myself disposed to echo the verdict of the three obnoxious children in the Saki story mentioned above:

"The story began badly," said the smaller of the small girls, "but it had a beautiful ending."

"It is the most beautiful that I ever heard," said the bigger of the small girls, with immense decision.

"It is the *only* beautiful story I have ever heard," said Cyril.

THE DIVINE POET AND THE
ANGELIC DOCTOR

IT was formerly the critical fashion to imply that the *Comedy*, theologically considered, was little more than a versified paraphrase of the *Summa*. Recently, energetic efforts have been made to show that in many respects Dante was anything but an orthodox and obedient Thomist. Augustinian and Aristotelian, Franciscan and Dominican have shed their ink freely in the battle for his allegiance, forgetting perhaps too readily those words in which Molière proclaimed the roving acquisitiveness of all poets: *"je prends mon bien partout où je le trouve"*. There are many "influences" with which we have to reckon when reading Dante: Boethius and the Victorines, the lyricists of Provence, and also the *roman courtois* and the whole of that *matière de Bretagne* to which the *Commedia* is in many ways more closely affiliated than to the Virgilian epic which Dante himself acknowledged as his model. It is, indeed, at the point where the *Comedy* touches the poetry of courtly love that it departs furthest from St. Thomas. As Charles Williams has remarked: "It seems likely that St. Thomas would have found some difficulty in apprehending Dante's whole Beatrician theme." [1] For St. Thomas agreed with Augustine that, if it had not been for the necessity of propagating the human species, another man would have made a much better companion for Adam than Eve ever could. Dante did not take this view, and I cannot help thinking that our civilisation might have been spared many unfortunate mistakes if we had, in this connection, paid a little more attention to what Dante was trying to tell us. But this is not part of my subject: I only mention it as a reminder that Dante was not so exclusively dominated by St. Thomas that he could not take a line of his own on occasion—and on very important occasions. There was no reason, in the beginning of the fourteenth century, why Dante, or anybody, should have been dominated by Aquinas, who was at that time not by any means the official theologian of the Roman Church, but, on the contrary, a rather dangerous "modern" who had incorporated a pagan scheme of philosophy into Christian dogmatic teaching, somewhat to the scandal and alarm of the old-fashioned orthodox. This was St. Thomas's supreme

[1] *The Figure of Beatrice*, p. 191.

38

achievement and it was this masterly triumph of synthesis that took hold of Dante's imagination and made it possible for him to present in the *Divine Comedy* his great orderly and architectural image of the universe. Never did two great minds so fit together hand and glove in a single undertaking. The impact of the Ancient World upon the New in the First Renaissance might have shaken Europe to pieces if St. Thomas had not shown theology how to baptise the old into the new, and if Dante had not shown Poetry—and, in a sense, the other arts— how to effect a fusion of the two. The later Renaissance did shake the world, but not so badly as it might have done if these two strong iron girders had not already been run through its structure. At that later date there was neither theologian nor poet with the necessary mental equipment for making a new synthesis; but at least nobody could undo the thing that had been done. The *Summa* and the *Comedy* still stood there, not only as completed achievements, but also as models and reminders of the kind of synthesis which might be effected, and of the right way to effect it. In our present distracted age, we most desperately need an Aquinas—and perhaps more desperately still a Dante—with the range and the grasp adequate for perceiving the universal complex as an orderly whole and presenting it to us in an adequate argument and an adequate image. In particular we require someone who can do for the inductive method of scientific reasoning what Aquinas and Dante between them did for the deductive method of Aristotelian logic, by bringing it into relation on the one hand with revealed Christian truth and on the other with personal, emotional, and—in the wider sense—political experience. To get either theologian or poet by himself would be a great thing—to get both at once might be salvation: but it is probably too much to expect that such an astonishing conjunction of major planets should occur a second time within a thousand years.

In the meantime, however, nobody can rob us of Dante and Aquinas themselves, and for all our progress we have not out-run them yet. Indeed we have scarcely caught up with them. As the Red Queen rudely remarked, "it takes all the running *you* can do to stay in the same place". We have to peg along pretty fast if we are not to fall behind such very great minds as these. And I am not sure that Dante—or St. Thomas and all the rest as mediated after Dante's manner—has not even more to offer to the world's present necessities than St. Thomas unmediated. For the language, and indeed the whole frame of discourse, of the schoolmen is difficult and alien to the generation which has learnt its thinking along different lines; but the great poetic images are timeless and changeless. True, the images themselves often have to be interpreted, when they are images of something that the reader has not experienced. But where there is experience, the image does its own interpreting. A man may remain impervious to argument or proof, or may simply not understand what you are driving at; and then some poetic image which does not attempt to prove but merely *shows* him the thing as it is, may get home, and he will say: "My God, yes!—that's it—that's me!" That is one of the reasons why, at the beginning of the *Comedy*, when Dante is lost in the Dark Wood, Beatrice cannot herself go to rescue him. She sends Virgil. "I fear I have risen up too late to help him, he is so far astray. But go thou—lift up thy golden voice, use every means to reach him." He is dead to grace, dead to religion and dead to theology, but even at the lowest level, even at the mouth of Hell, poetry can still touch him. That is, in itself, a poetic image of an important and very subtle truth.

We do not know a Dante uninfluenced by Thomas Aquinas. The *Vita Nuova* does indeed deal with the earlier part of his life, before the death of Beatrice made a break and turned his mind to the consolations of philosophy and the doctrine of the Schools; but the book itself was not written until after he had become acquainted with St. Thomas. From the *Vita* we get the impression of a rather moony and sentimental young man, engaged in making more or less serious love to various young women, staring them out of countenance in church, circulating sonnets among a small circle of friends, attending parties, and weeping a great deal over a passionate attachment which subjected him to a certain amount of ridicule among his acquaintance. He displays himself in these attitudes with a sort of humorous compassion—for, except in the period of his life covered by the *Convivio*, Dante was always ready to laugh at himself—but also with an overpowering conviction that in his vision of what Beatrice was he had got hold of something of enormous importance—some experience which held the clue to *all* experience, if only he could get it across to us. Even so—preoccupied as he was with this experience—he leaves many things out of his self-portrait. Nobody would guess, for instance, from reading the *Vita* that while (as the B.B.C. announcers would say) "all this was going on", a war was also going on, and that he served in it, if without special distinction at any rate without discredit. Nor does he say what, if anything, he studied at this time, beyond the reading and writing of love-poetry. But we do know that, after Beatrice's death in 1290 and before the writing of the *Vita*, his studies in St. Thomas had begun. The first effects of this might seem to be a little unfortunate. The *Vita* itself is, in form, a prose framework in which are inset a number of poems written to and about Beatrice, and all of these he feels himself bound to analyse in the manner of St. Thomas in his commentaries upon Aristotle, so that a perfectly straightforward and not very remarkable sonnet is followed up by a ruthless dissection, in this manner:

This sonnet can be divided into four parts: in the first I say and propound that all my thoughts are of love; in the second I say that they are diverse and I recount their diversity; in the third I say in what they all seem to accord; in the fourth, etc., etc. . . . The second part begins here: *And have in them*; the third: *And they only accord*; the fourth: *Wherefore I know not*.

The reader, impatient with so much elaboration of the obvious, may be excused for wishing that Dante had left St. Thomas alone. And yet, I don't know. Dante's style of versifying—*il dolce stil nuovo*—was considered modern and advanced in his day, and may have presented more difficulties to his contemporaries than it does to us. When I look at the works of our own younger poets I could find it in my heart to wish that—for example—Mr. Dylan Thomas had been a fervent Thomist and had condescended to furnish us with an analysis saying plainly what his poems are about, and what they say, and at what point they begin to say it.

It is clear at any rate that by this time Dante had fallen in love with a method—one often falls in love with an author's method before falling in love with his matter—and possibly what he had fallen in love with was method and order for their own sakes. His later work, the *Convivio*, also a set of poems with much longer and more elaborate analysis and commentary, is a very orgy of method. It was intended to be a kind of popular compendium of the philosophy and science of the period; and its arguments are set out with so many firstlies and secondlies, so many divisions, subdivisions and recapitulations, and such a display of syllogistic ingenuity, that modern editors, in order to disentangle its dialectic, find themselves using several sets of numerals and at least a couple of Greek and Roman alphabets in their efforts to follow its intricacies down the margins. Rather mercifully, perhaps, Dante abandoned the *Convivio* when only four of the intended treatises were completed. He had discovered that his true vocation was indeed to present the world with an orderly scheme of the universe, but in the form, not of an argument but of an image. He discovered, in short, that he was a story-teller. But the practice of orderly method had done his work for him. It was because he had learned to schematise his arguments that he was able to build the forty-four great circles of Hell and Purgatory and Heaven, and to hold together the threads of his tremendous story and its fourfold allegorical interpretation without omissions, without internal contradictions and without disproportion. Compare, for instance, Virgil's underworld, with its melodious, suggestive, but vague and random evocation of great names and images, with the massive and orderly intellectual architecture of the *Inferno*. See how the great rivers which stray through the fields of Tartarus, Melchisedek-like, without beginning of descent or end of days, are by Dante canalised into their three great circles—broad Acheron, marshy Styx, and burning Phlegethon, till, steaming between the dykes across the Abominable Sand, they cascade over the Great Barrier to form the ice of Cocytus. Economy, precision—the mere assigning of place and function, work here, not to diminish the poetry, but to enhance the image to an enormous scale of magnitude.

It was, I think, to Aquinas that Dante owed not only his passion for order, but his grasp of the universe, and of history, as something orderly, which made sense all through. I have seen foolish criticisms of Dante which said, sneeringly, that he inhabited a "narrow little clockwork universe". Dante's universe is not narrow or small, but he did see it as ordered; and this is what offends an age accustomed to see reality as disorderly and inconclusive. We have become antagonistic to the very idea of order—although, rather inconsistently, we are accustomed to put a good deal of faith in "planning". The physicists have disturbed us with the information that matter is not ordered—it merely tumbles about till it happens to tumble into patterns. Dante, of course, did not know that—the science of his day only saw the patterns and supposed that they were made intentionally; for us it is necessary to go a step further back and inquire why matter is made of such a kind that patterns result from its tumbling, or why we are so made that we perceive randomness as pattern. We have been further disturbed by the biologists, who, being some fifty years behind the physicists, are still unable to come to any conclusion about the patterns exhibited by organic matter—having more or less abandoned the theory of randomness and being still unwilling to accept the notion of diathesis. The psychologists have caused the worst disturbance by arguing that the conscious reason is fallacious—though this result, being reached by their own conscious reason, is presumably fallacious along with the rest. At any rate, they leave us uncertain whether we ought to suppress the conscious and let the unconscious take control, or, on the contrary, merely investigate the unconscious with a view to bringing it more perfectly under the control of the conscious. About this, neither Dante nor Aquinas would have had any doubts at all: they believed that the *virtus* of man consisted in the exercise of the conscious reason—the intellect as they understood it. The damned, said Dante, are precisely those who have "lost the good of the intellect". Only we must remember that for him "intellect" did not mean something that was the exclusive possession of "intellectuals" in Oxford or Bloomsbury; it meant all those powers characteristic of man, which make him so oddly different from all his fellow-animals—it included the intuitions and the imagination.

For Dante and Aquinas, then, the universe meant something; it made sense; it had order. And the order was a Christian order. This order God Himself had revealed. But how was one to fit into this ordered scheme, based on revelation, the findings of the natural reason, as arrived at by the great pagan philosophies? Obviously, something had to be done about it. Either one must say, with Tertullian, that all human reason, and consequently all philosophy, art, and literature not supernaturally revealed, was nothing and worse than nothing—which was the position later taken up by the Calvinists and the modern Barthians, and also by one school of modern psychologists (who, of course, reject revelation as well). Or one must find a means of reconciliation, which would fit all these human activities into the revealed order of things, and permit Christianity to follow the way of Affirmation along with (though not necessarily instead of) the way of Negation. This was the second great crisis at which the Church had been faced with this choice, and for the second time she decided against Tertullian. She decided to include rather than to exclude. She made it possible to sanctify the reason and the arts. For the second time in her history she set free and blessed all the images.

For this happy—though perhaps dangerous and adventurous—decision we are above all grateful to St. Thomas. And those who love Dante have especially much to be grateful for. I will not say that without this decision there would have been no *Divine Comedy*, but the poem would have lacked much of what we chiefly love in it. We should have lost, for instance, the grandiose conception of the twenty-four circles of Hell, with their three main divisions, on the Aristotelian plan, into the sins of Incontinence, Violence and Fraud. This might not have mattered much—Dante would have been quite capable of analysing sin for himself; but the structure which he extracted from the *Ethics* had at least one great poetic advantage for him, in that it allowed him to use a classification of sins which (thanks to St. Thomas's vindication of Aristotle) had authority, and yet was not the ecclesiastical division into the Seven Capital Sins, which he needed for the structure of Purgatory. Again: we should have lost all the classical monsters with which the *Inferno* is so pleasingly diversified—for he could hardly, I think, have accepted the classic myths as true images, even of sin, if he had felt obliged to deny *all* validity to classical thought. His Hell would have been much more like that of the Apocryphal *Apocalypse of Paul* (from which he did borrow some images of torments), in which the tormentors are all simply "devils". This would have been, poetically, a very sad loss. But the greatest loss of all and one which typifies and sums up all the rest would have been that we should not have had Virgil—the most beloved and the most tenderly drawn of all Dante's vast gallery of human portraits. Some angel, or personified abstraction, would have had to escort Dante through Hell and Purgatory; but no angel or allegorical figure could be what Virgil is—not only Dante's "gentle father", his "*duca, signore e maestro*", but *our* Virgil, the sweet singer of Italy, who is not only poetry but Rome, and in whom Rome's great past joins up with Christian Rome and with the Christian era, of whom the Middle Ages held him to have been a prophet. The denial of the entire pagan past which Tertullian's position involves would have had this particular consequence for Dante's poem, and robbed it of some of its greatest beauty, its most delicate comedy and its most piercing pathos. Nobody who has ever read the *Comedy* with any sort of feeling for its poetry has been able to resist the charm of Virgil; and the sense of banishment and exclusion which pervades the whole of Hell is made deeper because Virgil is there in everlasting and nostalgic exile.

It is by seeing just what Dante did with Virgil that we can best understand how he translated St. Thomas's synthesis into his own imagery. A great deal of misconception hangs round this whole matter in people's minds—very largely because so many readers merely skim through the *Inferno* for the picturesque passages and the juicier tortures, neglecting the other two books which complete the imagery and set Dante's conception of Hell in its right relation to the rest. That is an injustice to Dante. I think moreover that a better understanding of Dante's image might have saved us a good deal of heartburning and

confusion in this business of reconciling heathen and Christian philosophies and accepting the pagan *preparatio Evangelii*; and it might also
have saved certain reproaches that are made against Christianity
because of the doctrine of Hell. That doctrine seems harsh and is stern;
but an intelligent reading of Dante should have saved us from ever
supposing it to be arbitrary or vindictive.

To take the first point first—that is, the relation between the pagan
philosophies (or natural religion, or the ethics of reason) and the
Christian revelation. A misconception about this is shown very clearly
in a sentence in Roden Buxton's on the whole excellent little book
Prophets of Heaven and Hell. I quote this because I have the book
handy, but I have met the same misrepresentation elsewhere, so I suppose the error to be fairly common. Roden Buxton says:

> [Dante's] conception of the Earthly Paradise is that human wisdom and
> virtue [i.e. Virgil], unaided by Revelation, can lead man to a certain per-
> fection, which he reaches at the summit of the Purgatorial Mountain; it is
> the "identical garden which Adam and Eve inhabited before the Fall".

And he says that Dante got this conception from Aquinas, who
"placed Reason side by side with Revelation as one of the twin sources
of Truth".[1]

Now this sweeping simplification goes further, I fancy, than Aquinas
meant, and it is certainly not in the least what Dante wrote. He had,
indeed, written something very like it in the *Convivio*; but the *Commedia* is not merely a development of the *Convivio*, it is also a retractation.

To begin with, Virgil (as representing human wisdom and art and
virtue) does not, of his own initiative, lead Dante even through Hell;
he is *sent* by Beatrice. It is true that, in Hell, he is left, so to speak, to
act on his own and conduct the expedition as it pleases him. "Thou art
my lord," says Dante, "and knowest that I depart not from thy will."
Virgil has been through Hell before and knows the way from top to
bottom, and in Hell he exercises authority and can command and quell
the spirits with words of power. Yet, even so, there is one great exception: he cannot, in his own power, get Dante past the gates of the
City of Dis, which are shut against them by the fallen Angels, and
guarded by the Furies and the Gorgon. They have to wait for the
promised aid, the mysterious messenger from Heaven, who comes down
with a noise like thunder, shaking all Hell and scattering the spirits

[1] Roden Buxton: *Prophets of Heaven and Hell* (C.U.P., 1945), p. 77.

like frogs as he passes the Stygian marsh. He strikes the gates with his wand and they fly open. If we remember that, in Dante's allegory, Hell is only literally the place of spirits after death, but in its allegorical—
—i.e. its most real—meaning, the descent into the hidden deeps and evil possibilities in the soul, we see that Dante was insisting on, and embodying in a mighty image, a very important limitation of human wisdom. It cannot, of itself—reason cannot, and even poetry cannot— get the soul past the Furies (the futile remorse which can only tear and rend without bringing repentance) or the Gorgon (the obduracy which petrifies the will and makes it obstinate in its own perversity). At the gates of Dis, which lead from the sins of Incontinence, or failure of will, to the Nether Hell in which the will is actively involved in the sin, the soul exploring its own darkness has only two alternatives: to turn back if it can, and so wander for ever in the illusions of the Dark Wood and the purlieus of Upper Hell, or to continue through the gates till it has died to the worst possibilities of the self and faced the principle of destruction at the bottom of them. To pass that point, rational Human- ism is helpless; as indeed we see clearly enough, in the failure both of the heathen philosophies and of the Humanism of our own time, which have never been able to cope with the Furies and the Gorgon. A direct interference by Grace is necessary—though it may come, as Dante's angel comes, in a disguise terrifying, alien, and almost hostile.

After the passage of the gates, Virgil takes charge again, and leads Dante safely to the bottom of the Abyss—with only one perilous moment, due to under-estimating the sheer motiveless malice of the evil will—an error to which Humanism is always a little prone. And so, climbing up again by a hidden way, the two poets emerge at the Antipodes, on the shores of the island of Mount Purgatory.

But here there is a great change. Virgil has never been here before and does not know the way—he has to ask at every turn. He uses no words of power, he exercises no authority—he is under authority him- self. At the entrance to Purgatory proper he is challenged by the Angel of the Church, and it is only when he learns that the pilgrims are sent to him by St. Lucy that this "courteous porter" consents to receive them. From here to the top of the ascent of repentance, Dante and Virgil are under the authority of the Church—that is, of revealed religion. Human wisdom—and this is where Aquinas and Dante part company from Tertullian—human wisdom can, under God, rescue the soul from destruction and can, with Divine assistance, be its guide through and out of Hell; it can *accompany*, and assist, the soul right up the hill

of repentance to the point where the lost Paradise of original righteousness is regained, but not in its own strength or by its own right. After
that, it can do no more, and go no further.

And here we begin to see how Dante's image clarifies the relations
between the human and the Divine Wisdom. It was, I believe, St.
Thomas who defined the doctrine of Limbo, which he divides into
two parts—the Limbo Patrum, from which Christ brought out the
souls of Adam and Eve and the Patriarchs at the Harrowing of Hell;
and the Limbo Paganorum, in which the souls of the just Heathen
dwell, neither blessed nor tormented. In the Sixth Book of the *Aeneid*,
which (owing to St. Thomas's synthesis) he was free to draw upon,
Dante found the souls of the virtuous and heroic dead occupying the
Elysian Fields, which lie beneath the earth, and the entrance to which
lies adjacent to the entrance to Tartarus, a great Pit running away to
a depth below the earth equal to twice the height of Heaven. By two
great strokes of the imagination he welds these two conceptions
together: he equates the Limbo Paganorum with the Elysian Fields,
and he makes that place part of the topmost circle of Hell. And this is
the image that defines the relations between the realms of human and
Divine Wisdom. He concedes to Humanist and pagan philosophy all
that it conceded to itself; he allows it full validity in its own place, and
he endows it with the nature and degree of immortal blessedness with
which it had endowed itself. And he looks at it and sees that, even at
its best, it is only the upper circle of Hell; the whole Christian experience is piled above it.

And this throws light on the second point I mentioned—the
question about the nature of Hell. Dante insists over and over again
that nobody is ever *sent* to Hell. Men go there of their own will. Hell
is the state in which the will remains fixed eternally in that which it
insisted on having; the torments it endures are simply the sin itself,
experienced at last, without illusion, as that which it really is. If you
are determined to go to Hell, then you must. In desolating phrases
he speaks of the entrance to Hell: "On that door no bars remain for
ever"; "the gate whose threshold is denied to none"; "the wide-open
door". One is reminded of Maritain's sentence: "It is a fearful thing
to fall into the hands of the living God, for they give to every man
that which he has desired." And having desired Hell, the souls still
desire it, though they detest it. They long to pass Acheron, for "the
heavenly justice goads them so that all their fear is changed into desire".

And so, when it comes to the good pagans, Dante was himself

tormented by their exclusion from Heaven, and indeed went so far as to define the means by which some of them might actually attain a Christian bliss. But in the main, he is obliged to acquiesce in their remaining suspended in Limbo. "I lost Heaven", says Virgil, "for one thing only: that I had not faith." True, he did not know the Christian revelation. But faith is imagination actualised by the will. What was lacking in the heathen philosophies was precisely the imagination of bliss. They had not, so to speak, sufficient faith in the good intentions of the universe. All through the *Inferno*, the heathen sinners are judged by their own standards. Capaneus blasphemes against Jove, and Virgil comments: "He held, and still holds, God in disdain"—meaning by that, precisely, "God". Dante has placed no heathens in the Circle of the Suicides, for suicide in itself was not necessarily held sinful by pagan thought—indeed, Cato, who killed himself for the sake of justice, is given a privileged place as the guardian of Purgatory. Throughout Hell, we find twofold invocations of power: Christian and pagan—as when Virgil says to the demons in Malebolge: "Do you think I could have come so far had I not been led by Divine Will and Fates propitious?" So, the greatest and most virtuous of the heathen are judged by their own standards and "have what they desired". They suffer only from knowing that it is inadequate—but then, they always did know it to be inadequate, only they had not the faith to imagine better.

One does not, I think, quite realise the meaning of this, and the accuracy of Dante's judgement, till very much later in the poem. I have said that Dante equates the Limbo of the pagan heroes and sages with the Elysian Fields, and I think there is no doubt that he meant to do this. As we pass through the sighing shades—"the wood", says Dante, the *nemus*, "where souls stand thick as trees"—we come to a light, which makes a glowing hemisphere, a serene radiance:

> *Largior hic campos aether et lumine vestit*
> *purpureo, solemque suum, sua sidera norunt.*[1]

We meet the great poets and are taken to a noble castle, surrounded by a sevenfold stream—a mediaevalisation of the

> *Cyclopum aducta caminis moenia.*[2]

---

[1] Therein a more abundant heaven clothes all the meadows' face
With purple light, and their own sun and their own stars they have.
Aen. vi. 640–641 (trans. W. Morris).

[2] . . . the walls in Cyclops' furnace wrought.
Aen. vi. 630–631.

and the grove where

> *plurimus Eridani per silvam volvitur amnis.*[1]

Within, on an "enamelled green", we meet all the Trojan heroes and the great philosophers. Dante does not say what they were all doing; but, to be fair to the ancients, we can supply this from the *Aeneid* itself:

> *pars in gramineis exercent membra palestris,*
> *contendunt ludo et fulvâ luctantur harenâ;*
> *pars pedibus plaudunt choreas et carmina dicunt . . .*
> *stant terrâ defixae hastae, passimque soluti*
> *per campum pascuntur equi . . .* [2]

It is beautiful—everybody knows it is beautiful. But if one happens to come to it, as I did accidentally the other day, immediately after reading the *Paradiso*, the shock is indescribable. Dante's Christian Heaven pulsates with a passionate energy, a sheer, superabundant intellectual ecstasy. It is *un riso dell' universo*—the laughter of the universe—joy bubbles and spills over as the souls wheel and dance with the wheeling spheres. Dante uses the word *ebbrezza*—it is an intoxication of delight that is communicated to him—until in the height of the Empyrean, "the still point of the turning world", all is merged into the intense rapture of contemplation—contemplation of the *eterna fontana*, the eternal Fountain of all being. The great song goes soaring up, shrill and sweet as a skylark—*quale allodetta*. The poet's power, says Dante, fails the high vision, yet he could imagine this, and sustain and communicate his imagination. And it is from this that we look down on the Elysian Fields and see them for what they are—the *inania regna*— the empty kingdoms. The bodiless games, the shadowy and pathetic horses, even the choric odes and the conversations of philosophy— there is nothing here to give everlasting satisfaction to the passionate intellect. This is the best of Virgil's imagination—and it is all touched with the eternal futility and the eternal melancholy which is Hell.

---

[1] The full flood that Eridanus athwart the wood doth pour.
Aen. vi. 659.

[2] Here some in games upon the grass their bodies breathing gave;
Or on the yellow face of sand they strive and play the play;
Some beat the earth with dancing foot, and some, the song they say . . .
. . . stand the spears in earth, unyoked the horses are,
And graze the meadows all about . . .
Aen. vi. 642–644; 651–653.

The Catholic Church does, of course, recognise the efficacy of "baptism by desire". It has, I believe, been argued that Dante did not know of this, but on what grounds I do not know, since he could have read of it in the *Summa* (III. 1. xviii. 2). In any case, he gives us, in the Heaven of the Just, something which corresponds to it, and extends the conception to its extreme limit. Trajan, being recalled to life by the prayers of St. Gregory, "believed and in believing was kindled to such fire of true love that upon his second death he was found worthy to come to this bliss". Rhipeus, living many centuries before Christ, loved justice with so passionate a love that, says Dante, "God opened his eyes" (note the figure—for the eyes are the organs which perceive *images*; they typify imagination)—"God opened his eyes to our future redemption". To behold and love the face of Justice is to behold and love the face of Christ. Thus, through their faith and hope and charity Trajan and Rhipeus

> . . . died not heathen, as thou deemest it,
> But faithful Christians, clinging, he and he,
> To the passion-pierced, to the yet-to-be-passible feet.[1]

But for Virgil Dante dared not invoke this possibility; he dared not, quite apart from the fact that the unbaptised and unredeemed Virgil was necessary for the purpose of his poem. For he had before him the record of Virgil's best imagination, and he knew it to be inadequate. Virgil has to remain in his Elysian Fields—thus equated with the Limbo Paganorum—where they live "in desire without hope", suffering (as the Church, with St. Thomas, had decided) no punishment of sense, but only that nostalgia which is the privation of the vision of God.

Such, then, is the image which Dante found for the Thomist synthesis. So far as they go, human wisdom is valid, art is valid, science and philosophy and natural ethics, and even natural religion are valid; they can avail to preserve the soul from the lowest deeps—they can by proof and reason establish an overwhelming case for theism, and, under the authority of religion and in the power of Grace, they can sustain and fortify the soul for a long way on its journey. But they do not form a substitute for the redeemed life in Grace; of themselves they can climb no higher than the Elysian Fields, and in any case they can get no further than the Earthly Paradise—the Heavenly Paradise belongs to another universe of discourse altogether. I believe that, if this image

[1] *Para.* xx. 103–105.

had been kept more closely in mind, there need not have been, at the Reformation, so sharp a split between the followers of Aquinas and the followers of Tertullian—between the way of Negation and the way of Affirmation.

In Paradise, Dante meets the spirit of St. Thomas. It is significant that the Heaven of the Doctors in which he finds him—the sphere of the Sun—should be characterised rather especially as a Heaven of Reconciliation. The reconciliation—the synthesis—between Aristotelianism and Christianity is not discussed there;[1] what we see or hear in that Heaven is the union in joy and charity of the various schools of theologians and the various ecclesiastical orders. On earth, they may have been often in dispute: here they are at one. Disputation ceases; they delight in praising one another. Aquinas the Dominican extols the holiness of Francis of Assisi; Bonaventure the Franciscan extols the holiness of Dominic. The Angelic and the Seraphic Doctors exchange these celestial compliments, Bonaventure saying charmingly as he concludes his panegyric on Dominic: "To emulous speech of so great a paladin the enkindled courtesy—*l'infiammata cortesia*—of Brother Thomas and his judicious and learned discourse—*il discreto latino*—moved me, and moved this company with me." In that "company"—in that halo of rejoicing souls—St. Thomas shines and circles side by side with Sigier of Brabant, whose opponent he was in the schools, and with them too is Joachim of Flora, who is pointed out to Dante by his opponent Bonaventure. Other theologians, whose doctrines were not always held to be strictly orthodox, are here too, such as Boethius and Rabanus Maurus. I think that Dante, who possessed a most delicate sense of comedy, probably amused as well as delighted himself by thus proclaiming the heavenly concord of the doctors, for he must have known as much as most people of the disagreement of theologians. He does not express in so many words his personal debt to Aquinas, but he acknowledges and pays it in his own way: significantly, he makes St. Thomas the first soul to greet him on his arrival in the Sun; when he is troubled by theological perplexities St. Thomas solves them; it is into St. Thomas's mouth that he puts the famous and lovely eulogy of the Lady Poverty. Here in the Heaven of the Sun we see all the Doctors rejoicing together, and, says Dante:

As the horologe that calls us, what time the bride of God rises to sing

[1] It is, however, hinted at, cf. *The Paradoxes of the Comedy, Introductory Papers*, p. 179.

matins to her Spouse that He may love her, wherein one part drawing and thrusting another gives out a chime of so sweet a note that the ready spirit swells with love; so did I see the glorious wheel revolve, voice answering to voice in a harmony and sweetness that may not be known, except where joy makes itself eternal—

se non colà dove gioir s'insempra.

(Aquinas Society
1946)

DANTE'S VIRGIL

I HAVE called this paper *Dante's Virgil*. For a complete study, the title might well be "Dante's Seven Virgils", for one can, without confounding the persons or dividing the substance, distinguish at least that number in the poetic manifold which Dante evokes by the name "Virgilio", and every one of them merits a lecture to himself. Where the material is so rich, one can only select rather arbitrarily. I shall not attempt, for instance, to discuss at length the poetic use which Dante has made of Virgil's own works—for that would need a better Virgilian scholar than I am; neither shall I say very much about the concept of the Empire, which has of late received a great deal of critical attention. I shall try to deal briefly with two of the points which are most likely to exercise the minds of those who love Virgil: his symbolical significance in Dante's allegory, and (arising out of this) the necessity of his damnation, which has, I suppose, at some time troubled all of us, as indeed it troubled Dante. And finally I shall try to indicate how the symbolic significance dictates and is woven with the character and actions of Virgil as he appears in the first two books of the *Comedy*.

I shall make no apology for speaking from the Christian and theological point of view, still less for concentrating on the allegorical aspect of the poem. One of the most remarkable developments in contemporary literature and criticism is the return to meaning, which has brought with it a striking revival of allegorical form. We have passed through a period in which it was fashionable to despise or ignore the intellectual content of a work of art, and to endeavour to find its poetic significance in its form alone, arbitrarily separated from its matter. I need scarcely say how this unnatural disjunction of inseparables would have shocked and horrified the Schoolmen, not to say Dante himself; and the total inappropriateness of the doctrine of "Art for art's sake" to any intelligent appreciation of the *Commedia* may be clearly seen in the desperate struggles of the Crocean school of critics to find in the work a "poetic unity" distinct from its intellectual and ethical structure. Dante himself, in whom the passionate intellect is always integral with the emotions and the will, would have dismissed with a Gilbertian contempt both the criticism and the poetry of irrationalism, "which is pretty" (or, as the case may be, ugly) "but I don't know what it means". What Dante meant, he meant intensely; and a generation which, distracted by the loss of meaning, has learned to recognise its own distractions in the nightmare allegories of a Franz Kafka may well turn to Dante and once again read his poem as he intended it to be read: as a discovery of the eternal certitudes in the midst of perplexities, and a means "*removere viventes in hac vita de statu miseriae, et perducere ad statum felicitatis*".[1]

Allegory was, in Dante's time, what it shows signs of becoming again: the dominant literary form. For us, this form is made difficult and obscure by the loss, in a civilisation whose whole structure is being shattered and remade, of many of the great traditional archetypes, and by that increasing ignorance of the universal poetic sources which goes with a widespread superficial literacy. In the fourteenth century, these archetypes were still living in the structure of society—kingship, fatherhood, hierarchy, veneration, obedience, sacrifice, the order of nature, the unity of the city—such concepts still held a meaning for every reader, and their types were available to the poet's hand in the Bible, in the Classics, and in contemporary life. The allegorical form of the *Comedy* is consistently maintained throughout. Dante's handling differs from what may be called "standard practice", only by his very free use of modern historical personages as allegorical symbols, and by the fact that he uses a minimum of arbitrary, and the maximum of natural symbolism. About this we must say a few words.

A natural symbol is a particular instance of a universal truth. Merely by being what it is, it displays in its very structure a pattern which runs throughout space and time, so that by examining the symbol we become aware of the cosmic truth it symbolises. It is thus entirely different from the arbitrary or mathematical symbol [2] with which, in these days, we have perhaps grown more familiar. We may set down the opening formula of an equation: "Let X equal the number of unemployable persons in Middlesex"; but we might stare for hours together at the two crossed strokes of the X without learning anything from *them* about the disasters, diseases, and disappointments that make up the tale of human failure for which that symbol arbitrarily stands. If we want to know anything about unemployability itself—its essence, rather than its mere statistics, we shall do better to have a chat with the

---

[1]   to remove those living in this life from a state of misery, and lead them into a state of felicity.

Ep. to Can Grande.

[2] More properly called a "sign".

next tramp who calls at the back door. He—in his appearance, his
speech, his life-history, his desires, fears, sins and sufferings—is an
instance of that which he represents and its natural symbol. He is
himself the answer—or at any rate part of the answer—to the problem
of why certain people are unemployable; and the more intimately we
study him, the better we shall understand the problem. It is not that
his opinion on the subject is necessarily correct or valuable—very
likely he will have no opinion to give; it is he himself (including,
of course, his opinions if he has any) who displays to us, by *being* himself, the pattern of that abstract which we call "unemployability".

Now the characters in Dante's great allegory are, with very few
exceptions, natural symbols of what they represent. They are not
figures in what we may call the monumental style of allegory, where
a stout lady in a helmet stands for War, and another lady with an
olive-branch, who might be her twin sister, stands for Peace. They are
complex human beings, some legendary, some historical, some simply
and others more elaborately handled, who can be said to "stand for"
the vices and virtues with which Dante connects them—not in the
sense that they have no attributes beyond these qualities, but in the
deeper and more subtle sense that those vices or virtues have made
them what they are, coloured all their interests (and they have many)
and brought them in the end to the place in which we find them—
perverted, penitent, or glorified.

There is a further complication. Dante himself, in that letter to Can
Grande which combines the functions of Dedicatory Epistle, Analytical Commentary, and what we should nowadays call the "Publisher's
Blurb", has explained clearly and emphatically that his *Comedy* is to be
interpreted at more levels than one. In its *literal* meaning it is a poem
about "the state of souls after death"; but in its *signification* it is a poem
about this life, exhibiting at various levels that universal pattern of
Divine Justice of which the state of souls after death is at once the
crowning instance and the natural symbol. In an illustrative example
drawn from the Psalms, he invites our attention to three levels of
significance: the *allegorical proper*—which is the pattern as displayed
in history; the *moral*—the pattern as displayed in ethics; the *anagogical*
—the pattern displayed at the spiritual or mystical level. All these
significances are contained in the literal sense, which is in one way the
least important of the four, since it exists only for the sake of the others;
yet in another way is of supreme importance, since it is the concrete
and particular image by which we perceive all the rest. Doubtless there

are many other levels at which we might interpret the truth conveyed by the literal image, for its truth is ingrained, and wherever you cut it you will find the same immutable structure; indeed it is the very mark of greatness in an allegorical work that the more closely you examine and analyse it, the more levels of significance you find in it. Dante's own analysis is not necessarily exhaustive and probably was not meant to be.[1] It is important because it not only permits, but encourages and indeed commands us to find in his work all the richness of symbolical meaning that it is capable of yielding.

From these considerations it follows, I think, that we shall fall into a very great error if we try to over-simplify the significance of any of Dante's great images—particularly an image so important and so elaborate as that of Virgil. It is useless to argue passionately whether the Virgil of the *Comedy* "stands for" the Imperial idea, *or* Reason, *or* Poetry, *or* the Cardinal Virtues, *or* Natural Religion, or any *one* of a hundred other things. At different levels of interpretation he stands for them all. We have Dante's word for it that there are at least four Virgils—the literal, the historico-allegorical, the moral, and the mystical; and of these the literal Virgil, who contains and signifies all the rest, is as complex as any other personality in history or fiction. If we plump for an exclusively Imperial and Roman Virgil, his Romanity will not greatly enlighten us at the mystical level, and a Virgil conceived as "the embodiment of pure Reason" will have but a limited relevance at the historical level. If we are to find any phrase to sum up the total significance of Dante's Virgil at *all* levels, we must cast our net very much wider.

One need not, I think, experience much difficulty in doing this: the significance of Virgil is broad and deep but not obscure. Virgil is the Natural Man in his perfection—the best of which Humanity is capable, apart from the revelation and special grace of Christ. At the historical level, he is thus the idea of Empire, of the peaceably ordered World-State, governed by reason, administered with equity, freed from the evils of envy and competition, without exploitation either of men or of the land, prosperous by the exchange of honest commodities at a just price, hierarchic and secure. This is the kind of State which Plato desired, and for which we to-day are still nostalgically looking; the

---

[1] What he has done is to take over bodily the traditional three-level system of interpretation employed by the theologians for the exegesis of inspired writings, and boldly demand its application to that poem "to which Heaven and earth have set hand" (*Para.* xxv. 2).

State which Rome in the ancient world came nearest to realising; the State which Virgil sang "when in the world he wrote his lofty verse—*quando nel mondo gli alti versi scrissi*". At the moral level, Virgil is humanist ethics at its best—that traditional morality of moderation and reason and decency and duty which is sometimes conveniently and comprehensively called the Tao, founded upon the four Cardinal Virtues of Justice, Prudence, Temperance, and Fortitude. At the mystical level, Virgil is Natural Religion at its highest and best, confirming and sanctioning the moral virtues by the authority of the gods, serving these with reverence and piety, and prophetically, though unconsciously, pointing through its types and rituals and sacrifices to the true God, the true Church, and the one True Sacrifice of which all these things are the shadows. And at all these levels Virgil is the achievement of humanity, serving and embodying all its native ideals and aspirations in its works of knowledge or of inspiration: that is why Dante addresses him as "*Tu che onori e scienẓa ed arte*—thou that honourest all learning and art"—he both pays them honour and confers honour upon them.

We see that it is not arbitrarily that Dante has chosen Virgil to carry this symbolism. He can represent these things because for Dante he *was* these things. Dante had not to invent a figure or choose a name at random and attach all these significances to it. They were there already—he had only to look into Virgil's poetry to find them already there. "*Vagliami il lungo studio e il grande amore, Che m'a fatto cercar lo tuo volume*—may these", he says, "now avail me—the long study and the great love which put me to search your book." Everything which the liberal humanism of the last few centuries had in mind when it eulogised Man—his rationality, his ethical nobility, his scientific achievements, his creative powers, his tragic dignity, his *virtus* (in that expressive Latin phrase for which we have no exact equivalent)—everything which is predicated in the threefold allegorical Virgil is found in and explained by the literal Virgil, the poet of the *Eclogues* and the *Georgics* and the *Aeneid*. It is perhaps not accidental that the first words which Virgil speaks in the *Commedia* are: "*Non uomo, uomo già fui*." Dante, meeting him in the Dark Wood, asks him: "Are you ghost or very man?" He answers: "I am not, though once I was, a man." In the literal sense, it is a plain answer to Dante's question: "I am the shade of what was once a living man." But it is possible to take the Italian word *uomo*—thus written without the article—in the allegorical sense, and more generally: "Once I was Man; once all that Humanity is was perfectly summed up in me; now it is not so. There was a Man born, since whose coming mankind has been different. I am not mankind, only the ghost of what mankind once was." I do not know whether Dante deliberately wrote all that into the line, but certainly we can legitimately read it there. For Virgil goes on: "My parents were Mantuans. I lived in Rome in the time of the false and lying gods; I was a poet; I sang of the righteous son of Anchises"—all the great notes are struck one after the other: derivation, Romanity, poetry, justice; but the gods were false—*non uomo, uomo già fui*. Once again, the actual words are little more than the bare minimum needed to inform Dante of his identity: "I was born under Julius; I lived under Augustus; I wrote the *Aeneid*"; but once we realise what the central symbolism is, the whole passage vibrates under its weight of associative meaning. That is Dante's way, and the way of all great allegorists in so far as they are great: the allegorical sense is *in* the literal sense, and the literal sense is everywhere consistent with itself, so that what is right for the story is right for the allegory, and conversely.

May I offer a contrast, by way of making this plain, because, simple and even obvious as it may sound, the point is sometimes missed, both by the allegorists themselves and their interpreters. At the opening of *The Faerie Queene* Spenser—an excellent poet, but a very uncertain master of allegorical form—introduces Una to us thus:

> A lovely Ladie rode him faire beside,
> Upon a lowly Asse more white than snow,
> Yet she much whiter; but the same did hide
> Under a veil that wimpled was full low
> And over all a black stole shee did throw. . . .

And so forth, and so on,

> Seemed in heart some hidden care she had,
> And by her in a line, a milkewhite lambe she lad.[1]

Now the ass and the veil and the stole are all right—a lady errant must have clothes and something to ride upon; and if these things at the same time symbolise humility and modesty and grief, the allegory is helped and nothing is lost. But the lamb on the lead is mere allegorical furniture; it is only there, like St. Agnes's lamb in a stained-glass window, as an emblem of innocence. A more useless and embarrassing piece of luggage to take about on a long and adventurous trip one could

[1] *F.Q.* I. i. 4.

scarcely imagine. The lamb is entirely out of place in the literal story, and is, in fact, never mentioned again. But with Dante, every event, every object, and every word is tightly woven into the literal story he is telling, and the multiple allegorical significances are founded in the literal sense as the harmonics of a bell's music are founded in the actual note to which it is tuned. Thus, at every moment of the story, the three symbolical Virgils accompany the poetic figure of Virgil as he is literally presented to us—now the one and now the other predominating as the matter of the poem requires, but none being ever wholly obscured. And beneath and behind them all, we are aware of three other presences, whose voices sound below the verse as in bell-music the fundamental sounds below the nominal. There is the Virgil of real life—our Virgil, known to us as to Dante in his still-living verse. There is the Virgil of Christian tradition, "Maro the prophet of the Gentiles", whose name was touchingly remembered in a yearly Mass because in his Fourth Eclogue he wrote, unwittingly, words destined to a strange fulfilment which he himself could neither foresee nor find salvation in. And there is also the Virgil of mediaeval folk-lore, Virgilius Magus, the great White Magician, who could conjure the spirits, and who once at least, in the 26th canto of the *Inferno*, does very magnificently and in his own power conjure them.

Out of this sevenfold complexity is knit together the grave and beautiful personality which guides Dante through Hell and sustains him in the difficult ascent of Purgatory. Nobody, I suppose, who reads the *Divine Comedy* with any kind of understanding or sympathy, has ever failed to fall in love with Virgil. When, in the Earthly Paradise and in the presence of Beatrice, Dante turns to Virgil with a verse of the *Aeneid* upon his lips and finds him gone, he is overwhelmed: "Not all that our First Mother lost", he cries, "could keep my cheeks from darkening with tears"; and the reader is in much the same case as Dante. It was necessary to the plot that Virgil should go; but his is one of those characters which tend, as one says in the theatre, to "run away with the play", and Beatrice's self can, in that poignant moment, hardly compensate us for his loss. Virgil fills the first two books of the poem; and in making him so central and so lovable and in then rending him clean out of the story, Dante took a risk which only the very greatest of artists could venture or afford to take. The whole structure of the poem quivers under the shock, and stability is only restored by the intense and concentrated brilliance of the scene that follows between Dante and Beatrice, which so takes hold upon us that we are forced to attend to it. Even as things stand, one feels that it is touch-and-go; with the very slightest relaxing of the tension, with one shade less of sheer dramatic power, the poem might have fallen to pieces. And indeed, many readers and critics, especially during those centuries of Humanism which exalted the power and virtues of Man, have found it impossible to forgive Dante for his treatment of Virgil; or have invented the fiction that, in excluding Virgil from Paradise (and consequently from the *Paradiso*) Dante was doing violence to his own convictions.

But it is not so. To his feelings, Dante no doubt did violence, as is clear in many passages of piercing pathos, but to his convictions, never. He loves Virgil, honours and reverences him as master, leader, and lord, pours himself out in a passion of gratitude to him—and judges him. For the whole theme of the *Comedy* is that Virgil is fundamental, indispensable, and yet of himself inadequate. Man is inadequate. Natural Reason and Art, Natural Morality, Natural Religion, if without Grace, without Revelation, without Redemption, cannot at their best attain any higher state than Limbo. The Natural Man may—and indeed must—accompany the Redeemed Man upon his long and toilsome journey up the Mountain of Regeneration. Beyond that, his virtues, having served their purpose, become irrelevant and Man himself must become, in Dante's phrase, transhumanised. Art and Learning are not enough, Social Order is not enough, the four great reasonable Natural Virtues are not enough: the realm of bliss, which is the true end of Man's being, is, in the end, wholly other. That is why the relations between Dante and Virgil are ambivalent, and tense with a peculiarly moving paradox. For Dante represents himself always as infinitely Virgil's inferior—his pupil in the Grand Art of poetry, a child in wisdom as compared with him, a sinner where Virgil is virtuous, and moreover continually liable to be rebuked by him for cowardice, weakness, dawdling sloth, a prattling inquisitiveness, absence of mind, sentimentality and—on one famous occasion—downright vulgarity. Yet, because he is a child of Grace, he will arrive in the end where Virgil can never come; he will enter that heavenly Rome where Christ Himself is Roman; and they both know it. Not only Dante, but Statius and Sordello, whose whole poetic output is not worth one line of the *Aeneid*—Statius whose faith was so unheroic that he remained a crypto-Christian to the end of his life; and Sordello, a profligate in private and something very like a traitor in public life—they and all those souls who on the slopes of Mount Purgatory are expiating offences against every canon of morality, natural and divine—all these are preferred before Virgil. It might be said of him, as it was said of another: "Among men born of women there hath not arisen a greater than Virgil, yet he that is least in the Kingdom of Heaven is greater than he."

There is no reason to suppose that Dante did not, from the bottom of his heart, mean this; and we to-day are perhaps in a better position than our grandparents were to see what he meant and why he so emphatically meant it. The great illusion of the adequacy of Man is wearing thin, and it is less easy than it was to imagine that he can, in his own strength, achieve an Earthly Paradise, still less a Heavenly. We are aware, as the centuries of Humanist Enlightenment were not aware, but as Dante's tempestuous Middle Ages knew only too well, that only just beneath the crust of our civilisation the fires of Hell burn to an unimaginable depth, and that for the fruition of joy it is not sufficient to exhort men to be temperate and reasonable. To know the good is not necessarily to do it, as the heathen philosopher thought—nor even, perhaps, effectively to desire it. Our virtues stultify themselves, and "the evil that we would not, that we do". Dante, who in the *Convivio* had written of the attainment, here in this world, of the good life and the ordered state, has, in the *Comedy*, not abandoned hope of these things, but is concerned to warn us that they are, after all, a supernatural gift. As the souls of the Proud toil round the First Cornice of Purgatory, their backs bowed beneath the weight of their humiliation, they meditate the Lord's Prayer:

> Let come to us, let come Thy Kingdom's peace;
> If it come not, we've no power of our own
> To come to it, for all our subtleties;[1]

and every pronouncement that Dante makes upon the Natural Order and the Just Empire must be read in the light of that meditation.

This is the significance of that damnation of Virgil, which has so often been too narrowly explained, or even explained away. It has been said that Dante was forced into this position by the rigidity of his creed, and that his poem is a passionate protest against the exclusion of the good pagan from Heaven. The answer to that is simple. Neither the Bible nor Catholic theology necessarily excludes the individual good pagan from Heaven; and Dante himself set two pagans in Paradise. Nor must the piercing pathos of his poetry lead us to suppose that his sympathy affected his judgement. Dante, more than most poets, can

[1] *Purg.* xi. 7–9.

invest with an aching loveliness the very thing that he most sincerely condemns: the languorous love of Francesca, the intellectual adventuring of Ulysses—on these he has lavished all the glory of his verse. He has felt their seduction; precisely because they are his own sins he knows their delight at once and their danger. Here, most truly, he is Virgil's pupil. The agony that throbs through the Fourth Book of the *Aeneid* is only the more tenderly handled by the poet for his certain knowledge that the man whom God has chosen must not forget his vocation in the embrace of the dark Eros. When Virgil wrote of Dido, he taught Dante how to write of Virgil.

It is necessary to understand of what, exactly, Dante accuses Good-Paganism, and what sort of eternal dwelling he assigns to it. In the second canto of the *Inferno*, Virgil offers only the, as it were, formal and technical explanation of the presence in Limbo of himself and the other souls that dwell "suspended". They are those who are neither of the Old Covenant nor the New—the unbaptised and the men who, living before Christ's coming, did not worship God in the right way. No opportunity of salvation, it would seem, was afforded them. But later, in the seventh canto of the *Purgatorio*, Virgil expands this statement: he and his are lost, he says, for no other fault than that they had not faith—"*per non aver fè*". This is ambiguous, and reflects back a certain ambiguity upon the *Inferno* passage. Are we to understand, specifically, "lack of the Christian Faith" or, in a wider and more absolute manner, "lack of the quality of faith"? And again, is it "failure to worship God in the way appointed by the law of Moses" or "failure to conceive a right way of worshipping God" that has undone the Good Pagans? Virgil goes on to say:

> And there dwell I, with those who ne'er put on
> The three celestial virtues, yet, unsinning,
> Knew all the rest and practised every one.[1]

The "three celestial virtues" are faith, hope, and charity; the sole pain of Limbo is that "without hope they live in desire". We begin to glimpse the outline of eternal justice: in eternity they are deprived only of that which in life they refused—for it is of the essence of heaven and hell that one must abide for ever with that which one has chosen. The ambiguity concerning faith is resolved along similar lines. "It is madness," says Virgil,

[1] *Purg.* vii. 31–33.

Madness—that reason lodged in human heads
  Should hope to traverse backward and unweave
  The infinite path Three-personed Substance treads.

Content you with the *quia*, sons of Eve,
  For had you power to see the whole truth plain
  No need had been for Mary to conceive;

And you have seen such great souls thirst in vain
  As else had stilled that thirst in quietness
  Which now is given them for eternal pain;

I speak of Plato, Aristotle—yes,
  And many more . . . [1]

Could they have seen, they would have been satisfied. But the celestial virtue takes a more generous risk: "*Credo ut intelligam*", says Anselm —"I believe in order that I may see"; and Christ: "Blessed are they that have not seen, and yet have believed."

Charity is the third holy virtue, and this, at first sight, it is difficult to deny to Virgil. He has, and in perfection, that reasonable form of it which we call "kindness". Kindness is, indeed, characteristic of Humanism—that is why a humanist age lays so much stress on tolerance and good manners. And up to a certain point, Virgil has at least an intellectual grasp of a more ardent fire of charity, as he shows by his first great discourse on Heavenly Love in the 15th canto of *Purgatorio:*

The infinite and unexpressive Good
  Up there, so speeds to love as the ray speeds
  To bodies with clear lucency endued;

Lavish of self, all fires it finds it feeds;
  And thus, as charity yet rifer runs,
  Rifer thereby the immortal vigour breeds.

The more enamoured souls dwell there at once,
  Ever the better and the more they love,
  Each glassing each, all mirrors and all suns. [2]

He adds: "If my words are not enough for thee, thou shalt see Beatrice, and she will make all plain." Dante is about to reply that he is satisfied, when he is caught into a trance, and there sees a vision of St. Stephen praying for mercy upon his murderers. That is the true measure of the heavenly love, weighed against the good pagan's best

[1] *Purg.* iii. 34–44.   [2] *Purg.* xv. 67–75.

conception. The natural reason can grasp the exchange of love for love; the exchange of love for hatred is irrational: it belongs to another frame of discourse.

What is lacking to good-paganism, to the Tao, to the planned state, to the morality of "myself and my duty", to rational humanism, is precisely the self-abandonment, the all-or-nothingness, the ecstasy of the three great paradoxical virtues: to trust when all is betrayed, to hope when things are desperate, to love the unlovable. Justice, prudence, temperance and fortitude are indeed indispensable, and have their own austere and stoic beauty; but they are virtues which find it difficult to be meek, and therefore they do not inherit the earth, nor storm the gates of Heaven. To those who practised them perfectly, Dante assigns that noble place in Limbo which is, in fact, the Elysian Fields. This was the best that the good pagan hoped for from eternity; a reasonable self-control inhibited him from trusting the universe any further—either he could not, or he dared not, imagine an eternity of bliss. If there could be the imagination of delight, the disciplined will could make no assent to it. Therefore, according to his imagination, so it is to him. Dante describes the good pagans as he sees them, in Elysium:

> mighty shadows of the dead,
> Who in their mien nor joy nor grief displayed. . . .

> Persons with grave and tranquil eyes, and great
> Authority in their carriage and attitude,
> Who spoke but seldom, and in voice sedate.[1]

Such men are always with us, and our affection and reverence goes out to them. And it not infrequently seems to us that the sweet sobriety of their Elysium is not only the best that can be expected, but the best that can be imagined. We are ready, after a life of duty conscientiously performed, to sit with Anchises and the heroes by the streams of many-watered Eridanus, or to discuss philosophy with Plato and Aristotle in their tranquil castle in Limbo. Indeed, the thing which in modern literature most reminds us of it is Henry James's "Great Good Place"—though in James there is a faint touch of vulgarity, as of a very expensive and well-run hotel, which is foreign to Dante and Virgil alike. But we feel the charm of such states. We are in love with a gentle melancholy, and perhaps do not hear—perhaps do not want to hear the great exultant note which goes crashing across the last cantos of

[1] *Inf.* iv. 83–84; 113–115.

the *Paradiso*:

> "To Father and to Son and Holy Ghost"
> All Heaven broke forth, "be glory!" till I grew
> Drunk with the sweetness of the singing host,

> And everywhere I looked I seemed to view
> One smile of all creation, ear and eye
> Drinking alike the inebriate rapture through.[1]

Perhaps we neither trust in that kind of thing nor hope for it, nor even greatly desire it. But to read the *Paradiso* immediately after reading the Sixth *Aeneid* is to discover, in a difference of *tone*, the gulf that opens, for Dante, between Virgil and Beatrice, between man's best imagination and (if we may so call it) God's imagination for man. Or—to take the thing at a more intimate and familiar level, we may compare the love of Dido—or even, for that matter, Plato's noblest passages upon love—with what Dante as a young man, wrote of Beatrice:

> I say that when I saw her coming from any direction, then, through the hope I had of receiving her wondrous salutation, no enemies were left to me, but rather I was filled with a fire of charity which made me forgive every one who had ever done me injury; and if at that moment I had been asked about anything whatsoever, I could only have answered *"Love"*, with a countenance clothed in humility.[2]

Once again, the *note* is unmistakable: the towering passion of the enkindled imagination and the humble assent to it of the enraptured will. And it is, for Dante, this passion of the imaginative will which exalts the souls of Trajan and Rhipeus to the Heaven of the Just. Trajan is called back from the dead by the "living hope" which put might into St. Gregory's prayer, so that "his will might have power to be moved . . . and his soul believed in Him who had power to aid it and, believing, kindled into such a flame of very love . . . that it was worthy to enter into this great mirth."[3] The story, though not the interpretation of it, is legend; but the story of Rhipeus is Dante's own, founded on nothing more than a line and a half of Virgil:

> *Rhipeus, justissimus unus*
> *Que fuit in Teucris, et servantissimus aequi.*[4]

---

[1] *Para.* xxvii. 1–6.   [2] *Vita Nuova*, xi.   [3] *Para.* xx. 109–117.
[4] Rhipeus, the one most righteous man that was in Troy and most observant of justice.   *Aen.* ii. 426–427.

"He," says Dante, thus at last summing up his mature judgement on the relation between Grace and the Natural Man, "by that grace which wells up from so deep a fountain that no creaturely eye ever yet pierced down to its first wave, set all his love below on righteousness (*drittura*), wherefore from grace to grace God opened his eyes to our redemption yet to come. Whereat he believed." [1] Grace moves, and love responds; Grace, working upon love, opens the eyes of the imagination, and the will responds by faith; and, says Dante, the celestial virtues themselves stood sponsors to Rhipeus, "a thousand years and more before baptism".[2] This is the answer in Paradise to the lament that went up from Limbo: "We were lost because we had not baptism."

Rightly or wrongly, and certainly to his own grief as well as ours, Dante does not find the ecstatic and Paradisal note in Virgil. The only place, perhaps, in which he could have found it is in the Fourth Eclogue; but the mass and weight of Virgil's work, especially of the *Aeneid*, is of a different temper. His epic—his "high tragedy" as Dante, with a sure critical instinct calls it—is tinged throughout with melancholy, and closes on a sombre note. If in the Eclogue the prophetic imagination glimpsed a more ecstatic truth, the mature will did not assent to the imagination. We cannot be sure whether Dante knew that Virgil on his death-bed wished to destroy the *Aeneid*; nothing in the *Commedia* betrays any such knowledge. Nevertheless, the Virgil that Dante has drawn is of a piece with the Virgil of real life: he carries with him into eternity that sense, which haunted him in death, of frustration and insufficiency; enlarged to the measure of his full symbolic stature, it throws its shadow across the world. Virgil is the best of all that Man by his own nature has and is; and it is not enough.

It is not enough; but on the other hand it is fundamental. Nature itself is the work of Grace, and without Nature, Grace cannot operate. In nothing is Dante so Catholic as in his insistence upon the necessity and goodness of Nature. To sin and the Fall he gives their due weight; but he has no use at all for any doctrine of the Total Depravity of human nature. It is by a profound and beautiful symbolism that when Dante is lost in the Dark Wood and upon the brink of destruction, Beatrice is unable to reach him and is obliged to call upon Virgil for help. A man may be alienated from God and have sent his spiritual self to sleep, so that he is deaf to the voice of Beatrice, who is Grace; but there is always hope for him so long as he may be reached at the natural level: poetry, reason, traditional morality, common decency

[1] *Para.* xx. 118–124.   [2] *Para.* xx. 127–129.

or even common prudence. But if he is deaf to the voice of Virgil, he is far lost indeed. Therefore Beatrice sends Virgil: "Go thou; lift up thy golden voice, find him, reach him, use any means to bring him back." Grace is, ultimately, prior to Nature, and Virgil receives his commission from Beatrice; yet Grace perfects Nature and does not violate it; Beatrice does not order Virgil to go—she entreats him, and leaves the manner of his going to him. Stately compliments are exchanged:

> "O courteous Mantuan soul, whose skill in song
> Keeps green on earth a fame that shall not end
> While motion rolls the turning spheres along." [1]

So Beatrice begins; and Virgil replies:

> "Excellent lady, for whose sake alone
> The breed of men exceeds all things that dwell
> Closed in the heaven whose circles narrowest run,
>
> To do thy bidding pleases me so well
> That were't already done I should seem slow. . . ." [2]

"We should have been fortunate", observes Charles Williams, "if the ministers of religion and poetry had always spoken to each other with such courtesy as these." [3] So Virgil goes, and finds Dante in the desert, terrified by the wild beasts that are the externalisation of his own—or of our, or of society's—corruptions, and so near the death of the soul that even that golden voice is faint to him at first. "Have pity on me, whatever you are, ghost or man!"—"Man I am not, but I once was man. I was poet, Roman, I wrote the *Aeneid*—what are you doing here?"—"What! you are Virgil!" and in a passionate outbreak of admiring love, Dante takes the first step on the road of self-knowledge by acknowledging his own derivation: "You are my author and my maker. You taught me all I know, from you I learned the style for which I am honoured." [4] Of this flattering and impassioned outburst Virgil takes no notice whatever; and it is difficult to say whether, at this point, Dante's symbolical intention or his dry and delicate humour is uppermost. Few things are more irritating to an author's feelings

---

[1] *Inf.* ii. 58–60.
[3] *Figure of Beatrice*, p. 112.
[2] *Inf.* ii. 76–80.
[4] *Inf.* i. 65 *seq.*

than to be gushed over by some young aspirant to fame and to be informed that he has modelled his style upon one's own. There are things for which no one is anxious to be made responsible. Virgil merely answers Dante's appeal to be saved from the She-Wolf: "You must go by another road if you are ever to get out of this place," he replies aloofly, "looking upon me", says Dante, "as I wept." Virgil's first impression of Dante is not particularly favourable. There is truth to human nature there—and also a deeper truth. The older culture, the urbane and sophisticated natural civilisation, looks upon the beginnings of the spiritual man and finds them raw, clumsy, foolish, timid and childish. I remember very well hearing a theologian say: "One has to admit that when one comes from reading the great classical poets and philosophers and turns to the early Christian Fathers, it is like reading the awkward efforts of schoolboys or barbarians." Nor does Dante improve his position by first eagerly consenting to follow Virgil through Hell and Purgatory, and then getting cold feet, and shuffling, and inventing a thousand excellent reasons why he should not follow in the other-world footsteps of Aeneas and St. Paul: "I am not worthy, I might make a fool of myself, it might be out of the frying-pan into the fire, people would think it odd." To all of which, Virgil replies "Cowardice";[1] and we are aware of the familiar, faintly contemptuous attitude of the sturdy-minded natural moralist for the agitated half-baked Christian—for his fear of death, of eternity, of self-examination, for his tendency to "lie awake in the dark and whine about his sins". Dante, nevertheless, has some excuse, for the journey he has to take is the journey into the darkness of the self. He must fathom the deeps of his own corruption, and that is a bitter undertaking, even with reason and poetry and philosophy to help one.

At length, however, they set off together, through that underworld so thickly peopled with figures who have stepped out from the Sixth *Aeneid* and become curiously mediaevalised and fantasticated in the process. We cannot follow all their footsteps in detail, nor even enlarge upon the ingenious economy with which a hint or a name offered in the Latin epic is seized upon, expanded and fitted into place until the whole 3,000-mile shaft of Hell is decorated with these Virgilian images. We must be content with taking a small selection of the agreeable company which Aeneas finds gathered together in the "vestibule" of Hell:

[1] *Inf.* ii. 10 *seq.*

multaque praeterea variarum monstra ferarum
Centauri in foribus stabulant, Scyllaeque biformes,
et centumgeminus Briareus, ac belua Lernae
horrendum stridens, flammisque armata Chimaera,
Gorgones, Harpyiaeque, et forma tricorporis umbrae.[1]

The idea of the "vestibule" is seized on; but the place is appropriated to the Futile, who, excluded from Hell and Heaven alike, run there for ever after a shifting banner, stung by hornets and attended by "worms"—unspecified monsters—which lick up their blood and tears. The Centaurs are in the First Ring of the Violent, with a whole office and episode to themselves; Briareus with the rest of the Giants and Titans has gone down to stand at the rim of the well at the very bottom of Malebolge; the Gorgon has gone off to guard the barbican over the gates of the City of Dis, assisted by the Furies from a few lines higher up, who have reclaimed their viper-locks and bloodstained fillets, borrowed by Virgil, a little unscrupulously, for Discord. The Harpies are in the Wood of the Suicides, sitting and shrieking in the Bleeding Trees imported from *Aeneid III*; the fire-breathing Chimaera has become a fire-breathing dragon, and may be found perched on the head of Cacus in the Bolgia of the Thieves; and the *forma tricorporis umbrae* has turned from a three-bodied giant to a monster with a man's head, a bear's forelegs and a serpent's body, and carries Virgil and Dante on his back over the edge of the Great Barrier between the Circles of Violence and the Circles of Fraud. Only the *Scyllae biformes* and the *belua Lernae* have no specific mention in the *Inferno*, but the latter is probably present among the mixed collection of reptiles which adorn the Seventh Bolgia. Dante wastes nothing; neither does he use his material at random. The creatures all have their symbolic uses: the half-human, half-bestial monsters belong to the circle where violent passions make men into brutes; Cerberus, sop and all, not only guards the entrance to the Third Circle but is an image of gluttonous appetite. In the same fashion, but more profoundly, Dante recalls and modifies the Virgilian image of the souls who cluster on the bank of Acheron

[handwritten margin notes: Polydorus / Ovid: Doris' daughters / Daphne]

---

[1] Withal most wondrous, many-shaped, are all the wood-beasts there;
   The Centaurs stable by the porch, and twi-shaped Scyllas fare;
   And hundred-folded Briareus, and Lerna's Worm of dread,
   Fell hissing; and Chimaera's length and fire-behelmed head,
   Gorgons and Harpies, and the shape of that three-bodied Shade.
                              Aen. vi. 285–289 (Morris).

like autumn leaves, *tendebantque manus ripae ulterioris amore*,[1] giving
to their action and gesture a signification as much more terrible than
the Virgilian pathos as the Christian Hell is more terrible than the pagan
Hades. "They press to pass the river" because they are in love with
their own corruption; "therefore their fear is changed into desire".

The Classicist, as he follows Dante and Virgil on their pilgrims'
progress, is probably most struck, and at the same time perhaps irritated, by the mediaevalising of all the classical figures. The Mediaevalist,
on the other hand, is more apt to be struck by the classical restraint of
the handling. (Here, by the way, Dante is doubtless right in attributing
his own "noble style" to the influence of Virgil—for he would scarcely
have learned restraint from Statius, still less from Lucan, or even from
Ovid, his other models in epic narrative.) The fourteenth-century
illuminators, true to contemporary notions of the matter, always
depict Virgil in the costume considered appropriate to a magician—a
tall cap and a mantle trimmed with fur, faintly reminiscent of the Three
Magi in an Epiphany picture. And it is true enough that all through the
Inferno we are conscious of the presence with us of Virgil the Sorcerer.
But of the tawdry marvels of the Virgilian folk-lore there is no trace.
The poet of the *Aeneid* need not blush for the august words of power
which bear down the resistance of Charon and put Minos to silence:
"Thus it is willed where will and power are one; ask thou no more";[2]
nor yet at the great discourse on Holy Luck, which, unexpectedly
equating the Roman Fortuna with the Christian Providence, moves
from a majestic opening to the lovely and lyric close:

> Lo! this is she that hath so curst a name
>   Even from those who should give thanks to her:
>   Luck, whom men senselessly revile and·blame;
>
> But she is blissful and she does not hear;
>   She, with the other primal creatures, gay
>   Tastes her own blessedness and turns her sphere.[3]

With words of wisdom and words of power, Virgil leads his pupil
through those outer suburbs of Hell in which the sins of Incontinence
find their eternal fulfilment. But at the Gates of Dis, which enclose the
sins of the obdurate and hardened will, there is a check. The demons
and fallen angels slam the gate in Virgil's face, and the Furies, scream-

---

[1] were stretching forth their hands with longing for the further shore.

Aen. vi. 314.

[2] *Inf.* iii. 95–96; v. 23–24.   [3] *Inf.* vii. 91–96.

ing from the summit of the red-hot tower of iron, threaten to bring
out Medusa to turn Dante into stone.

> "Quick, turn thee back and seal thine eyelids tight—
> If Gorgon show her face and thou thereon
> Look once, there's no returning to the light."

> Thus cried the Master; nor to my hands alone
> Would trust, but turned me himself, and urgently
> Pressed my palms close and covered them with his own.

> O you whose intellects keep their sanity,
> Do you mark well the doctrine shrouded o'er
> By the strange verses with their mystery.[1]

The mystery, puzzling to the age of Reason, is, or should be, less
puzzling to us. The journey into self-knowledge is a perilous one, as
priests and psycho-analysts know well; and there is always the possibility that, at the deeper levels, the soul may encounter the Erinyes of
a futile remorse and become paralysed by a stony despair. We have
been watching this happen on a scale more than nation-wide; the whole
civilisation of the West is at the moment standing before the Gates of
Dis, terrified of itself, and clinging with desperation to Virgil while it
awaits the coming of the Angel. The hands of Virgil can hold us steady
and preserve us for a time from total collapse; but something more
energetic and more positive is needed to smash down resistance and
lead us on to tackle our spiritual troubles at the source. Virgil is the
best of ourselves; but salvation must come from beyond us. The
allegory holds true at all levels, but it is perhaps easier for us to see it
at the historical level and on this colossal scale. In the same way, recent
political experience may enable us to understand that other episode,
when Virgil allows himself to be tricked by the plausible devils who
guard the Fifth Bolgia. The thing that Liberal Humanism finds it
most difficult to understand or cope with is the riddle of the evil mind,
practising a purposeless malignity for its own sake. The love of evil
is sub-rational, as the Divine charity is super-rational; and the golden
mean of reason is as incapable of the one as of the other.

Apart from this incident, and once the Gates of Dis are passed,
Virgil is mighty in Hell. His relations with his pupil become more
intimate and more cordial—though one feels that Dante is perhaps a
rather trying companion, and that one would like to know what sort

[1] *Inf.* ix. 55–63.

of report Virgil gave of him to Homer and Ovid and Horace and the rest when, his mission fulfilled, he returned to the Elysian Fields. The comments of Horace, "the great satirical", would also be of interest, if we were but privileged to hear them. Throughout, the relations between the great shade and the living man are handled with peculiar charm, and with Dante's most exquisite, delicate and slightly dry humour. What could be more enchanting than the little exchanges of dialogue in the Sixth Circle, when, after the Angel has opened the gate for them, they find themselves among the burning tombs of the Heretics. "O sovereign power," begins Dante politely, "you who guide and turn me as seems good to you through these circles of evil, could we not look into these tombs? The lids are open and there is no one on guard." "The lids", says Virgil, "will stand open till they are sealed at the Day of Judgement; and", he adds, knowing well that Dante is anxious to see the great Florentine patriot, Farinata, who was a follower of the Epicurean heresy, "this part of the circle contains the tombs of Epicurus and his disciples. So your wish may be fulfilled, and also that other wish which you have not thought fit to mention to me." "Oh, sir," protests Dante, "I would never dream of concealing anything from you—but you have several times told me not to talk so much, so I said nothing about it." So far, the honours are with Dante; but at that moment he is suddenly hailed by a voice from one of the tombs and huddles up to Virgil in a fright. "Come, come," says Virgil, "what are you doing? That's Farinata. Look! he has lifted himself erect and you can see him all from the waist up." And since Dante still seems rather taken aback at this unexpected fulfilment of his wish, Virgil firmly pushes him along to Farinata, saying: "Go on; speak to him; but do keep to the point." Needless to say, Dante does not keep to the point. He expatiates—apparently at some length—upon his own ancestry, embarks upon an argument with Farinata, entangles himself in a conversation with Cavalcante Cavalcanti, interrogates Farinata about the knowledge which the lost souls have of the future, and has to be summoned away by Virgil. Not that he comes—no; "I now heard my Master calling me," says he, "and therefore asked the spirit, with the more haste, to tell me who else was in that cemetery." Since the cemetery stretches to an immeasurable distance in both directions, and is closely packed with tombs, each of which may hold anything up to a thousand souls, Farinata shows some tact in mentioning only two people and promptly vanishing. It is greatly to Virgil's credit that when Dante rejoins him (not at any great speed, but "pondering as he goes"), he makes no comment on this behaviour.[1] One is glad to note that the next time Dante is allowed to go exploring on his own he hurries back of his own accord "in order to please him who bade me lose no time"; though on this occasion there was the less temptation to linger, since the Usurer whom he was interviewing limited his conversation to making offensive remarks and putting his tongue out.[2]

There are many other delightful pictures of Virgil: Virgil standing by the great Centaur Chiron, his head about reaching to "where the two natures join", and explaining, with a touch of self-consciousness, his appearance in this "novel appointment" as bear-leader to a living man, who will have to be carried across Phlegethon on the back of somebody's horse-part; Virgil the poet pointing out Eurypylus the Augur in the Bolgia of the Sorcerers, and observing negligently: "My great tragedy mentions him somewhere or other—you will know the passage, since you have the whole poem by heart." (Dante's original compliment did not, perhaps, fall on wholly deaf ears.) Virgil, in the same Bolgia, rebuking Dante for his tears of sentiment: "Here, pity has no place; accept God's judgement." Virgil anxiously working out a way by which Dante, encumbered with his mortal body, may climb up the ruins of the broken bridge from the bottom of the Sixth Bolgia, "try this stone—now that—do make sure before you step on it that it will bear your weight". Virgil, when poor Dante has laboured to the top and flung himself down on the hard rock to pant his heart out, exhorting him with a certain severity: "Get up—there is a longer stair to climb; sprawling on feather-pillows and idling in bed is no way to fame." Virgil, in his own power and by the magic of his own great verse, compelling the spirit of Ulysses in the speaking flame, and pronouncing the formulae of conjuration; Virgil, in some of the loveliest verse Dante ever wrote, telling the story of the statue of the Old Man of Crete and the source of the Four Rivers of Hell, and the story of the founding of Mantua, with its melodious description of the course of the Mincio from Val Camonica to its junction with the Po.[3] Virgil standing dignified and aristocratic amid the squalors of the Bolgia of Disease, while Dante listens and gloats, horribly fascinated by the sordid wranglings of the dropsical Adam of Brescia and the fever-ridden

[1] *Inf.* x. 4 *seq.*
[2] *Inf.* xvii. 37 *seq.*
[3] *Inf.* xii. 76 *seq.*; xx. 112–114, 26–30; xxiv. 19 *seq.*; xxvi. 76 *seq.*; xiv. 94–120; xx. 52 *seq.*

Sinon of Troy. "Go on," he says, "feast your eyes; a little more, and I shall quarrel with you." Dante, flushing hotly all over, stammers out his excuses:

> "Less shame would wash away a greater crime
>   Than thine has been;" so said my gentle guide;
> "Think no more of it; but, another time
>
> Imagine I'm still standing at thy side
>   Whenever Fortune, in thy wayfaring,
>   Brings thee where people wrangle thus and chide;
>
> It's vulgar to enjoy that kind of thing." [1]

Urbane Virgil! But it is in Purgatory that his charm is most potent and most moving. For here he is no longer on his own ground. To this place he could not come except in company of a Christian soul; he can accompany Dante and advise and sustain him, but he is ignorant of the way and has no words of power to speak. His first encounter is with Cato of Utica—a highly-moral but not very lovable personality—who holds (a little oddly, perhaps) the office of guardian of the lower slopes of the Mountain. Him Virgil approaches with a long, elegant and complimentary address, which is poorly received: "There is no need of all this flattery," says Cato, coldly: "if a Lady from Heaven sent you here, there is nothing more to be said. Take this man, and wash his face, which is filthy—and you need not come back this way." [2] Virgil accepts reproof meekly; only to get into trouble with Cato again for lingering with the other spirits to hear Dante's friend Casella singing one of Dante's own songs in the unearthly dawn-light after the arrival of the Ship of Souls at the island.[3] Art and culture are all very well in their place, but they must not impede the soul's progress. Doubtless this is true; but our sympathy is with Virgil every time. It is just after this that as they hasten up the hill together with the rising sun behind them, Dante is startled to see only his own shadow cast upon the ground, and thinks for a terrified moment that Virgil has deserted him. "What, even now mistrustful?" says Virgil. "Do you not believe that I am with you and guide you still?

> *Vespero è già colà dove è sepolto*
>   *Il corpo dentro al quale io facea ombra;*
>   *Napoli l'ha, e da Brandizio è tolto."*

---

[1] *Inf.* xxx. 142–145.   [2] *Purg.* i. 52 *seq.*   [3] *Purg.* ii. 115 *seq.*

> " 'Tis vesper-tide already, where the tomb
>   Yet holds the body in which I once cast shade,
>   Naples received it from Brundisium." [1]

The elegiac note, so tenderly and musically struck, is in our ears all through the *Purgatory*. The higher the poem ascends into the atmosphere in which Nature cannot walk alone, the more exquisite is the courtesy shown to it by all the characters in the *Comedy*, and the more gracious is the poet's touch upon the personal Virgil. Beautifully balanced against this is Virgil's own increasing modesty as he draws near the time when his pupil will pass out of his hands, and as the spirits with whom the pilgrims have to do approach more nearly to their final state of perfection. To Sordello, already a "spirit elect", but not yet admitted to Purgatory, Virgil announces himself plainly: "I am Virgil", and when Sordello "embraces where the inferior clasps the superior" he lets him have his way.[2] But when they meet Statius, his purgation already accomplished and ready to enter the Earthly Paradise and be made fit for Heaven, Virgil signs to Dante not to betray his identity; and when, through Dante's indiscretion, it is nevertheless betrayed, he prevents Statius from falling at his feet: "Brother, see that thou do it not." [3] Continually he refers Dante away from himself to Beatrice; and when he delivers his second great discourse on Love, on the staircase to the Fourth Cornice, we have an enchanting picture of him, as he looks anxiously into Dante's face to see whether he is making himself understood, which somehow conveys, in a line and a fleeting gesture, how far we have come since the moment when they sat side by side behind the tomb of Pope Anastasius while Virgil explained the lay-out of the Infernal Circles. On that occasion, the Master was a trifle tart with his pupil:

> "What error has seduced thy reason, pray?"
>   Said he; "thou art not wont to be so dull;
>   Or are thy wits woolgathering miles away?" [4]

But now he is all gentleness: "Neither Creator nor creature, my son, was ever without love, and this thou knowest." And, as he "looks intently" in Dante's face, Dante, still wanting to know more, is silent, thinking, "Perhaps I am worrying him with asking too many questions" —and goes on, "But he, my true father, perceiving the timid desire which hesitated to disclose itself, spoke, and encouraged me to speak."[5]

---

[1] *Purg.* iii. 25–27. [2] *Purg.* vii. 1–15 [3] *Purg.* xxi. 94 *seq.*
[4] *Inf.* xi. 76–78. [5] *Purg.* xviii. 1–9.

It is the scene at Farinata's tomb over again, but mellowed and softened with affection, and with the consciousness of the changing relations between the two.

Yet, although Nature cannot ascend Purgatory without the aid of Grace and in company with a soul in Grace, Virgil has a right to be there, and the ascent cannot be made without him. For at the summit of the Mountain is the Earthly Paradise, and what is restored there is, precisely, Nature. The end and aim of the long journey through Hell and up the Mountain is to bring Man back to the perfection of Nature which was lost by the Fall; journey's end is, literally, Paradise Regained. As Dante mounts up to the last circle, he is accompanied by Virgil and also by Statius, who, like Virgil, is of the old Roman culture. Nature unredeemed and Nature redeemed, old Rome and new Rome, Classical Humanism and Christian Humanism—these are the guides and sponsors who bring him through the Barrier of Fire which economically does double duty as the purgation of the Lovers and as the fire of the Cherubim that flamed like a sword to bar out Adam and Eve from the lost Garden. It is they who guard his sleep on the last staircase, lying one above and one below him; in Dante's charming image: "as the goats that have been capering wildly about the hills before feeding-time grow quiet and ruminate, silent in the shade when the sun is hot, guarded by their hersdman . . . such were we then all three, they the herdsmen and I the goat."[1] And when the Garden is reached, and Nature restored to what it should and would have been if Adam had not sinned, with a will perfect and free to turn of itself to God, needing neither Church nor Empire to hold it to its spontaneous obedience, it is Virgil who, as of right, salutes and ratifies that perfection:

> "No word from me, no further sign expect;
>   Free, upright, whole, thy will henceforth lays down
>   Guidance that it were error to neglect,
>
> Whence o'er thyself I mitre thee and crown." [2]

That is Virgil's last word. The whole *praeparatio evangelii* in the secular state finds its end and fulfilment in the making of the City of God; the whole natural revelation is taken up into the Christian revelation; the whole Way of Affirmation leads at last to the point where it must be negated before it can be reaffirmed in different terms: Virgil makes way for Beatrice and St. Bernard, for Mary and for the Beatific

[1] *Purg.* xxvii. 76–86.   [2] *Purg.* xxvii. 139–142.

Vision. He saves others; himself he cannot save. "By thee," says Statius, "I was a poet; by thee a Christian. Thou wast as one who walks by night and carries a lantern behind him, so that it avails not himself but lights the way of others." [1] For the theme of his poem, Dante could not say otherwise; he was bound, not by any external law but by the poetic necessity of his own symbolism. We, however, are not bound—as neither was he—to accept this conclusion literally as the judgement of Christianity upon the personal Virgil. Love, gratitude, prayer can operate backwards in time as well as forward. Charles Williams, in his poem, *Taliessin on the Death of Virgil*, imagines the devoted love of those Christian followers for whom Virgil had held the lantern as rushing in from the future ages to support him with the gift of their own faith in the moment of passing:

> In that hour they came; more and faster, they sped
> To their dead master; they sought him to save
> From the spectral grave and the endless falling,
> Who had heard, for their own instruction, the sound of his calling.
> There was intervention, suspension, the net of their loves.
> . . . .
> Virgil was fathered of his friends.
> He lived in their ends.
> He was set on the marble of exchange. [2]

(Virgil Society
1948)

[1] *Purg.* xxii. 67–69.
[2] *Taliessin through Logres* (O.U.P., 1950), *Taliessin on the Death of Virgil*.

DANTE'S COSMOS

I CAST about a good deal for a way to begin this talk, and after rejecting several very dull openings I decided that, before we looked at Dante's Cosmos, it might be amusing to let him have a look at one of ours. So I took down Eddington's *Nature of the Physical World*, which happened to be handy, and which seems specially suitable because it approaches its subject, not from the factual but from the philosophical side—a method familiar to Dante. So let us imagine that the late Professor Eddington—now, to the regret of his colleagues and readers, released from the limitations of the space-time continuum—has hastened, at a speed exceeding that of light, into the fourteenth century. He is clothed in that aerial body with which (as Dante has told us) spirits are endued between death and the Last Judgement, and he has taken with him (though about this Dante would have been more dubious) an aerial copy of his book. He is reading it aloud in the room where Dante lies dying of malaria—in the house provided by the generosity of Guido Novello da Polenta. It is a feverish dream, perhaps, on the border of two worlds; but Dante's insatiable curiosity is still unquenched. Except when I quote their *ipsissima verba* I shall be bound to misrepresent both of them—but not, I hope, the one much more than the other.

Eddington has begun at the beginning—the now famous introduction about the two tables—and has broken off to say:

"Of course you understand, Messer Dante, that these lectures were of a popular nature—intended for an audience, not of experts, but of average people."

DANTE: I understand perfectly. I began a treatise myself of a similar kind. But in the end I put all I had to say about the cosmos into a great poem. Are you a poet, sir?

EDDINGTON: No; I am a scientist.

DANTE: The two callings are not incompatible. But please go on.

EDDINGTON: I had got to the familiar table which is "a commonplace object of that environment which I call the world".

DANTE: Do you mean by that the totality of sensibles?

EDDINGTON: Well, yes. (*He reads on*) "How shall I describe it? It has extension; it is comparatively permanent; it is coloured; above all, it is *substantial*. By substantial I do not merely mean that it does not collapse when I lean upon it——"

DANTE: I should think not indeed! Why do you have to warn your audience against an error so ridiculous?

EDDINGTON: Because in our time the word "substantial" has come to be used as a synonym of "solid".

DANTE: How lamentable a corruption, when its proper meaning is almost the direct opposite! ... Are you interested in the development of the vulgar tongue? I began a treatise on that also.

EDDINGTON: I am a physicist, not a philologist.

DANTE: Does the one necessarily exclude the other?

EDDINGTON: There is no time in our century to pursue half-a-dozen studies at once. ... "By 'substantial' I mean that it is constituted of 'substance' ... It is a *thing*; not like space, which is a mere negation, not like time, which is—Heaven knows what! But that will not help you to my meaning because it is the distinctive characteristic of a 'thing' to have this substantiality and I do not think substantiality can be described better than by saying that it is the kind of nature exemplified by an ordinary table. And so we go round in circles."

DANTE: Forgive me; but in *my* day we were taught not to argue in circles. And a "substance" is not necessarily a thing like a table. The word means only an individual subject—as distinct from a universal (like "plant-life") or a quality (like "redness" or "honesty") inhering *in* a subject.

EDDINGTON: That is more or less what I mean when I say it is "a thing" ... As you seem a little restless, I will skip some observations about the notions of the common man and go on to my "Table No. 2, my scientific table", which "does not belong to the world previously mentioned—that world which spontaneously appears around me ——"

DANTE: In short, it is not sensible.

EDDINGTON: Quite—though if I used that word many people would think I mean that it was not rational or prudent—that, in short, it was lacking in common-sense.

DANTE: But the common sense has no connection with prudence. It means——

EDDINGTON (*hurriedly*): I am afraid a great many philosophic terms have changed their meaning since your day—"My scientific table——"

DANTE: By "scientific" as opposed to "sensible" or "visible" do you mean "conceptual"? Because, if so, the word "science" has changed its meaning too.

EDDINGTON: Not exactly. I think I mean, "The only table about which we have any accurate knowledge." But you will see as we go on. "My scientific table is mostly emptiness. Sparsely scattered in that emptiness are numerous electric charges rushing about with great speed; but their combined bulk amounts to less than a billionth of the bulk of the table itself" . . . I fear, Messer Dante, the nature of an electric charge is unfamiliar to you.

DANTE: It is something altogether new. But since it has motion and bulk, I conclude that it belongs to the world (as you call it) of sensibles. Though now I come to think of it, you have just implied that it does not. But the apparent contradiction will doubtless quickly resolve itself.

EDDINGTON (*reading*): "It supports my writing-paper as satisfactorily as Table No. 1, for when I lay the paper on it the little electric particles keep on hitting the underside, so that the paper is maintained in shuttlecock fashion at a nearly steady level."

DANTE: Particles! then we certainly have to do with sensibles. And a shuttlecock——

EDDINGTON: Is a kind of projectile made of feathers and cork, with which people play at racquets.

DANTE: A thing like a hawk's lure. Are you fond of hawking, Professor?

EDDINGTON: That sport has gone out, I am afraid . . . "If I lean upon this table I shall not go through——"

DANTE: One moment. Are you not illegitimately confusing two different orders of things—your phenomenal paper and phenomenal body with your scientific table?

EDDINGTON: I am coming to that; "or, to be strictly accurate, the chance of my scientific elbow going through my scientific table is so excessively small that it can be neglected in practical life".

DANTE: You mean that your paper and elbow are also composed of the sparsely distributed electric particles whose nature is still to be disclosed?

EDDINGTON: That is the whole point. Does that surprise you?

DANTE: Of course not. That was to be expected . . . Your audience is familiar with electric particles?

EDDINGTON: They all know how to use electricity in practical affairs, though they have not all a thorough understanding of its scientific composition.

DANTE: They know it in its effects, though not in its nature. That is likely enough . . . But I interrupt you too often.

EDDINGTON: Not at all. "There is nothing *substantial* about my second table. It is nearly all empty space——"

DANTE: How would that prevent it from being a "substance" as defined. Or by "substantial" do you mean "solid"?

EDDINGTON: No—no—you will see presently . . . "space pervaded, it is true, by fields of force, but these are consigned to the category of 'influences' not 'things' ".

DANTE: "Influences?" That is not an Aristotelian category—it is an astrological phrase. Are you an astrologer?

EDDINGTON: God forbid.

DANTE: He has forbidden it.

EDDINGTON: Astronomy, on the other hand, belongs to my subject. It is part of physics. But when I say "influences", I refer to a nexus of relationships——

DANTE: Between what?

EDDINGTON: Perhaps if you would let me finish the paragraph, you would see that your question is irrelevant . . . "Even into the minute part which is not empty we must not transfer the old notion of substance. In dissecting matter——"

DANTE: In dissecting WHAT? You have hitherto said nothing about Matter.

EDDINGTON: That is true—perhaps I ought not to have introduced that term so sud denly. But I refer to my phenomenal table—that is, to the material—I should say to the composition of my phenomenal table . . . "In dissecting matter into electric charges we have travelled far from that picture of it which first gave rise to the conception of substance, and the meaning of that conception—if it ever had any—has been lost by the way."

DANTE: Why? However far you dissect a particular portion of matter, you will never resolve it into a universal or a quality. Besides, a "substance" need not be material: a human soul is a substantial form, and so is an angel, who is a pure intelligence with no matter to be dissected.

EDDINGTON: That is the very point I am making. I go on: "The whole trend of modern scientific views is to break down the separate categories of 'things' and 'influences', 'forms', etc., and to substitute a common background of all experience."

DANTE: That is indeed a sweeping statement—if you mean literally that *all* experience—joy and grief, will and affection, humility and pride, sin and grace—can be resolved into electrical charges, or the relations between them.

EDDINGTON: The experiences you mention belong rather to the Department of Psychology——

DANTE: And you are not a psychologist. I must try to remember your self-imposed limitations. But perhaps you mean no more than did Thomas Aquinas when he said: "*Nihil in intellectu quod non prius in sensu.*" [1] After all, your book in its title claims to deal only with the physical world. But if you mean that the whole of physical nature is only a nexus of arrangements and relationships of the same material substratum, then what you have just said was a commonplace of philosophy long before my day.

EDDINGTON: I have defined a little further. I have said, "Whether we are studying a material object, a magnetic field, a geometrical figure, or a duration of time, our scientific information is summed up in measures."

DANTE: Well, I see you have cautiously avoided the question of psychological experience. And you restrict that which is knowable to that which is measurable. But there must, after all, be something to be measured—or else, what you call your physical world is purely conceptual and not a physical world at all. Or perhaps you are simply saying that although we may know *that* things exist, and *how* they influence one another, and even to some extent *why* they are as they are, we can never in this world attain to perfect knowledge of the thing-in-its-essence—the thing as it exists in itself.

EDDINGTON: I am not sure that either "thing" or "existence" has any clear scientific meaning. I have said as much elsewhere.

DANTE: "Content you with the *quia*, sons of Eve,
         For might you have beheld the whole truth plain
         No need had been for Mary to conceive;

         And you have seen such great souls thirst in vain
         As else had stilled that thirst in quietness
         Which now is given them for eternal pain;

         I speak of Plato, Aristotle—yes,
         And many others."
                                    Purg. iii. 37–44.

I gave those lines to Virgil. But we are Christians, and we may hope

[1] [there is] nothing in the intellect which was not first in the senses.

to know that which is not knowable to us now, though not in itself unknowable. For God knows it, and His knowledge of it is its whole existence. But you will say that this is Theology, and that you are not a theologian. But tell me—What folly in me to ask! for I am dying to know this world of matter and measure, and soon I shall know even as I am known—and yet I still want to be told things—tell me more about these electric charges, or particles, or fields of force you speak of, because there I believe you can satisfy a curiosity that has tormented me half my life.

EDDINGTON: With pleasure.

(*The reading is resumed, and proceeds without much interruption until the structure of the atom is made clear.*)

DANTE: Thank you—thank you a thousand times. What you say fills me with excitement beyond measure, and your scientific instruments can find no yard-stick to set against my gratitude. For it appears as though you had come very close to perceiving the first form of the prime matter, out of which the whole visible universe is shaped. Further than that first form you cannot go, for matter without form is unintelligible. Pardon me for using the language of my own philosophy—there is not time now to learn yours. I mean by "form" that which makes anything what it is—without form there is no "what"—there is only that bare, undifferentiated potentiality which we call the prime matter. In my younger days I doubted whether that was intelligible even to God—but I think now that He must know it, because He made it. You say you find it elusive—you cannot simultaneously measure its position and motion—you are not even sure whether to call it matter or mind-stuff. That is why I feel so sure that you have pursued it very nearly to its first form. . . . It is all most wonderful. . . . Wonderful, too, is what you tell me about the Heavens and the multiplicity of universes—though I am almost glad I did not know it earlier.

EDDINGTON: Would it have disturbed your faith?

DANTE: Why should it? No, but I should have had to re-write my poem—and it would be a great labour to reduce so vast and complex a scheme of creation into a few thousand lines of verse. Yet I am sorry I did not know that the attraction (if it is not yet wholly out of date to call it so) of all bodies is mutual. It would have suited my allegory well—since I know it is so in the metaphysical world of the heavenly Movers, where from the highest to lowest "*tutti tirati sono e tutti tirano*"—"all are drawn and draw". And a central sun about which all the planets move with their proper motion—the nearer the faster—

that would have pleased me well. For so in my vision I saw their angels move, and it troubled me that it was not so also in the world of sense.

EDDINGTON: Yet 300 years after your death, the churchmen condemned Galileo for saying that the earth went round the sun.

DANTE: Did they? Or I should rather say, will they? Yet it is a very ancient opinion. I mentioned it in my *Convivio*; but Aristotle, as we all thought, had disproved it on philosophical grounds. By your mathematical science, it seems Aristarchus was right about it after all.

EDDINGTON: Right by the Euclidean geometry we still use on Mondays, Wednesdays and Fridays. By the relativist geometry we use on other days, one may choose one's centre to suit one's own convenience.

DANTE: As you say. But I do not know why the Church should concern herself to confute Aristarchus—except that in my day the schools were almost obsessed by Aristotle.

EDDINGTON: Galileo's opinion was thought to run contrary to Scripture.

DANTE: The Scriptures are not a mathematical treatise. The blessed Augustine himself warned us against the childish habit of interpreting them too literally, for the Spirit speaks in parables and allegories.

EDDINGTON: Does not our modern cosmology overthrow your notions about the location of Heaven and Hell?

DANTE: It seems I shall have written in vain. Did I not make it sufficiently clear that Heaven has no location?

> "There and there only every longing has
>   Final attainment, perfect, ripe, and whole,
>   And there each part is where it always was,
>
> For it is not in space and has no pole."
> *Para.* xxii. 64–67.

And again:

> "Nor has this heaven any other 'where'
> Than in the mind of God."
> *Para.* xxvii. 109–110.

And in another place I speak of the Divine mind,

> "Where centres every *where* and every *when*."
> *Para.* xxix. 12.

As for Hell, it is where we make it, for it is nothing but the rejection of reality, as Heaven is the immediate knowledge of the sole Reality which is absolute. And in that knowledge, the nature of time and causality (which trouble your philosophers as much as they troubled ours) will also be known, for we shall see that nothing is *pre*-determined, but all is determined there where it is. And effects will be seen to proceed from their causes, not sequentially, but essentially, as all mathematical relations spring from the integer. For eternity is related to time as a solid to the plane figures of all its sections. You cannot construct a solid out of plane figures—no, though you should build them to infinity. Yet it contains and exhibits them all. Nevertheless, it knows them, not in sequence but simultaneously . . . But you and I are still in time, and I am detaining you too long from your purgation. Pray for me when you reach the summit of the stair.

EDDINGTON: You are forgetting. You will be there before me.

DANTE: Prayer is not subject to your second law of thermodynamics. The arrow of God's time flies both ways. We will pray for one another. Thank you, and farewell.

From this imaginary conversation, two or three points will, I hope, have emerged. The first is a difference of vocabulary. The constant modification of the meanings of words, under the pressure of association and misuse, is a standing grievance with scientifically-minded persons. Invent a technical word and define it as carefully as you will, it keeps its specialised meaning only so long as it is preserved in the hands of specialists. Release it into common use, and it at once begins to collect associative meanings as a caddis-worm collects sticks and shells. Once the journalist, the popular novelist and the cocktail-party chatterer have got hold of it, it becomes so damaged by downright mishandling as to be perilous in any argument. Look what has happened within living memory to phrases like "allergic", "sadistic", and "inferiority complex". Horrified by these results, some philosophers have tried to fall back upon the use of verbal symbols of the mathematical type, whose rule shall be "one word, one meaning". But they are caught upon the horns of a dilemma—either they must remain powerless to communicate with their fellow-creatures, or they must communicate by either releasing their symbols into common use or translating them into common words; and all is to do again. In this respect, the philosophers of our own time are much worse off than their mediaeval counterparts, for they are surrounded by an enormous public which is literate only in the sense that it can read print, and which has for the most part never undergone the linguistic discipline of the mediaeval Trivium. The average modern man is not trained either to understand the grammatical structure of language, or to express his meaning with precision, or to detect fallacies in argument. (Children are indeed encouraged to "express themselves"—but that is a very different matter, and "themselves" is about all that they express.) In view of all these difficulties, it is the more important that no one should form—much less give utterance to—any opinion on the thought of another age unless he understands its vocabulary and is able to translate it accurately into that of his own. The word "substance" is a notorious case in point. The triumph of nonsense may be seen in its full glory when any argument about transubstantiation crops up in a popular paper. But it is fascinating to see how even with an educated writer like Eddington, who has actually begun by defining "substance" more or less correctly, a sort of aura or flavour of "solidity" still clings about the word. We noticed also the sudden intrusion into the argument of question-begging words like "matter" and "material" without previous definition; and the use of long, verbose, and "atmospheric" phrases such as "that *world* which *spontaneously* appears around me when I *open my eyes*", where a mediaeval writer would have said "sensibilia", "observables", or simply "phenomena".

Not only the vocabulary, but the whole method of argument of a mediaeval writer is alien to us. Many statements are by the superficial labelled "unintelligible", "obscure", "crabbed", "superstitious", or (most detested of words) "quaint", which, when translated, turn out to be quite familiar conclusions. Thus, in the 11th canto of the *Inferno*, Dante asks Virgil why Usurers should be classed as violent offenders against God's bounty, and set to dwell upon the sterile and burning sand along with the Sodomites who violate Nature, and the Blasphemers who defy God. Here is Virgil's reply:

> "Not in one place", said he, "but many a time
>   Philosophy points out to who will learn,
>   How Nature takes her course from the sublime
>
> Intellect and Its Art; note that; then turn
>   The pages of thy *Physics*, and not far
>   From the beginning, there shalt thou discern
>
> How *your* Art, as it best can, follows her
>   Like a pupil with his master; we may call
>   This art of yours God's grandchild, as it were

By Art and Nature, if thou well recall
    How Genesis begins, man ought to get
    His bread, and make prosperity for all.

But the usurer contrives a third way yet,
    And in herself and in her follower, Art,
    Scorns Nature."   *Inf.* xi. 97–111.

The first clue to the rigmarole is the word "art", which here means the work of Man in para-creation, as Nature means the creation of the natural world by God. God creates Nature by His sole bounty; Man para-creates by his art things in imitation of Nature: his works are therefore para-created at two removes from their origin, as a grandchild is procreated at two removes from his grandparents. We then look up the opening chapters of Genesis, and find that in his time of innocence Man was "put into the Garden of Eden to dress it and to keep it"— that is, he was given natural resources and told to cultivate them. These (says Dante) are the only sources of real wealth: Nature and Art—or as we should say, Natural Resources and the Labour of Man. But the Usurer has found a third way (that is, of procuring wealth): he makes money breed money; and its results are injury to the earth and the exploitation of man—dustbowls and sweated labour in twentieth-century language, but in Dante's language, violence to Nature and Art. And injury to Nature is a crime against the bounty of God who made Nature. So that there emerges in the end, fortified by the authority of Aristotle and Scripture, a conclusion which we recognise as a very orthodox piece of economics,—one which we have proved of late by bitter experience. Possibly, if we had studied Dante (not to say Aristotle and Genesis) more receptively, we might have avoided the hard and experiential way of proof—I cannot say. In any case, what seems orthodox and even commonplace to us did not appear so to the men of the nineteenth century, by whom the conjunction in one condemnation of unmentionable vice and the most respectable kind of banking was felt to be rather worse than odd.

This brings me to another point: that in many respects our thought is nearer to Dante's to-day than perhaps at any period in the six intervening centuries. I believe, for instance, that at any time between the twelfth and the fourteenth centuries the astronomy of Galileo or the evolutionary theory of Darwin would have created far less outrage among Christian theologians than they did in the seventeenth and nineteenth centuries respectively. Two things had happened in between

—first, the Reformation, which tended to substitute the authority of an infallible Book for that of a living and infallible Church; followed by the Counter-Reformation which tended to make doctrine a more rigid and inelastic thing—to objectify and pigeon-hole it, and to take, as one may say, "the poetry out of it". Secondly, there was a growing obsession with scientific method, leading men to discount all values which were not (in the modern sense) "scientific", so that no truth was held to be true if it could not be tested in the laboratory.

A third point, which needs no labouring, is the increasing segregation of specialists in their own specialities, so that the scientist is not expected to study theology nor the theologian to study science, nor either of them to be an artist or a poet. This would matter less, of course, if they did not sometimes burst into print or speech upon one another's subjects, each interpreting the other man's pronouncements in terms of his own vocabulary, and producing inextricable confusion in the mind of the common man.

Fourthly: between one period and another there is a disparity of interest, which accounts for much that the latter age is apt to put down to ignorance and stupidity in the earlier. Not all, of course. In every branch of learning, for instance, that depends upon the accumulation of experiment and the perfecting of instruments of precision, the later age (unless, as Dante says, a barbarous time should intervene) shows a genuine advance upon the earlier. Dante's embryology, for instance, which derives directly from Aristotle, is defective, since no microscope had yet discovered sperm and ovum, not to say genes and chromosomes. Seven planets and no more were visible to his eyes, neither had any telescope beheld the satellites of Jupiter nor posed, much less solved, the conundrum of Saturn's rings.

But, allowing for all this, differences of interest and emphasis remain between one age and another, as between one contemporary and another. If I think my neighbour ignorant because he has not read the *Divine Comedy*, I ought to remember that he thinks me abysmally and contemptibly ignorant for not knowing the name of a single international football player. The average educated modern pities the mediaeval for his ignorance of the new cosmology, but is not in the least abashed that he cannot pick out and name all the constellations of the Zodiac, and is completely flummoxed by the visible heavenly motions among which Dante's verse moves with ease and fluency. In fact, he skips the astronomical bits, and is not ashamed to do so. We call the Middle Ages dirty, because they did not understand sanitation;

I do not know what mediaevals would have thought of the Industrial Age, with its rivers polluted by chemical refuse, and its skies veiled permanently with fumes and soot.

Or, to take another instance: we pride ourselves upon a "sense of period"—we are interested in differences and relativity; mediaeval men cared little for "period"—they were interested in likenesses and permanence. Yet it is in no way true to say that they had a "static" view of history; they could not, for they were Christians, and history to them was a process and development, directed from the beginning of time towards a central historical event, and proceeding thence by a steady unfolding towards the accomplishment of a supreme purpose. The whole idea of "progress" was unknown to the ancients; it is purely Christian. But the mediaevals did not admire progress for its own sake—they believed in progress to a goal. If anybody had read them the last speech of Lilith in *Back to Methuselah*, or informed them that it "was better to travel hopefully than to arrive" they would have replied that he was talking nonsense, and that the only rational hope on any journey was precisely the hope of sometime arriving.

Indeed, if I were asked to name the one particular in which the mediaeval spirit differed most profoundly from our own, I think I should have to reply, "its faith and hope in fulfilment". It believed that desire could be satisfied, that knowledge could be made perfect, that progress would some day cease because every potentiality had been fully actualised. It believed in happiness—we, for the most part, only in the pursuit of happiness.

Let us now take a brief view of Dante's cosmos, bearing these things in mind. Physically, it is much smaller than ours. In its centre is the Earth, and at the centre of the earth, perhaps, lies hell. (Those who say that the mediaeval universe is "man-centred" are mistaken—a poor view was taken of man, but not so poor as all that.)

The dimensions of the earth were known to within a few hundred miles, though mediaeval geography was sketchy, and the Americas, of course, undreamed of. The northern hemisphere was mostly land; the southern practically all water. Wrapped about the earth was the sphere of air, and beyond that, the sphere of fire—this disposed of the four elements. Incidentally, in coping with the vagaries of ancient science, one should be careful to distinguish between its good observations and the fantastic conclusions sometimes drawn from them. To have realised that matter exists in four principal forms—solid, liquid, gaseous and radiant—was sound enough. Similarly, the fixed mediaeval belief in the possibility of transmuting metals is now seen to be justified; and the pitying scorn once poured upon the search for the Philosopher's Stone should be confined to the means used, which were ill-adapted for their purpose, and not extended to the object of research itself. A long time-lag was of course necessary before scientific instruments and experiment could catch up with this ancient piece of insight, and the search was, in any case, undertaken for the wrong motive. But I want to come back to that later.

Circling about the earth were the seven planets, each carried upon a transparent sphere which performed its revolution from East to West every 24 hours, and each moving by its proper motion from West to East in a series of complicated epicycles—except the Sun, whose proper movement was simple and circular.

The distance of the Moon was exactly known, since, owing to its nearness, its parallax could be measured without instruments. Educated people in the thirteenth century did *not* believe that the tallest mountains on earth touched the Moon's orbit—though I have seen this implied by one of those writers who like to appear superior to their forefathers.[1]

Beyond the spheres of the planets was that of the Fixed Stars; beyond that, the crystalline sphere, or Primum Mobile, whose speed could not be measured, though (or because) it imparted speed to all the rest and was the measure of their movement.

Beyond this, physically, there was nothing, for, as Dante has already pointed out, the true Heaven or Empyrean "is not in space and turns upon no pole". So far, then, the Dantean cosmos is, compared to ours, as a pinhole to Diocletian's Palace.

But if we consider its metaphysical aspect, we shall find our ideas somewhat enlarged, for we must now take into account the hierarchy of Being.

Of Absolute Being, there is One and One alone—God, the sole Reality, the only true Existence, the Prime Mover, the First Intelligible, Pure Act, who Is all that He Has. We need not waste time piling up the technical phrases; the important thing is to remember that for

---

[1] What some mediaeval astronomer may have said is that the "Sphere of Air" surrounding the Earth was deemed to cease at about the height reached by the tallest mountains, and that the transparent sphere carrying the Moon and her epicycle was calculated as beginning at that point. It was, however, more usually held that the "Sphere of Fire" intervened between the Sphere of Air and the Sphere of the Moon. (See *Paradiso* i. 7 *seq*.)

mediaeval Christians (as indeed for all instructed Christians) God alone is Self-Existent. All other existence derives from Him and is contingent. He alone knows all things in their essence—that is, as they are in themselves—because He made them. All relations are relative except the relations within the Trinity of Godhead, and the relation between creature and Creator. All knowledge is relative except the Divine Knowledge and that which the Angels and the Blessed know in Him. Nothing can be understood of the mediaeval cosmos, unless we *begin* with God and understand that He is conceived—not as an external ruler,—but as the sole Reality and source of all contingent realities.

Having thus postulated God, we come to the order of creation, which extends in a continuous chain from highest to lowest. Highest are the nine Angelic orders—pure Intelligences, created in the mode of eternity, not changing nor developing, but possessed in the everlasting moment of eternity each of the fullness of his bliss. These nine orders are the Movers of the nine celestial spheres. At the lowest end of the scale is the Prime Matter, which we have already discussed—an almost-nothing, distinguished from the nothing out of which it was created only by its bare potentiality for receiving form, and so becoming a something.

These, together with the human soul and the body of the First Man, are (according to Dante) the only creatures directly made by God. In the making of all other creatures, the Intelligences co-operate. If the first few verses of Genesis were translated into the language of mediaeval theology, they would run something like this:

In His timelessness, Being called into being the Intelligences and the Prime Matter. And the Prime Matter was without form and unintelligible; and space lay in darkness. And the Power of the First Mover moved upon the unmeasuredness of space. And Act expressed Itself in the creation of light. And the movement of the light was the beginning of time.

If we ask why God should make a creation, Dante has his answer ready. It was not that creation could add anything to God, since He is and has everything in Himself; but that His splendour, shining back to Him, might be able to declare "I am"—"*subsisto*". The intention of creation was to create, that is, a joy that could rejoice in its own being, each creature after its own manner, and reflect back to God the joy and gifts that He bestowed upon it. It is thus right and proper for creatures to have an individual existence—the end of each is not (as in some

Oriental religions) to be re-absorbed into the One, but each to remain its true self—the self that exists in God and is centred upon God.

Between the Prime Matter and the Intelligences come in ascending order: first, inorganic matter, which has existence but no life; then plants, which have existence and life but no consciousness; next the animals, which have existence, life, and consciousness, but no self-consciousness. All these creatures are produced, or developed, or evolved through the operation of the Intelligences, or, if we like to call them so, the Forces of Nature, who on each case stamp upon the predisposed matter the form which makes it what it is. Mediaeval opinion differed as to whether these stages of development were originally successive, as the Aristotelians thought, and the Six Days of Creation would suggest, or whether, as St. Augustine thought, the whole creaturely Universe was the result of a single simultaneous act. Dante, who is rather more Aristotelian than Augustinian, is at any rate perfectly aware of the recapitulation of the race-history in the embryo.

Above the animals comes the rational animal, Man—the only species of that order known to Dante or so far to anybody. Up to a certain point, the human organism too is the work of natural forces; but, as soon as "the articulation of the brain has been completed in the embryo:

> Then the First Mover turns to it, full fain
> Of Nature's triumph, and inbreathes a rare
> New spirit, filled with virtue to constrain
>
> To its own substance whatso active there
> It finds, and make one single soul complete,
> Alive, and sensitive, and self-aware."
>
> *Purg.* xxv. 70-75.

This new creation, made directly by God, without the co-operation of natural forces, is by Dante correctly called "spirit", and not "soul". Observe, too, that he speaks of its "substance". It is not a quality or a universal, but has individual existence. Note too that it has virtue (i.e. power) to "compel to its own substance" all the active principles it finds already existing (i.e. life and consciousness) and so make "one single soul complete". This compound is the rational soul, and we must observe three things about it. First, it is a *compound*—it is not a "portion of the universal spirit" temporarily lodged in an animal container, like brandy in a bottle: it is inextricably fused with the vegetable and animal life and consciousness to make "one single soul complete". Secondly, the spirit is a "substantial form" and compels the rest to its own substantiality. Consequently, although for its entire completeness the soul needs its full physical animality, it is able to subsist after death, while awaiting the resurrection of the body. But in separation from the body its perfection is impaired and not increased. That is why the doctrine of the immortality of the soul, though Christians do in fact believe it, is not particularly characteristic of Christianity, nor even vital to it. No Christian creed so much as mentions it, and theoretically, it would be quite compatible with Christian belief if soul as well as body had to undergo the experience of death. The characteristic belief of Christendom is in the Resurrection of the Body and the life everlasting of the complete body-soul complex. Excessive spirituality is the mark, not of the Christian, but of the Gnostic.

To return to the rational soul. It is this that gives Man his unique position in the hierarchy of being. He is the junction of the physical and the metaphysical. In his bodily part he subsumes all physical nature, from animal consciousness to bare brute matter. By his rational soul he is akin to the angels, who also are substantial forms. His specific virtue—that which characterises him as man and distinguishes him from the rest of the creation—is the possession of a possible (or potential) intellect. Animals have no *intellectus* though all have an instinct and some have intelligence. The angel has an intellect, but in an angel all the powers of the intellect are always fully actualised. Only man has a *possible* intellect, containing powers some of which are unused or undeveloped, and capable of learning by experience. Man belongs also to the side of the angels by reason of the freedom of his will.

The loose assertions one hears made to-day to the effect that mediaeval people believed the entire cosmos to have been created for the benefit of Man are thus seen to be quite baseless. The cosmos was made for its own sake; and Dante takes it for granted that the Angels are nearer and dearer to God than the rest of creation.[1] The importance of Man lay in the fact that he occupied a key-position, and that, by misusing his freedom, he disturbed the order of the universe and was the occasion of God's great act of redemption.

The nature and consequences of sin are too large an issue to discuss here. Briefly, the doctrine is that the first rational man, by repudiating his creaturely status and centring his will upon self instead of God, introduced into the psyche of his species what we might nowadays describe as a hereditary trauma, transmitted in the act of generation to

[1] *Purg.* xi. 1–3.

his whole posterity; and that release from this condition could be expected only through the agency of the Incarnate Godhead. The mention of this brings us to mediaeval psychology, which is more properly a part of our subject.

The first thing that strikes us is one of those fundamental divergences of interest which open so large a gap between one generation and another. One question that has bulked large in our eyes for the last century or so attracted little or no attention six centuries back. The Middle Ages had practically no psychology of the sub-conscious. They were not altogether unaware of the existence of the dim regions beneath the threshold; but they were not interested. This was in a way unfortunate; for it involved them in much speculation about the trans-mission of hereditary guilt which an examination of the sub-conscious might have cleared up. The examination was eventually undertaken by a generation of scientists to whom the whole concept of original sin had become alien; and its results were received rather with alarm than alacrity by a Church which had lost her eager mediaeval curiosity, and did not quite realise that a new argument for her traditional truth had actually been presented to her.[1]

But the reason why the Middle Ages did not seize their opportunity is, I think, fairly obvious. Their minds were otherwise engaged. The psychology of the conscious, and the thorough investigation of the processes of conscious thought, absorbed them to the exclusion of everything else in the psychological field. Emerging from the Dark Ages, when learning had only been kept alive in the West by the dogged persistence of isolated communities, cut off from almost all literary sources except the Scriptures, the Schoolmen were intoxicated by the heady draughts of the new—or rather the old—learning which came to them from the East—chiefly, of course, in the form of Latin translations of Aristotle. The *Organon*, which was widely available all over the West by the middle of the twelfth century, provided them with what they had never had before,—an apparatus of orderly thinking; and the stream of volumes, spreading across Europe, brought to them more and more exciting materials on which to whet and exercise their wonderful new intellectual tools. A century or so later—that is, by the time Dante was born—almost the whole of the Philosopher's works were in their hands. It is scarcely surprising that they had little attention to devote to anything else. Especially as, while

[1] For an interesting restatement of the doctrine of the Fall in terms of modern psychology, see B. G. Sanders' *Christianity after Freud* (Bles, 1949).

coping with all this abundant new material, they had also to wrestle with the task of accommodating it to the revealed doctrine of Scripture. That task had been familiar to Augustine in the fourth century and his Platonic tradition still survived; but now it had to be undertaken all over again.

Nothing, I think, should give us more respect for the mediaeval churchmen than their courage and versatility in the face of this problem. When shallow people say that, at this period "education had got into the hands of the Church" they usually say it with a derogatory implication—as though one should say that the liquor trade had got into the hands of racketeers. It is really more like saying that the shipwrecked crew had got into the hands of the lifeboat-men. The Church was concerned to advance learning in the universities and likewise to gain a rational understanding of her own doctrines—but the new weapon added to her armoury was double-edged. For one could not disguise from one's self that it had been forged by heathen hands, and that the Aristotelian learning took no account of the truths of Revelation.

Let us be clear what this means. By "revelation" in this context is meant, primarily, not inspiration and prophecy, but a unique historical event of shattering importance. It was not the fault of Aristotle that he had lived before the time of Christ—but there it was. Since he wrote, an event had occurred which had changed the whole orientation of philosophy, history, and ethics. Whatever was, in fact, true, remained true; the general revelation given to all men by the light of reason could not, ultimately, be irreconcilable with the especial revelation given in Jesus Christ; but it must, in the nature of things, be imperfect. And to trust to it implicitly would be dangerous.

Let us put it this way. You would probably hesitate about entrusting your children and friends to a hospital, however well-managed and well-arranged, which took no account of any developments in medicine later than the time of Hippocrates. Similarly, the mediaeval Church was dubious about entrusting her children to a philosophy that was, literally, out of date in the Year One. Yet something had to be done about it, for the books went on arriving, and nothing could keep them out of the universities. Various attempts were made to prohibit them from the syllabus until such time as the text could be expurgated and commented for the elimination of heathen error; but all was in vain. We find the University of Toulouse sending out an advertising circular, one of whose attractions was, "Come to Toulouse and study there those books of Aristotle which are forbidden to be read in Paris." In Paris itself, violent uproars and demonstrations took place; the University was split from top to bottom, and Masters of Faculty had to be sternly prohibited from taking part in torchlight processions and singing songs on the quays at night. The Church girded up her loins and charged two great Masters with the task of constructing a synthesis. The work of Albertus Magnus was followed by the great *Summa* of Thomas Aquinas, and peace was established between reason and faith for several centuries.

The struggle of the Church at that time was thus not primarily with science, but with a pagan philosophy. Her method of tackling it suggests that if only she had been in a position to tackle Copernican astronomy, Darwinian evolution, Freudian psychology and Einsteinian relativity in the same spirit, much distress and heart-burning might have been saved. But for various reasons, her reactions in later centuries could not be so prompt or so elastic. I believe that all these ideas, if they could have been presented to twelfth- or thirteenth-century theologians, could have been accommodated with comparatively little trouble, and in some cases perhaps even welcomed as confirmation of that which in later times they seemed to contradict.

However, it is not possible for everything to happen at once. We are left with our mediaeval psychology, which was, of course, faculty psychology—shrewd and penetrating enough to have influenced our common thought and speech to this day. Indeed, we still talk mediaeval psychology in practical life just as we talk Ptolemaic astronomy. We speak of will and judgement as we speak of sunrise and sunset.

The problem of free will and free judgement naturally preoccupied the mediaeval psychologist a good deal, closely bound up as it is with the whole subject of ethics on the one hand and of determinacy on the other. Generally speaking, the man of the Middle Ages held that *nature* was strictly determined, due allowance being made for the operations of what the Ancients called "chance" and Christians call "Providence". Man, on the other hand, was determined as regards his natural physical make-up, but free as regards his will and judgement—free, that is, in so far as sin had not subjected his higher to his lower faculties. One of the main operations of Grace was precisely to restore to the will and judgement that full freedom which sin had impaired. To this complex of freedom and determination in Man's nature, mediaeval writers return over and over again: frequently, as in the 16th Canto of *Purgatorio*, their treatment of it takes the form of an argument as to whether or not destiny is ruled by the stars. On the lips of a well-instructed man like Dante, this phrase stands, of course, for the determinacy of the physical world: the spheres, which are moved by the Intelligences, govern the motions of every material atom in the universe: if the system is so tightly locked that *everything* is rigidly ruled by these movements, then no choice is possible, and the whole cosmos is mechanistic. (Astrology in the sense of fortune-telling was frowned on, then as now, by right-minded people; and Dante places astrologers with witches and sorcerers in the lower reaches of Hell.)

The following speech from *Purgatorio* xviii gives a good summary of sound Aristotelian teaching on this question of freedom. Virgil is the speaker, and he begins by disclaiming any ability to speak about the work of Grace in this connection. Dante has asked whether the attraction of the soul to a beloved object is irresistible; because, if so, we can neither be blamed for pursuing an evil object nor praised for pursuing a good one. Note the reference in the first lines to the "substantial form" and its composition with the material body: and to Man's "specific virtue", which is the potential intellect.

> To each substantial form that doth compound
>   With matter, though distinct from it, there cleaves
>   Specific virtue, integral, inbound,
>
> Which, save in operation, none perceives—
>   It's known by its effects, as, in the plant,
>   Life manifests itself by the green leaves.
>
> So how his intellect's made cognisant
>   Of the prime concepts, or what guides his aim
>   Toward the first appetibles, man's ignorant;

[Because, that is, these things are the necessary postulates of all operations of the intellect.]

> Such things are instincts in you, much the same
>   As is in bees the honey-making bent;
>   This prime volition earns nor praise nor blame.
>
> Now, to keep all volitions else well blent
>   With this, you have a counsellor-power innate
>   Set there to guard the threshold of assent:
>
> That is the principle to which relate
>   All your deserts, according as its fan
>   Is strict to purge right loves from reprobate.

They who by reasoning probed creation's plan
Root-deep, perceived this inborn liberty
And bequeathed ethics to the race of man.

Grant, then, all loves that wake in you to be
Born of necessity, you still possess
Within yourselves the power of mastery;

And this same noble faculty it is
Beatrice calls Free Will.   *Purg.* xviii. 49-74.

The threshold at which the Censor sits is not, of course, the threshold of consciousness, but what we might call the threshold of intention—the point at which some desire which you cannot help entertaining either is rejected, or assented to and embraced by the will. The presence of a similar Censor at the lower level was not then suspected.[1]

I am not sure what attitude Dante and his contemporaries would have taken to the idea of indeterminacy in *nature*, which is put forward by some physicists in connection with the orbit-jumps of the electron. It would probably have startled them more than the complementary efforts of some psychologists to show that the human will is determined. The latter was, after all, a heretical notion to which they were accustomed. I am inclined to think that orthodox persons would have opposed the concept of an indeterminate nature; they would undoubtedly have thought poorly of the pathetic efforts of certain modern churchmen to allege physical indeterminacy as a proof of God's existence. They would probably have said either that the orbit-jumps would, on further examination, turn out to conform to a law: or, that their unpredictability was certainly another manifestation of the hidden working of "Holy Luck" or Providence, but no more a proof of the Divine existence than the predictable laws. I do not think they knew much about statistical laws or the laws of probability. That problem, like the problem of the transmutation of metals, exemplifies the importance, in the development of any science, of having the right sort of interest of the right sort of people directed to a subject at the right time. So long as transmutation was studied only in a commercial spirit by investigators who wanted to fabricate wealth quickly, no result was produced. Similarly, down to a comparatively short time ago, the laws of probability engaged the attention chiefly of insurance companies and persons pursuing their scientific studies at

[1] For a more extended commentary on this passage, see below, *The Cornice of Sloth*, p. 124 *seq.*

Monte Carlo. The "systems" for betting on the red, and the mediaeval "systems" for wedding sulphur and mercury in an alembic to propagate gold have a sinister family likeness of fantasy. The subjection of scientific inquiry to the requirements of political ideologies presents a disquieting likeness to both. Some odd biological theories have issued from both German and Russian universities—I do not know what may be happening nearer at hand. One is reminded of the violent protests made by the Averroïsts of the thirteenth century against the procedure of St. Thomas, who was, they complained, distorting Aristotle in the interests of Christianity. I do not think St. Thomas was himself doing this; but some authorities in the Paris University undoubtedly were, and in fact shamelessly instructed the Masters of Faculty to that effect. The protest was at any rate an honourable one, and gained for the Averroïst leader, Sigier of Brabant, a place among the Doctors in Dante's *Paradiso*.

Another modern cosmological theory which one would like to have seen presented to a mediaeval mind is that recently broadcast to an astonished world of the continuous creation of matter out of nothing. It certainly conflicts with Genesis ii. 2, but not more so than the continuous creation of new souls. On the other hand, it contains nothing *per se* incompatible with the nature of a God who is pure Being and pure Act, and it might even have been welcomed as proof of that nature. It would at any rate have been much more philosophically pleasing to the mediaeval mind than the notion, so dear to the eighteenth-century Deist, of a clock-making Divinity who, having once wound up His creation and set it going, retired into apathy and took no further interest in its proceedings. On the whole, and once the preliminary shock had been absorbed, I think the mediaevals might rather have liked it. But all this is speculation.

The distinguishing marks of the mediaeval cosmos were hierarchy, order, and purpose. These were reflected in the political ideals of the day: church and state, with their ascending ranks of honour, founded upon function and status; the steady effort to bring code and canon law into conformity with natural law; the tenacious belief in the ultimate establishment of a perfect universal state that should usher in the reign of the Kingdom of God on earth. This ideal, like the cosmos upon which it was modelled, wins little admiration from an age which prefers equality to hierarchy, and contract to status; which seems to have almost abandoned hope or belief in purpose; and whose conception of order wavers between totalitarian bureaucracy and a catch-as-catch-can individualism. The contempt for mediaeval sociology sometimes extends itself, in an odd way, to the cosmos itself: I have seen Dante mildly sneered at in a popular organ, for "living in a neat and narrow cosmos"—as though it were somehow easier to be virtuous and intelligent in a cosmos not too cluttered with nebulae. Perhaps it is: "the silence of these infinite spaces terrifies us"; we cringe under the menace of mere size and number, we are disturbed by our inability to discern any central purpose, we do not know whether this unwieldy, many-dimensional, expanding and evolving multiplex has any order or not. It is the *silence* of the spaces that is terrifying: we no longer believe in the celestial Movers.[1] Or is it, perhaps, the other way round? Does Man make a cosmos after his own image? Is it, either way, a coincidence that the rather terrifying pronouncement, "randomness always increases", seems at the moment applicable alike to the microcosm and the macrocosm?

It would almost seem as though, in their pre-occupation with astronomical numbers and distances, the mathematicians of the new age had lost grasp of the eternal and the infinite, to which all size and number are equally indifferent.

[1] It is entertaining to set side by side two passages, written at an interval of almost exactly three hundred years. The first celebrates the passing of these "superstitious" beliefs which subjected Nature to the control of "Fantastical Forms", with the result that "men began to be frighted from their Cradles":

> But from the time in which the Real Philosophy has appear'd there is scarce any whisper remaining of such horrors: Every man is unshaken at those Tales at which his Ancestors trembled: *The course of things goes quietly along, in its own true channel of Natural Causes and Effects.* For this we are beholden to Experiments; which though they have not yet completed the discovery of the true world, yet they have already vanquish'd those wild inhabitants of the false world, that us'd to astonish the minds of men.
>
> Thomas Sprat: History of the Royal Society, 1667.

From the second it would appear that though "Experiments" have considerably enlarged the scope of discovery, men remain oddly liable to be frightened and astonished, even in the absence of "wild inhabitants" and "fantastical forms":

> It seems to me that religion is but a blind attempt to find an escape from *the truly dreadful situation in which we find ourselves. Here we are in this wholly fantastic universe* with scarcely a clue as to whether our existence has any real significance. No wonder then that many people feel the need for some belief that gives them a sense of security.
>
> Fred Hoyle: The Nature of the Universe (Blackwell, 1950).

Italics mine in both cases. One would hardly think that the two men are speaking of the same universe.

O Grace abounding, whereby I presumed
   So deep the eternal light to search and sound
   That my whole vision was therein consumed!

In that abyss I saw how love held bound
   Into one volume all the leaves whose flight
   Is scattered through the universe around;

How substance, accident, and mode unite
   Fused so to speak together, in such wise
   That this I speak of is one simple light.

Yea, of this complex I believe mine eyes
   Beheld the universal form—I feel,
   Even as I speak, such springs of rapture rise.
                         Para. xxxiii. 82–90.

Thus Dante; and again:

The glory of Him who moves all things soe'er
   Impenetrates the universe, and bright
   The splendour burns, more here, and lesser there.
                         Para. i. 1.

                         (Royal Institution
                         1951)

THE EIGHTH BOLGIA

THE DIVINE COMEDY—and let us not forget it—is a poem which tells a story. It is easy enough for superior persons to scorn the story-teller's art and patronise his unsophisticated audience. Story-telling (so they say, and I will not deny it) is a knack often possessed by very vulgar and illiterate writers; the eagerness to know "what happened next" is (no doubt) a mark of the eternal child in all of us. Good story-telling often results—discreditably—in popularity and large sales, and is therefore a thing to be condemned of the high-minded; and it is all the more disconcerting to discover that good story-telling is one of the conditions of earthly immortality. Without it, no long narrative whether in prose or verse has ever been able to survive, save in the sheltered libraries of culture; with it, many works which by academic standards ought to have died before they were born live on, indomitable and irrepressible, from one generation to another.

The good story-teller is born, not made; and this is perhaps the reason why his art is despised by the learned, for learning can neither bestow it nor account for it. It can, of course, be analysed; and those who already have it can improve it by pains and practice; but those who by nature are without it cannot acquire it—it is a gift, like a turn for writing stage dialogue. Yet, like every other gift, it is mightiest in the mighty: by itself, it can produce the minor immortality of a *Sherlock Holmes* or a *Three Musketeers*; in the hands of a great poet it produces the major immortality of an *Odyssey*, a *Paradise Lost*, or a *Divine Comedy*. And, whether we like it or not, we have to acknowledge that the whole vast structure of Dante-study and Dante-criticism—theological, philosophical, historical, philological, poetical and what-not—beneath which the book-shelves of Christendom sag, is carried upon the sturdy bones of a narrative, as the reality of all the universe once endured to be carried upon a donkey.

Dante is an incomparable story-teller. For sheer skill and mastery in the art of putting a narrative poem together, I do not think there is anyone to touch him—particularly when one takes into account the number and variety of the threads he has woven together to make his vast allegorical tapestry. I shall not in this paper attempt to appreciate the grand architectural outlines of the poem as a whole; I propose to take only one little section of it and examine that in detail, showing from time to time how it is related to the over-riding narrative scheme. Of the two cantos devoted to the Eighth Bolgia I have selected the first (Canto 26), which is the most beautiful in the *Inferno*, and which displays Dante's craftsmanship on two different scales: on the large scale, in his management of the general movement of the poem; on the small scale, in the inset narrative of the voyage of Ulysses.

We shall, for this purpose, approach the subject, not primarily from the Christian, historical, or political point of view (though we cannot avoid all allusion to Dante's purpose in writing), but chiefly from the literary point of view, to see how a major poet copes with the fundamental task of telling a story in verse.

Let us begin by remembering exactly where we have got to. We are more than two-thirds of the way down Malebolge, the grim grey funnel of stone that shelves centrewards from the Great Barrier below the Abominable Sand to the lip of the Well where the Giants stand, and Nimrod blows his horn in the everlasting twilight. Round Malebolge run the ten great pits of damnation, carved in the eternal rock and bridged by the colossal spurs, like the spokes of a cartwheel, along which Dante and Virgil, and we with them, have painfully clambered upon our perilous journey. Between the fifth and sixth *bolge* the bridges are all shattered by the earthquake that accompanied Christ's Harrowing of Hell, and here the monotonous gloom of the descent was broken for us by a burst of ghastly merriment, when Ciampolo the Barrator played his trick upon the demons and two of them fell, "chewing and clawing" one another, into the boiling pitch. There was a moment of terror and excitement when the angry devils turned on the poets, and Virgil had to slither over the bank, carrying Dante to safety in his arms. There was the long and difficult climb up from the *bolgia* of the Hypocrites to the arch of the Seventh Bridge. Then came the verminous horror of the *bolgia* of the Thieves, where man and reptile hideously interchange and blend their shapes. (I well remember that when, without previous knowledge or preparation, I first read that passage the hair rose on my head, and even now that I have become familiar with it by translating it, it still keeps its dreadful fascination.) We have lingered in this revolting chasm for two cantos, and we are about to pass on to the bloody mutilations of the Ninth and the filthy diseases of the Tenth chasm, which lose nothing of their repulsiveness for being described with Dante's grisly humour and dry precision of detail. If we are to go on without being made almost physically sick, there must be some change of tone, to afford us time for recovery. It is for this reason, I think, that Dante has lavished his art to fill the Eighth Bolgia with an austere and moving beauty. Torment is there, but grief is stressed rather than torment; the lovely simple verse, suiting itself to each variation of mood as easily as a kid glove to the hand, maintains itself more consistently in the grand manner than in any other part of the *Inferno*; the humour, modulating from tragic irony to tender absurdity and thence to a devilish mockery, never touches the coarse and brutal notes which bray and blare in the Fifth Bolgia, for example, or the Tenth; of the two cantos devoted to the Counsellors of Fraud, the second tells a human story, painful in the extreme, but suffused all through with the dark passion of Dante's pity; the first, almost purged of horror by the sheer magic of the narration, has, set within it, the strange, romantic tale of the Last Voyage of Ulysses—a wonderful piece of swift, direct story-telling, and the supreme example, I suppose, that literature has to offer of the perfect fusion of classic outline and mediaeval colour.

This is the canto upon which we are now to concentrate. I remember very well how, when I had translated it as well as I could, I read the result aloud to a couple of friends who knew little of Dante, and had, until then, endured my mania for the *Comedy* with sympathetic interest rather than a whole-hearted answering enthusiasm. When I had done, they remained silent for a few seconds, and then exclaimed with one voice: "Great heavens! I had no idea that there was anything like that in Dante!" Even the thick veil of an English rendering could not muffle the free and splendid stride of the narrative. I will now take the magical thing apart and try to show, so far as it can be shown, how beautifully it is put together, and with what a cunning hand. Analysis may sometimes be a bad thing—we have had only too much, in late years, of the white-ant school of critics, who niggle out the pith of a man's work, leaving only a hollow shell and a little heap of dry dust. Yet there is much to be said for a return to that more ancient critical modesty which was content, while analysing, to point out such felicities as the running reader might perchance have over-looked, and to record its marginal judgement that the creator's work is very good. So let us begin. We are standing on a shelf of rock part-way down (I think) on the lower wall of the Bolgia of the Thieves, among whom Dante has recognised no fewer than five of his fellow-Florentines. To continue our journey we shall now have to scramble back up the bank, and thence up the side of the rocky spur which will eventually bring us on to the crown of the bridge from which we overlook the Eighth Bolgia.

The canto opens with a terrible ironic salute to Florence [1]—less savage than the satire which closes the great denunciation of Italy in the 6th Canto of the *Purgatorio*, but no less bitter and still more heavily charged with personal feeling. It echoes the dreadful cry in the *Convivio*—"*O misera, misera patria mia!*" [2]—the broken-hearted reproach of the man who loves his city and knows that she is doomed and deserves her doom, and whose love is full of anger and hatred both of her doom and her. For Dante, "who", says Browning, "loved well because he hated", love was always, one way or another, the "lord of terrible aspect". Only his love for Beatrice, and through her for all women, was completely taken up and resolved in the love of God, so that he remains for us the poet in whom, almost uniquely, sex is without either sentimentality or bitterness. Otherwise, his love —whether for Florence or for Italy or for his fellow-men—was of the fierce and ravaging kind: he scourged all those whom he received. But why—since it is his art and not his character that we are discussing— why is this great desolate cry placed precisely here at the opening of this canto?

First and foremost, because it is a *great* cry. Look how it immediately sets the scale and tone of what is to follow. The 25th Canto closed on a quiet, almost colloquial note with the identification of the Florentine thieves. Now the voice jumps, as it were, a whole octave and rings out high and loud: "*Godi, Fiorenza, poi che sei sì grande*"—and then follows the simile of huge wings "beating over land and sea": the great words, the big image—vastness, wideness, space—and the sudden plunge into the depths—"*e per l'inferno il tuo nome si spande*". [3] Then, by a quick turn, the whole movement is controlled, gathered up and turned inward to himself—"I am ashamed"—and he adds, with deadly meiosis: "it will raise thee to no great honour". And again he expands—this time into a new kind of vastness, the dim borderland of vision and prophecy: "if near the morning"—in the vague

---

[1] The references, where not otherwise indicated, are to the canto under discussion.

[2] O my country! my wretched, wretched country!
Conv. IV. xxvii.

[3] Florence, rejoice, because thy soaring fame
Spreads its broad wings across both land and sea,
And all the deep of hell rings with thy name!
Inf. xxvi. 1–3.

shadowland that comes before dawn—"men dream true dreams"—why then, Florence is doomed; and he once more contracts the thing and focuses it in upon himself: "Well, then, let it come—'twere well it were done quickly—the older I grow the heavier it will be to bear."

We are looking at *him* now—so cleverly has our eye been brought back from its wanderings—looking at Dante as he stands wrapped in melancholy meditation on the bank, and now we see him suddenly pull himself together and get back to the job in hand. "We departed thence," he says, abruptly; "my guide remounted the cliff and drew me up after him." Yes, of course. It was Virgil who roused him out of his brooding—Virgil, who was always a little fretted by Dante's tendency to dawdle and dream, and had frequently to speak sharply to him about it. We see the whole action as though it were shown on a screen: Virgil moves off—Dante, with a start, remembers what he is doing and turns to follow. Three lines describe the climb and contrive to pack a long extent of time and space into that brief compass. The figures of the two companions show like climbing insects against the background of that "*via solinga*",[1] piled with crags and boulders, up which Dante, encumbered with his heavy body, scrambles slowly and painfully, using hands as well as feet. At last they are up; and the unhappiness for which he had not time while he was climbing comes flooding over him in a fresh wave. "I sorrowed then—I sorrow now when I think of what I saw"—grief, and a warning. Most commentators take the next lines as applying only to what he sees in the Eighth Bolgia, but I am inclined myself to interpret them as looking both forwards and back. "*Those* men were Florentines, brought up like me in the 'great city by Arno's lovely stream', sharing with me her art and culture, sharing my opportunities; and *these* were men like me, sharing my intellectual powers and my political interests; Heaven grant me humility, for well I know I lack it—and there but for the grace of God go I."

But now for the second time he shakes himself out of his musing, this time with a still more abrupt transition. "*Quante il villan, ch'al poggio si riposa . . .*"[2] he suddenly lifts us right out of the stuffy, enclosed atmosphere of Hell and perches us on an Italian hillside. Hell is hot, and the hillside is hot too, for it is summer—but the iron-grey

[1] solitary way.
[2] . . . as the peasant at rest
On some hillside . . .
        Inf. xxvi. 25–26.

rocks have vanished: we are looking down over a quiet pastoral landscape. The peasant has done his day's work and is resting (in Hell nobody ever rests—it is all one treadmill round of ceaseless, meaningless activity—but the peasant is resting); and it will soon be cool, because the sun is going down—it is the hour when the fly yields to the mosquito. (I take Dante's word for it that there is such an hour; my only experience is of Venice in August, and there was then no moment of the day or night when the mosquito was not triumphant; but that is very likely due to the canals and the close neighbourhood of the *laguna morta*—Venetian mosquitoes are celebrated for their ferocity.) At any rate, it is evening; the peasant is contemplating a homely and familiar scene, "the valley where he tills the fields and gathers grapes", and there he sees the fireflies glittering along the valley beneath him—"So numerous," says Dante, "I saw the eighth *bolgia* gleam with fires"; and we realise that we have got to the crown of the bridge and are looking down into the pit below. (Ten times, as the poets progress down Malebolge, the poet has to indicate this moment of arrival; and we may note this skilful variation, to avoid monotonous repetition.)

Having struck the note of beauty in this serene and charming simile, which seems, so far as we are concerned, to take the heat and torment out of the flame and leave it pure light, Dante proceeds to strike it again in a second simile. This time it is not from daily life, but from literature—he goes back to the Old Testament. Here occurs the one line which the modern reader might, perhaps, wish away from this canto: the story about the children who mocked Elisha and were promptly eaten by bears seems to us both comic and repulsive, and we do not much care to be reminded of it. We must remember that it probably did not worry the mediaeval mind in the same way. Dante no doubt wished to avoid confusion between the names Elia and Eliséo; what was more important, the word "orsi" offered a convenient rhyme for the word "levorsi". "*Quando i cavalli al cielo erti levorsi*"— "when the horses rose upright to Heaven". I do not know how, nowadays, we should visualise the departure of Elijah's fiery chariot—most likely we should see it skimming away horizontally and gradually rising, like an aeroplane taking off. But Dante evidently saw the horses "*erti*"—rearing erect. And that is exactly how you will find them in the illuminated margin of the Winchester Bible. It is rather pleasant to think that here, perhaps, is a picture fixed in Dante's mind from the days when, as a child, he pored over the gay and gilded miniatures of

the family Vulgate. But after this, he does his own visualising. He sees
the chariot as it goes up and up, soaring into the sky till the form of
man and horses is lost and the straining eyes of Elisha can see nothing
but the flame *"si come nuvoletta, in su salire"*.[1]

So, back from the quiet earth and the open sky to the stone circles of
Hell: "even so the flames moved through the gullet of the pit, for each
holds a stolen sinner and none betrays the theft". This is the last stage
of the men who counselled Fraud; they filched away the integrity of
other men, laying stealthy hands on their purposes and wrapping them
up in a tissue of deceits; and so it is with them for ever. They can
neither be seen nor see—the enclosing flame shrouds and (as the
following canto shows) also deceives them; neither can they speak
directly with their own tongues, for that they never did. They used
other men's tongues to speak their lies for them; and now the flame
itself is the only tongue they have.

But we are running too far ahead. Dante has not yet told us all this;
in fact he does not yet know himself, and—good Heavens! what is the
man doing? He has scrambled up on to the spur and is craning over
so perilously that, as he says: "if I had not clung to a bit of rock I
should have gone over without being pushed". Well, really! And
suppose he did go over, with his heavy, vulnerably mortal body
bouncing from crag to crag and landing with a crash in the bottom of
the *bolgia*. Our hearts go out to Virgil, who, no doubt, would have
had to report this unfortunate accident to Beatrice.

Nobody has ever yet, I think, sufficiently considered this journey
from Virgil's point of view, or realised the anxiety he must have undergone in carrying out "this novel charge"—*"quest' ufficio nuovo"* as he
calls it to the sympathetic Chiron, with (one fancies) a small depre-
cating gesture and whimsical twist of the lips. Dante is so absurd and
so tiresome—always panicking when he most needs to keep his head,
and giving way to a lunatic heedlessness when he really ought to be
careful. The full flavour of this nerve-racking moment cannot be fully
appreciated till we realise how often this same kind of thing has
happened. Dante clambering down the broken precipice below the
Minotaur, for instance, and feeling the stones move beneath his unaccustomed weight. "I went bemused", he says—naturally; that is the
very moment he would select for going off into a brown study, at
the imminent risk of missing his footing and pitching head-first into the

[1] Like a little, shining cloud, high in the skies.
Inf. xxvi. 39.

river of boiling blood or under the hoofs of the Centaurs.[1] Then there is the scramble up by the shattered bridge out of the *bolgia* of the Hypocrites, with Virgil hoisting him from behind, telling him where to catch hold, and beseeching him in imploring tones—"Try this, test it first; make sure it will bear your weight".[2] There is the moment, high up on the bare narrow cornices of Purgatory when Virgil feels he really cannot take any more risks and moves over to walk on the outside edge, "whence", as Dante observes, "one may fall because there is no parapet".[3] On the present occasion his shadowy hand must surely have gone out to clutch his pupil's skirt; but with great self-command he keeps his feelings to himself. He merely observes that the spirits are hidden in the flames—"shrouded in their own torment" —as much as to say that it is not worth while breaking one's neck trying to see them: they are invisible and there's an end of it.

Dante—and it is perhaps his greatest charm—can always see his own absurdity. His vocation as poet and prophet he does indeed take very seriously, as he takes his soul's welfare seriously; what he does not take seriously is himself: throughout the poem he always treats himself with a delicate and disarming ridicule. In a sense, the whole *Comedy* is a story told against himself; and it is this genuine humility of his which captures our sympathy and makes his relations with Virgil and Beatrice so touching and so true. And without it, how could he show himself privileged to walk through deep Hell with living feet, to converse with the Saints, to partake before death of the Beatific Vision, and yet escape the charge of egotism? That charge has, in fact, been brought against him—unjustly as I think; and I think largely because the comic element in his own self-portrait has never been sufficiently appreciated. Sometimes it seems not to be even noticed. Commentators and translators, with misplaced reverence, have tried to smooth it away, under the impression that it has got there by accident. But we must not fall into the trap of supposing that because Dante is "mediaeval" he is therefore "quaint" and "naïve", producing funny effects without intending them. He is nothing of the sort; he is very great and a very subtle artist: when he amuses it is because he means to be amusing. Here and there, to be sure, in any work removed from us by a lapse of six hundred years there will be phrases or points of view which seem to us odd or incongruous; but a consistent comic presentation sustained over fourteen thousand lines is a different matter, and has nothing accidental about it.

[1] *Inf.* xii. 28 *seq.*   [2] *Inf.* xxiv. 22 *seq.*   [3] *Purg.* xiii. 79–81.

Why, then, has the poet placed this moment of comedy precisely here? The canto opened with a Dante in the grand manner—the inspired poet, the solemn voice of prophecy, the heartbroken patriot, the grave, middle-aged man foreseeing his own exile and the ruin of Florence. Now, that Dante is smilingly withdrawn from us, and instead we have the private and personal Dante, preposterously perched on a breakneck piece of rock, and pouring out questions like an eager and excited schoolboy. "Yes, Master; thank you for telling me—but I'd guessed that. Who is in the big flame with the cloven tip? *Diomede and Ulysses?* Oh, Master, please, *please* let us wait till it comes! Don't say no! You see how dreadfully badly I want to speak to it"—"*vedi che del disìo ver lei mi piego*"—"I yearn", but also, literally, "I lean" towards it—"lean" is the right word, under the circumstances; and if we had any doubts that Dante the poet was smiling at himself, his sly use of that word is sufficient to dispel them.

The reason for all this is plain enough. Dante is going to tell us the most marvellous piece of folklore ever imagined—a thing as simple as a ballad or a nursery-tale; a wonder-voyage, with the great names of Greece and Troy sounding through it, and with a touch of the Celtic mystery too—like the voyages of Bran and Maelduin: the other-world journey to the Western Isles, the uninhabited places, the world behind the sun. He does not want us to be clever and critical; he wants our minds emptied of all that kind of thing; he wants us to be receptive, like children. We are to identify ourselves with the eager, simple and childlike Dante who is pleading so excitedly to be allowed to stay— I nearly said "to stay up"—a little longer, and hear the story.

So Virgil smiles and consents. But before the story begins, the poet has another spell to bind. And here we come to a passage which has puzzled innumerable critics, though I cannot for the life of me see why. "I know what you want to ask," says Virgil; "so do you refrain your tongue and let *me* speak to them; for they are Greeks and might despise your words."

What made Virgil say that? Dante certainly does not mean that the Greeks would not understand Italian, because, in the next canto, he goes out of his way to inform us that Virgil in fact addressed them "in the Lombard tongue". Nor is it anything to do with Dante's being a "modern", and therefore an object of contempt to these ancient heroes. It is true that Virgil habitually takes charge of the conversation with classical personages, and usually (though not invariably) hands the modern people over to Dante; but in Canto 15, the Theban

Capaneus takes notice of Dante's remarks and replies to them. Still less is it, as one commentator has in desperation suggested, because "classical learning had been much neglected in Dante's time"; Diomede and Ulysses would not care much about that. No. But Dante was an Italian—that is to say, a descendant of the "noble seed of the Romans"; and the Romans, as Dante never wearies of reminding us, and does remind us in this very passage, are the offspring of Aeneas—they are of the lineage of Troy. But Ulysses and Diomede are the conquerors of Troy; to them the Trojans are beaten enemies. If Dante were to address them, it would be rather as though the shade of Winston Churchill were to be pestered by some twopenny-ha'penny poet descended in a direct line from Ribbentrop. Very well; but does not the same objection apply equally to Virgil? He too is of the seed of the Romans. Yes; but Virgil is different. We must not forget that to the men of the Middle Ages Virgil was a great White Magician. He could command the spirits. Where Dante could only request, Virgil could compel them to speak.

Look at the whole passage: there is nothing like it in the rest of the *Comedy*. The clue is given at once by the word *forma*—"I heard him (that is, Virgil) speak *in questa forma*". Most people translate this "in this manner", or "with these words"; but it is not that at all; it is specifically: "with this *form* of words", "with this formula"; and what follows is nothing more or less than a *formal conjuration*. We are not to suppose, of course, that Virgil is dabbling in what nowadays is properly called "magic", in the sense of unhallowed dealings with the powers of darkness: anything of that sort would have landed him not in Limbo but in the *bolgia* of the Sorcerers. But he has authority to command the spirits because he is the soul of a good and virtuous man, who, moreover, though he is not in the Grace of Christ, is yet in the favour of God and engaged on a Heaven-appointed mission. And further: he is experienced in these matters—"*persona accorta*" (Canto 3)—he corresponds to what, in the Christian Church, we should call a "trained exorcist". We notice that, since at this point he is only satisfying Dante's laudable curiosity and not protecting him against danger, he does not use any of the great "Words of Power" which he invoked to overcome Charon or Minos: he relies, this time, solely on his native authority. He invokes the bond of sympathy which provides a contact between himself and the spirits: he is a poet; he sang of them in his verse—not favourably, it is true, but he sang of them, and so kept their names in remembrance in the world. That is what the spirits in Hell so often and so nostalgically plead for: "Keep green my memory"—"speak of me in the world". So that is the tie by which Virgil now binds these proud spirits: "*S'io meritai di voi.*" It is often rendered "*If* I merited anything of you", but the English "if" is too weak in this context; it might be merely a plea. It should rather be translated "*as* I deserved", or "*by* what I deserved of you". Here, then, we have the *forma*, the *formula of conjuration*, consisting of an obsecration twice-repeated, followed by the command: "Stand; speak." So the flame stands still and Ulysses speaks. Notice that he never directly addresses either Dante or Virgil. He does not seem to be aware of them as persons. Under the compulsion the words reel off like a gramophone record and then stop. The spirit adds nothing on his own account; like a subject under hypnosis he speaks what the controlling power commands and no more. This is entirely characteristic. And what follows at the beginning of the next canto is proof positive that we have here to do with a conjuration; for the spirit, unlike any other in the *Comedy*, remains bound and cannot move until Virgil gives permission. Dante uses here what is, I think, a technical term; *licenza*—"the licence to depart"; and a few lines later he duly supplies the actual *forma*—the "formula of dismissal": "*Issa ten va; più non t'adizzo*"—"Depart now; I vex thee no further."

This is interesting in itself: but the thing we have to admire is the consummate narrative skill by which we are led from one mood to the other, passing from wrath and grief, through pastoral serenity to laughter and excitement and so to a childlike simplicity and receptiveness, and are then, literally as it were, bespelled. And all the time, the melody of the verse follows the mood—now big and strong and ringing, now stooping to an easy colloquialism, now lifting again to recapture the "grand manner" at another level; and always with a perfect flexibility and smoothness.

Thus conjured, then, the spirit of Ulysses speaks. Notice in passing the loving care which Dante always uses to get the machinery of his story convincing. He is never slapdash like (for instance) Spenser, who will describe how Britomart's steed is cut in two in the middle of a fight, and then, a few stanzas later, cheerfully make the whole party remount and go on their way, as though no shortage of horse-power had arisen. Dante would have made somebody ride pillion: he never loses sight of what he is doing; never presents us with a result without providing the means. Thus, in the Wood of the Suicides, where the spirits are turned to trees, he is at pains to tell us how they manage to speak. When a branch is broken, it bleeds, and the voice comes whistling out together with the blood, "as", says he, "when you burn one end of a green brand, the other oozes sap and sizzles with the escaping air".[1] Nothing could be more plausible. So here. The tall flame comes along; it stops; it roars like a bonfire, and the tip of it quivers *come fosse la lingua che parlasse*.[2] Everybody has noticed that resemblance—in fact we speak of a "tongue of flame". We have no difficulty in getting the picture; and in the following canto Dante explains how the words the spirit speaks down at the root of the flame are first translated into "fire's native speech"—an inarticulate roaring— and then re-translated into words when they reach the tip: much on the principle of the telephone, by which sound-waves are transmitted as electric vibrations and turned back into sound-waves when they reach the receiver. (How Dante's scientific mind would have enjoyed that!) There is the further convenience that the words uttered down in the bottom of the *bolgia* are shaken out much nearer the level of the bridge on which Dante is standing, so that he can hear them more easily.

And now at last—I say "at last", because it has taken us a long time to get there; but in fact the whole complicated progression has taken fewer than a hundred lines—at last the story begins. And here the magic almost defies analysis. Its secret lies in its complete simplicity; it is austere almost to bareness; its beauty is that of flawless structure and proportion. It has a strange, almost fairy-tale atmosphere of its own, but this "romantic" quality (so to call it for lack of a better adjective) is all conveyed by suggestion: there are no decorative words or heavily surcharged epithets. There is nothing like Keats's:

> *magic* casements, opening on the foam
> Of *perilous* seas in *faery* lands *forlorn*

or Tennyson's:

> Through *scudding* drifts the *rainy* Hyades
> Vext the *dim* seas

where the adjectives are expressly chosen for their spell-binding associations. When we look at the lines that charm us, we see that they are all strictly functional: their ostensible job is simply to tell a story.

---

[1] *Inf.* xiii. 40–42.
[2] like a speaking tongue.
Inf. xxvi. 88.

They define a geographical position:

> *dalla man destra mi lasciai Sibilia,*
> *dall' altra già m'avea lasciata Setta.*[1]

How does that produce its extraordinary effect of remoteness and mystery? One may say that it is due to the cunning play on the liquids and sibilants, and to the placing of the two names on the rhyme-syllables. So, no doubt, it is. The fact remains that it merely tells us, without a single poetic ornament, precisely where Ulysses had got to. Or take the extraordinary sense of lonely adventure, with its undertone of desolation and loss, that we get from the lines about the rising of the other pole and the disappearance of the Northern Stars. Without a single superfluous word they inform us just how much Southing the voyagers had made: "already night saw the other pole with all its stars"—*all* its stars: that is the operative phrase. For he means, I think, that not only was the South Celestial Pole visible, but that it stood high in the sky, with all the Antarctic constellations clear of the horizon; so that our pole was, in consequence, *tanto basso*, that it, and all the familiar constellations which here never set, there never rose. The Little Bear and the Plough and Cassiopeia have all gone, that would explain the strangeness and the desolation; yet we feel the emotional effect before we have worked out the reason for it.

The end of the story is pure ballad-poetry. The enormous mountain, *"bruna per la distanza"* [2] towering out of the sea—what is it? "It appeared to be the highest I had ever seen." Well it might. For though we do not know it yet, we shall realise later that this is the Mountain of the Earthly Paradise; of the Forbidden Garden, which, after Christ's coming, will be Mount Purgatory—that mountain which Virgil calls *"principio e cagion di tutta gioia"*.[3] There it stands, mysterious and remote, the only land in the Southern Hemisphere, lifting its seven great cornices high beyond the clouds, with Eden at the summit. Ulysses may glimpse that salvation far off, but he never can attain it; we shall recognise the echo as it goes sounding through other songs

---

[1] Ceuta I'd left to larboard, sailing by,
Seville I now left in the starboard seas.
Inf. xxvi. 110–111.

[2] dark with distance.
Inf. xxvi. 134.

[3] The cause and first beginning of all joy.
Inf. i. 78.

and later ballads:

> "O those are the hills of Paradise
> Where thou and I may never win——"

For the whirlwind comes leaping at them out of the unknown land
and they are caught, spinning helplessly "with all the waters", the
deep, dark, deadly funnel of the eddy sucking them down—and the
ballad-music sounds again:

> "And three times round went our gallant ship
> And three times round went she——"

Then, with a fearful suddenness: "the fourth time the poop rose and
the prow went down"—"*com' Altrui piacque*"—as pleased that Other
whom Hell does not care to name—

> *infin che il mar fu sopra noi richiuso.*[1]

It is all over; they are sunk without trace; and the calm surface of the
sea stretches out again, flat and shining, to the shores of that distant
island, "*di retro al sol, il mondo senza gente*".[2]

But now, why has Dante indulged himself and us with this piece of
romantic imagination? What is this incomparable story doing here?
It seems to add nothing to our knowledge of sin and Hell. Is it *mere*
decoration? *mere* refreshment and *sollazzo*?

It is that, of course. We began by saying that it was there to fortify
ours stomachs against the sickening horrors that come before and after.
Though while it does this, it intensifies those horrors by contrast. The
splash and sparkle of running water are never long absent from the arid
wastes of the *Inferno*: I have counted no fewer than 72 of these water-
images—sometimes only a passing word; sometimes a long, elaborate
passage like those which describe the origin of the infernal rivers,[3] or
the course of the Mincio, spilling over from the bosom of Benaco,
and running down "through verdant meads" to the marshes about
Mantua;[4] sometimes a vivid, nostalgic glimpse as in Master Adam's

---

[1] Till over our heads the hollow seas closed up.
Inf. xxvi. 142.
[2] the uninhabited world behind the sun.
Inf. xxvi. 117.
[3] *Inf.* xiv. 94 *seq.*
[4] *Inf.* xxiii. 61 *seq.*

terrible cry in the Valley of Disease:

> *li ruscelletti che dei verdi colli*
> *del Casentin discendon giuso in Arno,*
> *facendo i lor canali freddi e molli,*
>
> *sempre mi stanno innanzi—e non indarno. . . .* [1]

"*e non indarno*"—not for nothing; "their image", he says, "parches me more than the disease that wastes my face". So. That is one good poetic reason for the presence of these cool and liquid images, of which the Voyage of Ulysses, with its strong salt breath of open sea, is the most powerful and unforgettable.

Nor is it quite true that the story tells us nothing about sin. It shows the Counsellor of Fraud become, in his old age, the Counsellor of Folly. He has traded in false values, and his own values have become false. What sets him off upon the "witless flight" to the West? Nothing —an itching and aimless curiosity. What should have held him back? Piety, says Dante: his duty to his people; his duty to the City. And this from Dante, whose own intellectual curiosity burned like a fire in him! Although it is his own temptation, he can judge it; because it is his own temptation he can present it so alluringly as to capture all our emotional sympathy for Ulysses. In the nineteenth century, when the voice of intellectual curiosity was being listened to as though it were the Voice of God, Tennyson, that dutiful Victorian and excellent family man, wrote his famous descant on Dante's theme and reversed its moral. Follow knowledge—no matter at what cost or to what end: "it may be that the gulfs will wash us down" (or the atom bomb, we may add, blow us up) the great thing is to progress, to go on, "to strive, to seek, to find, and not to yield". Dante knew that urge and refused to endorse it; and Tennyson, before he died, had begun to wonder whether the voyage was altogether blest.

But the story does more than refresh the spirit, enhance by contrast the heat and drouth of Hell, or enlarge our understanding of self-deception. Structurally, it is a superb example of Dante's large-scale architectonics. In the first place, it links up the *Inferno* with the *Purga-*

---

[1] The little brooks that ripple from the hills
    Of the green Casentin to Arno river,
    Suppling their channels with their cooling rills,

    Are in my eyes and in my ears for ever,
    And not for naught——
                                Inf. xxx. 64–68.

torio. When we emerge from the murk of Hell upon the reedy, wind-swept shore beneath the Southern stars, it slowly dawns upon us that this, and no other, is the mysterious land that the voyagers beheld far off. Where Ulysses might not come, Dante will pass freely. By the right way and not the wrong; not by a *"folle volo"* but by the path of self-knowledge and the death to sin; not lured by idle curiosity, but sped by Grace and guided by Wisdom. His feet will tread the un-inhabited world, and climb the inaccessible mountain to the very top.

That is not all. There is a link also with the *Paradiso.* The long pilgrimage is nearly done, and Dante is standing with Beatrice in the Heaven of the Fixed Stars. The living flames that are the souls of the Redeemed are mounting past them to the Empyrean—

"As our air rains downward the flakes of frozen cloud when the horn of the celestial Goat is touched by the Sun, so did I see the ether adorn itself and rain upward the flakes of the triumphant exhalations that had sojourned there awhile with us. And the Lady, seeing me now set free from gazing upward——"

Are we already a little reminded of how, far away in time and space, he once gazed *downward* at bodiless flames moving like fireflies along a valley?

"—the Lady said to me: 'Plunge thy sight downward—see how far thou hast rolled.' Then I saw that since the hour when I had first looked down I had turned through the whole quadrant of the first Climate, so that I saw beyond Cadiz the mad course Ulysses took—*il varco folle d'Ulisse*".[1] The tale told in the Eighth Bolgia of the Eighth Circle is recalled in the Eighth Heaven; the numerical agree-ment may be a chance coincidence—but Dante was not the sort of man who leaves very much to chance. I fancy that the figure 8, scribbled as it were on the margin, is a kind of sign of his intention: "Look—*attento*! between the fires of Heaven and the fires of Hell, between the Counsel of Truth and the Counsel of Fraud, there is a terrible correspondence, and a single glance can embrace them." Then, having roused this associative and warning echo, he will not linger on the note, but passes on to complete the sentence:

> *e di qua presso il lito*
> *nel qual si fece Europa dolce carco.*[2]

---

[1] *Para.* xxvii. 67 *seq.*

[2]   and, near to it, the shore where Europa made herself a pleasant burden.   *Para.* xxvii. 83–84.

Dante is not merely a great artist, but also an artist on a great scale. Though one may dwell for hours together on the delicate finish of his "minute particulars", these are never allowed to obscure the balance and breadth of his outlines. Criticism may niggle over him, but he is no niggler. When we examine his work closely, we see how even the most casual-looking word is selected to produce the right effect. His style is pregnant and economical, suggesting far more than it states. Yet the general impression is of an extraordinary ease and freedom from strain—the solidity and repose which come from a perfect command over his material; the effortless mastery of a supreme story-teller at the very top of his form.

(Summer School of Italian Studies
Cambridge 1946)

THE CORNICE OF SLOTH

(*Purg.* xviii–xix. 69)

THE style of the *Purgatorio* is more mixed than that of either of the other two cantiche. Compared with it, the *Inferno* is all action and the *Paradiso* all discourse. But as we pant up the steep ascents of "Death's Second Kingdom", we pass continually, by sudden transitions, from swift action to leisurely discussion and back again—and the discussions, though less rarefied than Beatrice's theological analyses in the *Paradiso*, are carried on at a higher intellectual level than any that occur in the *Inferno*. That is why some people never get further in their reading of the *Commedia* than the first stage of the journey. They complain that, as soon as the travellers emerge from Hell, "the sermons begin".

The present passage is typical of the *Purgatorio*; for we start in mid-sermon, and afterwards are suddenly plunged into a very frenzy of action. For the narrative has brought us to the edge of the Cornice of Sloth, which (since here lukewarm love renews its ardour and the slackened oar is plied again) is naturally a very lively and bustling place—when we get to it. I say, "When we get to it", because it was just as Dante and Virgil were about to set foot on the topmost step of the stair leading up to it, that the sun sank, and the rule of the Mountain made itself felt: "No going upwards after dark." [1] This rule, for which, of course, it is easy to find an allegorical significance, is very useful in the mechanics of the literal story. When we first hear of it, we are on the lower terraces of the Mountain, and it provides us with an excellent reason for passing a peaceful night in the Valley of the Rulers. The key-note of the *Purgatorio* is always "Make haste! lose no time! work while the daylight lasts!"; but that the poem may not weary the reader by rushing forward at breathless and unbroken speed, moments of repose are provided for recollection and refreshment. On the present occasion, Dante very neatly works the rule in again just as we come to the purging of Sloth. Virgil has remembered it, and has told Dante to climb quickly. But they are just not quick enough, and there they are, stuck fast within a step of the goal—"*pur come nave ch'alla piaggia*

[1] *Purg.* vii. 43 *seq.*

arriva—just like a vessel grounding on a beach". That shows you what comes of being too slow. The thing would have looked a little forced and frigid if we had not heard of the rule till now, or if no use had been made of it before. As it is, we have heard of the rule, and accepted and acted upon it, though we have not yet actually seen it in operation. We have had time to forget about it; then we hear Virgil's warning, and have just time to become a little anxious when, suddenly, the worst happens.

So, when Canto xviii opens, here we are, immobilised at the top of the stairs, and Virgil has just concluded one of those long discourses with which Dante is always begging him to improve the occasion, and while away the time if any hold-up occurs on the journey. We remember that when they were shut out from the Gates of Dis, in *Inferno* ix, Virgil took the opportunity to offer a little topographical information about the City. Unfortunately, we shall never know what he said, because Dante was so distracted by the sudden appearance of the Furies that he was unable to pay attention.[1] Then there was a later occasion, in Ante-Purgatory, when Dante was out of breath, after scrambling to the top of the Second Terrace, and they sat down and had an astronomy lesson about why, in the Southern Hemisphere, the Sun's chariot drove upon the North. Dante heard that, and repeated his lesson so intelligently that Belacqua pulled his leg about it.[2] But this pause below the Cornice of Sloth bears the closest resemblance to the one in *Inferno* xi, where the poets take shelter behind the tomb of Pope Anastasius from the stinking wind of the Pit, and Virgil explains to Dante the lay-out of the Abyss.[3] The two passages correspond to one another, and are marked by various verbal parallels. Here, as there, Dante asks Virgil to speak in order that their stay may not be profitless. Here, as there, Virgil makes clear to him the arrangements of the circles they have already seen and those they are about to see. Here, as there, Dante pays Virgil a compliment on his clear way of explaining things, and asks for further enlightenment. This is the moment at which our Canto actually begins; and the closeness of the parallelism only serves to show how the relations between the two poets have altered since they set out upon their journey.

> Thus the great teacher closed his argument,
> And earnestly perused my face, to see
> Whether I now appeared to be content:

---

[1] *Inf.* ix. 31 *seq.*   [2] *Purg.* iv. 52 *seq.*   [3] *Inf.* xi. 10 *seq.*

While I, though a new thirst tormented me,
  Kept outward silence, and within me said:
  "My endless questions worry him, maybe."

But he, true father that he was, had read
  My timid, unvoiced wish, and now by speech
  Nerved me to speech; and so I went ahead.[1]

Neither at the beginning of the discourse nor now, is there any of the tartness with which Virgil once rebuked his pupil for being "less intelligent than usual", or for having forgotten "the teaching of his school". He has grown fond of this funny little man, and takes pleasure in what he once referred to with a touch of embarrassment, as his *"uficio nuovo"*—"this novel employment". And Dante has learned consideration and self-control. Although Virgil has not been short with him, as he was when Dante badgered him with questions at the approach to Acheron, it occurs to the questioner, of his own accord, that he is possibly being a nuisance. So he is silent, until Virgil encourages him to speak. Without a word of pictorial description, Dante has painted the two faces—the one filled with a timid eagerness, the other with a grave and gentle anxiety. For—it is the distinctive note of the new relationship—Virgil is no longer in his own eyes "master, leader and lord". He no longer speaks with the accents of authority, as he did in Hell, for he is on Christian ground where, without Dante, he could not come. He would like to satisfy his pupil's thirst for knowledge, but he cannot, and he knows he cannot—he can go only thus far and no farther. Dante is asking him about love—and there is an especial poignancy in that; for Virgil is damned for no fault save, precisely, that he never knew love, and the other two great, supra-rational Christian graces. The change of relationship is felt by Dante too: never for a moment does he admit this to Virgil or even himself, but his language becomes more tender, his courtesy more exquisite. He still says *"maestro, signore, duca"*, but far more frequently than before it is: *"padre"*, *"dolce padre caro"*. And all through the *Purgatorio* runs the agonising tenderness which springs from their knowledge that the time of their companionship is short.

Dante is going to Beatrice, yet he asks Virgil to define love for him. One might think the question unnecessary; yet a man may know love without being able to analyse it. Or—and this is the very lesson which

---

[1] The references, where not otherwise indicated, are to the passage under discussion.

the Mountain exists to teach—he may love a wrong thing, or love the right thing too little or too well. All Dante's pilgrimage is undertaken that he may learn what and when and how to love.

What, then, is this thing called "love", to which Virgil has reduced "all virtuous actions *and their contraries*"? Let us note in passing how he here affirms the theological doctrine that no sin or evil has any being in itself. It is a parasite, which can only exist by, and be defined in terms of, the good which it apes and perverts. Pure good can exist by, in and for itself; pure evil cannot. Truth is that which is, *simpliciter*; but there can be no error, unless there is some truth for it to be erroneous about.

Virgil, then, begins to define love. What he says reminds us of what Marco Lombardo said in Canto xvi, when he compared the soul, first to a little child attracted by some gaud and rushing in pursuit of it, and then (by a shift in the metaphor) to a horseman, whose steed needs to be controlled by the bridle. Virgil develops and completes this theme. Whereas Marco was most interested in external manifestations (the pursuit of happiness), and external controls (the discipline of Church and Empire), Virgil is concerned with the inward nature of love and the soul's control over itself. Two points in his exposition of love's nature call for special attention. He says:

> The soul, which is created apt for love,
> > The moment pleasure wakes it into act,
> > To any pleasant thing is swift to move.

> Your apprehension draws from some real fact
> > An inward image, which it shows to you,
> > And by that image doth the soul attract:

> And if the soul, attracted, yearns thereto,
> > That yearning's love.

Some *real fact* (*esser verace*) existing outside the soul, is apprehended by the senses; an interior image is formed; and it is this image which attracts the soul. This description is in conformity with mediaeval physiology and psychology: some exterior object—say a frying-pan full of bacon—is perceived in the surrounding landscape: the eye conveys a visual picture of it, the nose reports an appetising odour, the ear takes note of a pleasant sizzling sound, and from these external data a pleasurable interior *image* is formed, which attracts the mind and prods it into thinking about breakfast. The word "image" is important:

there are the various *physical* images—appearance, odour, sound—
which are combined into a *mental* image—an *imagination* of breakfast.
But the bacon itself is exterior to the mind. So, too, with nobler loves
—the love for a beautiful work of art, the love for another person, the
love for God Himself: all these are external objects really existing in
themselves. The image is not spun out of the mind, but represents
something real outside it. All love, that is to say, is love for a real other.
That is the first point. And Virgil adds:

> *"Quel piegare è amor, quello è natura,*
> *che per piacer di nuovo in voi si lega."*

This is a difficult passage. John D. Sinclair, rightly linking it up with
what Virgil has already said in Canto xvii about the natural love which
cannot err, comments succinctly:

> Natural love, which is instinctive and innocent, is confirmed by attainment
> and by pleasure in the thing loved; it makes for its object just as fire by its
> "form", its essential nature, ascends towards the sphere of fire, "its
> element".[1]

The reference, however, to *"natura che per piacer di nuovo in voi si*
lega"—"is bound anew in you" wakes a faint echo of that earlier phrase
in *Inferno xi* about the *"vinco d'amor che fa natura"*—"the bond of
love which nature makes". That, as we may remember, is the "natural
bond" of common humanity, which is severed by fraud: the bond
which links every soul to its other in a natural and instinctive love,
quite apart from special obligations deliberately undertaken.

And so (Virgil goes on), just as fire hastens to its native sphere—
where "it may best endure", so love seeks its object on which it may
feed and rest in joy. And he ends up with a crack at those people who
think that love—all love, any love—is a good thing in itself, whatever
its object, and whatever antics it may play. Since the Romantic Age,
it has become almost automatic to assume [2] that love, and certain other
things—such as freedom, and experience—are self-justified. But the

---

[1] John D. Sinclair: *The Divine Comedy of Dante Alighieri, with translation and*
comment (John Lane, the Bodley Head, 1939), comment *in loc.*

[2] Here, for instance, in a letter to the Press about the Church's attitude to
divorce, we find the assumption in its most naïve form: "And if a great and deep
love comes to these unfortunate [lovelessly married] people, not for each other,
but for another woman or another man, are they to believe that it comes not
from God but from the Devil?"—*Daily Telegraph*, 8.8.52. Contrast the crudity
of this with the subtlety of the scholastic analysis.

mediaeval mind, and the Christian mind in all ages, cannot allow so
large an assumption; but asks always: experience of what? the love of
what? freedom to do what?

So that here, very relevantly and very urgently in this connection,
Dante raises again the question of freedom, which had troubled him
when he was talking to Marco Lombardo. Then, he had asked whether
men were bound by a material determinism. Were they (as the Middle
Ages put it) subject to the stars? Or (as a modern determinist might
put it) was every atom in the universe so linked to every other atom
in an iron network of causality that no real choice was possible? To
which Marco had replied "No".

> If that were so, it would destroy free will
>   Within you, and it were unjust indeed
>   You should have joy for good and grief for ill.
>
> Promptings of motion from your stars proceed—
>   I say not all, but if I did, what then?
>   Light's given you to know right from wrong at need.
>
> And free will, so its stuff can stand the strain
>   Of its first tussles with the stars, will fight,
>   If nourished well, to win the whole campaign.
>
> For of a nobler nature, mightier might,
>   You're the free subjects—might which doth create
>   A mind in you that's no star's perquisite.[1]

In other words: the disposition of the material universe—all the
factors which go to make up the "world-situation" at any moment—
may predispose a man in this way or that; but he is endowed with the
ability to know right from wrong and the power to choose, in the last
resort, what he will make of the situation into which he is born. Man
is not the creature of the situation, but the handiwork of God, whose
service is perfect freedom.

But now the problem presents itself in another way and at a deeper
level. Man may not be the creature of mechanical forces, but is he the
slave of his own emotions? So Dante asks again:

> "If from without love beckons us to it,
>   And with no choice the soul's foot followeth,
>   Go right, go wrong, we merit not a whit."

Virgil's reply is most important, both for what he says and for what

[1] *Purg.* xvi. 70–81.

he does not say. He begins by warning Dante that his cannot be the
last word on the subject:

> *"Quanto ragion qui vede*
> *dirti poss'io; da indi in là t'aspetta*
> *pur a Beatrice, ch'opera è di fede."* [1]

The whole problem of free will, involving as it does in the end the
relation between omnipotent Will and the conditioned will of the
creature, can only be resolved at a level to which reason by itself can
never rise. The real clue lies in the words of Marco the Christian—"of
a nobler nature, mightier might, you're the free servants"; but how
this can be will not be seen until Dante stands in Heaven with Beatrice
and learns how God's will is the peace of the Blessed. It is a matter of
faith: and faith, as we know, was lacking in Virgil. Nor, indeed, can
he speak the last word about love, for the love that reason can analyse
is not the love that redeems the world. But reason can at least clear away
misunderstandings and lay bare the bones of the problem. So Virgil
begins; and his argument runs parallel with Marco's:

> "To each substantial form that doth compound
> With matter, though distinct from it——"

The "substantial form", in the technical language of the Schools,
is that essential being which makes a thing what it is—its "thisness",
in virtue of which it is this thing and not that thing. The substantial
form of man is the rational soul, which, though distinguishable from
his bodily "matter", is inseparably bound up with it. Man is not a soul
shut up in a body, like brandy in a bottle; the body-soul is a single
compound, of which the soul is the form of the matter—like a poem,
which is a compound of sense and sound, the sense informing the sound
and making a poem of it.

(Incidentally, it is this kind of thing which puts people off the
Purgatorio and the *Paradiso*. More than half the difficulty is, quite
simply, knowing what the technical philosophic jargon means. It is, to
be sure, no more abstruse than the technical jargon bandied about
daily among electrical engineers; and in the days when people were as
much interested in their souls as they are now in their radio sets, it was

---

[1] "So much as reason here distinguisheth
I can unfold," said he; "once past that ground
Look to Beatrice, for it's work for faith."
Purg. xviii. 47–49.

quite well understood by educated people. Dante, in fact, does not trouble to define the substantial form which he is talking about; he expects his readers to know that bit.)

Having got over this preliminary hurdle, we can go on.

> " To each substantial form that doth compound
> With matter, though distinct from it, there cleaves
> Specific virtue, integral, inbound,
>
> Which, save in operation, none perceives;
> It's known by its effects, as, in the plant,
> Life manifests itself by the green leaves."

A specific virtue or "power" is that which belongs to all members of a species and to them only. In the human species, this characteristic power is the discursive intellect (sometimes called the "possible" or "potential" intellect) which develops knowledge by arguing from the known to the unknown. This marks man off from animals, on the one hand, who do not argue from point to point in this way, and from the angels on the other, whose knowledge is intuitive and immediate. We cannot be aware of this discursive power directly: we only know it is there because we see its effects which show us that something is at work; just as we cannot directly *see* life in a plant, but infer its presence from the greenness of its leaves. Thus, with the discursive intellect, we infer its existence because we observe the process of argument going on. What no observation of the process will ever tell us is how the intellect gets the first data from which to start its argument. All we can say is that there appear to be certain axioms from which every intellect starts work: and these we call the "prime cognitions" or "primal concepts". There appear also to be certain basic desires implanted in every soul from the start: and these we call the "first appetibles" or "prime objects of desire". To put it as briefly as possible: all thought starts from the perception that some things are obviously true and some things obviously desirable; and however rigorously we reduce the content of this perception, we cannot do away with it altogether: otherwise the whole process of reasoning would be meaningless.

> "So how his intellect's made cognisant
> Of primal concepts, or what guides his aim
> Toward the first appetibles, man's ignorant;
>
> Such things are instincts in you, much the same
> As is in bees the honey-making bent;
> This prime volition earns nor praise nor blame."

This ground of inquiry and of desire is neutral and innocent. It is part of our natural make-up, and we are in no way responsible for it. The "prime volition" which it involves is simply an instinctive inclination: the "*amore di fuori a noi offerto*".[1] But what we proceed to do with it is very much our responsibility.

> "Now, to keep all volitions else well blent
>   With this . . ."

(in order, that is, that our conscious desires may remain innocent like our instincts):

> " . . . you have a counsellor-power innate
>   Set there to guard the threshold of assent."

This is the famous image of the Threshold and the Censor of which we have heard so much in recent years. Dante's use of it is not, of course, quite the same as Freud's; he is concerned here with a different threshold—or, if you like, a different step of the threshold. Freudian psychology is chiefly interested in the threshold of consciousness. Certain desires are so shocking to the self that harbours them, that the Censor will not allow us even to become aware of them. Dante makes no explicit reference to this, though, in fact, the whole of the *Inferno* may be looked on as the therapeutic process of dragging these hidden horrors into consciousness. The journey through the door "whose threshold is denied to none",[2] and into the "*segrete cose*",[3] is the exploration of the unfathomable mystery of iniquity within the heart. But in the passage we are considering, Dante is concerned with the threshold of conscious assent. Desires arrive in the conscious mind, impelled by the "prime volition"; we can then either assent to them whole-heartedly, repudiate them whole-heartedly, or (in the useful modern phrase) sublimate them. The God-given faculty which enables us to do this is usually called Free Will, and I have so translated it; but Dante's Italian is *libero arbitrio*, the Latin *liberum arbitrium*, which is literally "Free Judgement". That is why Dante calls it a "counsellor-power", "*la virtù che consiglia*".

There is an illuminating passage in Leslie Paul's book *The Meaning*

---

[1] the love which is offered to us from without.
    Purg. xviii. 43.

[2] *Inf.* xiv. 86–87.
[3] the hidden things.
    Inf. iii. 21.

of Human Existence, which might almost have been written as a commentary upon these lines. He is talking about the restoration of the personality effected through psycho-analysis:

> It is not [he says] simply the totality of the *experiences* of a person which causes him to act in this way rather than that, but the *judgment* of the experiences. And that there is this unique individual judgment is demonstrated by the fact that in the end the cure of the psyche is effected by a guided judgment—the patient is brought carefully to the point at which he can make a judgment in his own case, or revise a judgment about himself made on the occasion of an earlier incident in his life, and, most significant of all, his cure cannot be effected without this act, and no one else can perform it for him. The re-integration of the human personality sought by psycho-analysis is nothing more or less than the restoration of its power of free judgment.[1]

Psycho-analysis deals, of course, with minds that are sick. When the mind is whole, and the judgement free, the conscious will assents to the judgement, and the desire which has presented itself for consideration is either judged rightful and implemented, or judged wrongful and otherwise dealt with. The threshold thus guarded by the Free Judgement may be called the Threshold of Will, or the Threshold of Intention; and it is only at this point that man is held responsible to that "punishing or awarding Justice" of which the "counsellor-power" is the vicegerent.

> "That is the principle to which relate
> All your deserts, according as its fan
> Is strict to purge right loves from reprobate."

If man had not this faculty of judgement, which is peculiar to him, all codes of morality would be meaningless—as indeed they are, in any system of strict determinism. That, incidentally, is why the question of Free Will is first raised—unexpectedly, and as it might seem irrelevantly—on the Cornice of Wrath. For if a man is not responsible for his own actions it is clearly useless to be angry with him; so that in the absence of Free Will there can be neither "evil wrath" nor righteous indignation—there is only a nonsensical gesture. But in practice no philosopher is so determinist that he will not blame the cook if the toast is burnt; and all systems of ethics are founded on the presupposi-

[1] *Op. cit.* (Faber, 1949), p. 93.

tion that the freedom which we appear to have is more than mere appearance. So Virgil concludes his discourse:

> "They who by reasoning probed creation's plan
> Root-deep, perceived this inborn liberty,
> And bequeathed ethics to the race of man.

> Grant, then, all loves that wake in you to be
> Born of necessity, you still possess
> Within yourselves the power of mastery;

> And this same noble faculty it is
> Beatrice calls Free Will; if she thereon
> Should speak with thee, look thou remember this."

It is here, then, that Virgil hands over the subject to Beatrice. What is there for Grace to expound that Reason leaves unresolved? Two things chiefly. The first is the *means* by which the will is brought into conformity with the judgement. Granting that the judgement is and remains free, man does not always do what he judges to be right. Or if we say, with Plato, that this is not a defect in the will but in the judgement, and that if a man *really* knows what is best for him, he will do it, then it is the judgement itself that is diseased and in fetters. Wherever one chooses to locate the trouble, the bitter cry goes up: "*Video meliora proboque; deteriora sequor.*"[1] To this ugly gulf opening up between will and power, Virgil's philosophy can bring no bridge. For that, we must look to Beatrice—or to St. Paul: "For to will is present with me, but how to perform that which is good I find not. For the good that I would I do not; but the evil which I would not, that I do. . . . O wretched man that I am! who shall deliver me from this body of death? I thank God, through Jesus Christ our Lord."[2]

The freeing of the *arbitrio*, so that it and the *volere* become the "free subjects" of the "nobler nature" which is God, can only be accomplished by the union of the human nature with the Divine Nature "where will and power are one". Beatrice will, in the great Seventh Canto of the *Paradiso*, expound the nature of this atonement, made possible by the assuming of the human nature into the Incarnate Godhead. The love of God, and the answering love of man, are the bridge that spans the gulf, so that, in contemplation of the final mystery—

[1] I see and approve what is better; I follow what is worse.
                                 Ovid: *Metam.* vii. 20–21.

[2] *Rom.* iii. 18–19, 24–25.

... già volgeva il mio disio e il velle,
si come rota ch'egualmente è mossa,
l'amor che move il sol e le altre stelle.[1]

The will, that is, moves as easily and freely in its right motion as do
the inorganic spheres that have no will, or the intuitive wills of their
angelic Movers who need no process of reason. Perfect freedom and
perfect servitude reach the same end and are seen to be identical in
love. That is why Love and Free Will are here treated together as
aspects of the same subject.

But that "inclination of the soul to pleasurable objects" which is
Virgil's definition of love—what has that in common with the ecstasy
of the *Paradiso?* with the love that is like *"un riso del universo"*,[2] that
sets all the spheres dancing together, that kindles the delighted spirits
to a rosier fire of rapture, and rings out in the shouting *Gloria* so that
Dante, only to hear it, is "drunken with the sweetness of the sound"?
Little enough, we might think. The difference between the two is the
measure of distance that separates Limbo from the Empyrean, the
wisdom of this world from the rebirth of the spirit, Virgil from Beatrice.
If anyone is inclined to complain that the discourses of the *Purgatorio*,
however noble and reasonable, leave them cold, the answer is that
Dante knew what he was doing. The last word cannot be with Virgil;
(the nature of supernatural love is the second theme of Beatrice's
argument) and he does not wait for the *Paradiso* to make that clear.

For now, following upon the stately discourse occupying, in all,
123 lines, during which the movement of the narrative has remained
static, there explodes upon us with dramatic suddenness one of the
noisiest, swiftest, most exciting scenes in the whole poem. The golden
voice of Virgil falls silent, and, without transition, there comes one of
the beautiful sky-pictures by which Dante, in the *Purgatorio*, reminds
us of the passing of time:

> Retarded near to midnight now, the moon,
>   Shaped like a mazer new and fiery-bright,
>   Was making the stars appear but thinly strewn

---

[1] Yet, as a wheel turns equal, free from jars,
    Already my will and desire were wheeled by love,
    The Love that moves the sun and the other stars.
                    Para. xxxiii. 143–145.
[2] a smile of the whole universe.
        Para. xxvii. 5–6.

> As counter-heaven she ran by the road whose light
>   Flares red at night, when the sun, beheld from Rome,
>   'Twixt Corsica and Sardinia sinks from sight.

There are some problems here for the astronomers. Does "*quasi a mezza notte tarda*" merely mean that it was now so late as to be nearly midnight? Or does it mean that the moon, rising half an hour later every night, was by now "retarded to nearly midnight"? and, if the latter, does Dante refer to the hour of moon-rise? because, if so, "*quasi*" has a lot to carry, since the moon would actually have risen at about 10 o'clock. Or does it mean that the moon, retarded as she was, did not appear to Dante till about midnight, since before that time she would have been hidden behind the mountain? It does not, perhaps, matter greatly to the reader. I think it unlikely that Dante would have miscalculated the hour of moonrise; but I think he probably did intend a reference to the retardation of the moon which marks the time that has elapsed since he began his journey.

Time, on the Cornice of Sloth, is all-important. I fancy there is here a conflation of two ideas into a single phrase: "It was getting on to midnight, and the moon, rising later than she did, was now well up into the sky and already putting out the stars." That Dante is concerned with the change in the moon's motion and appearance is shown by his reference to her shape. She is "*fatta com'un secchione che tutto arda*". "*Secchione*" is, literally, a bucket—but the usual translation, "like a bucket of fire", is singularly unhelpful, suggesting as it does a common English bucket pierced with holes and filled with glowing coke, such as roadmenders use at night. Dante is thinking of one of the large hemispherical buckets, still to be seen in Italy, which are made of brass or copper; and the point is that the moon, which had been full in the Dark Wood, is now gibbous, and shining like metal that is polished, or (to use Shakespeare's word) "fire-new". The nearest English equivalent, in shape and material, though not in size, is the footless metal drinking-vessel known as a mazer.

There is a further problem about the moon's course: the fact being that, at the Spring equinox, the sun would *not* set on a line drawn direct from Rome to a point between Corsica and Sardinia. But mediaeval geography is apt to be as inexact as mediaeval astronomy is precise. What matters is the reminder of time and the moon's motion (like Coleridge's "the moving moon went up the sky"); and the evocation there on the other side of the world, of home and Rome, and of the sun flaring down into Mediterranean waters.

So there they sit, Virgil "disburdened" of Dante and his problems, and Dante, with his mind stuffed with information, doubtless "closing his eyes for a quiet think" and dropping off into a doze.

> When, all at once, and close behind our backs,
>   Startling me up, a throng came roundabout,
>   Wheeling towards us in their circling tracks.
>
> As on their banks by night a rush and rout
>   Of old Ismenus and Asopus spied
>   When Thebans to their aid called Bacchus out—

It is a shame to break the swing of the narrative—but look how the mere mention of Bacchus snatches the whole theme of love and will out of the philosophic calm of Virgil's discourse and plunges it straight into an atmosphere of fervour and excitement—these Christian souls are drunk with love, consumed with thirst for that Prime Appetible which is God, the goal of all desire.

> As on their banks by night a rush and rout
>   Of old Ismenus and Asopus spied
>   When Thebans to their aid called Bacchus out,
>
> So round that circle sweeping, stride on stride,
>   I saw them come whom love, devoutly vowed,
>   And glad good-will like horsemen spur and ride.
>
> Soon they were on us, for the whole great crowd
>   Were running at top speed; and there were twain
>   Who went before, and weeping, cried aloud:
>
> "Mary ran to the hills in haste!" and then:
>   "Caesar, to subjugate Ilerda, thrust
>   Hard at Marseilles, and raced on into Spain!"
>
> "Quick, quick! let not the precious time be lost
>   For lack of love!" the others cried, pursuing;
>   "In good work strive, till grace revive from dust!"

This is the "whip" which, as on the other cornices, urges the spirits on by great examples of the virtue which corresponds to their sin. The word "whip" is not here mentioned, but the image is of horses which good-will and right love "*cavalca*". Dante's verse jingles and jolts with great thundering rhymes—"*calca, falca, cavalca; venendo, correndo, piangendo; magna, montagna, Ispagna*"—and all the lines are end-stopped.

It has often been pointed out that on this cornice alone no prayer is provided for the spirits. An exhortation to "good works"—"*studio di ben far*"—takes its place. Perhaps these spirits had been too much inclined to relax into a "cosy piety". "Sloth", says the mystical writer Tauler, "often makes men fain to be excused from their work and set to contemplation. Never trust a virtue that has not been put into practice." So, on this cornice the neglect of the Active Life is purged; the souls remind themselves that to labour is to pray.

Virgil accosts them politely and inquires the way to the next stair:

> "*O gente, in cui fervore acuto adesso*
> *ricompie forse negligenʒa e indugio,*
> *da voi per tepideʒʒa in ben far messo——*" [1]

"*forse*" is charming. To the "*spiriti eletti*" of Purgatory Virgil always shows the most exquisite tact and deference, as though hardly liking to mention the faults of which their repentance now makes them so acutely conscious. And the spirit who replies, though in a desperate hurry, takes pains to excuse his apparent rudeness:

> "Come this way,
> Thou'lt find the pass if thou behind us run.
>
> Zeal to be moving goads us so that stay
> We cannot; if our duty seem at first
> Too like discourtesy, forgive us, pray."

He then adds the information for which Dante has not asked. Presumably he knows that it will be acceptable, and by giving it unasked he doubtless accomplishes his "good deed for the day".

> "San Zeno's abbot in Verona erst
> Was I, 'neath good King Barbarossa brave
> Who in Milan's still talked about, and cursed.
>
> A man there is with one foot in the grave,
> Shall for that convent soon have tears to shed,
> Rueing his influence and the powers it gave,
>
> Because he's set his own son, bastard-bred,
> Twisted of body and still worse in wit,
> To rule there in its rightful pastor's stead."

---

[1] "O people, now with eager haste renewing
The time, belike, that slipped in dalliance by,
Or sloth, through lukewarm fervour for well-doing."
                         Purg. xviii. 106–108.

> If more he spake, or ceased there, never a whit
> Know I; he'd fled so far beyond us both;
> Thus much I heard, and gladly noted it.

Who this Abbot may have been, we do not know; but the regrettable old gentleman who caused the scandal was Alberto della Scala, the father of Dante's friends and patrons, Bartolommeo and Can Grande. He died in 1301, a year after the date of the vision, and commentators have thought it tactless of Dante to throw out these sinister hints about what (at the time of writing) was presumably happening to him then and there in the after-life. But after all, Dante knew the della Scalas, and we do not. They may have powerfully disliked their unpleasant and illegitimate half-brother, and predicted that one day their papa would be sorry. And after all, Dante has threatened him with nothing worse than "tears"—which might be shed in Purgatory, or even on his death-bed. And if Dante represents himself as having "gladly noted" the information, it may have been, not out of malignant satisfaction, but because he thought it would please his friends to hear it. Or out of mere anxiety to oblige the speaker, who was taking so much trouble to pour out all this story as he fled away at top speed. At any rate, the voice coming clear and small through the still air, dies away along the mountain-side, and Virgil hastens to attract Dante's attention to the remaining spirits, two of whom have the task of applying the "bridle" to the sin of Sloth. I think *"dando di morso"* means this, rather than "biting at" Sloth; because this is exactly the place where one would expect the "bridle" to be mentioned. The image of Sloth as needing a bridle is, of course, an odd one; but this sounds less like a mixed metaphor when the name of sin is given as *"accidia"*. "Accidie" is the sin of not-caring, and may lead to rambling aside as easily as to mere sitting down and doing nothing, and so need the pressure of the bit.

The shades, in any case, cry out against the Children of Israel, who after their triumphant exodus from Egypt, roamed so long in the Wilderness [1] that, as the old rhyme says:

> Joshua the son of Nun
> And Caleb the son of Zephunneh
> Were the only two who ever got through
> To the land of milk and honey.

And they pour scorn on these companions of Aeneas who lost heart

[1] *Exod.* xiv. 10–20; *Num.* xiv. 1–39; *Deut.* i. 26–36.

half-way through the adventure, and settled in Sicily instead of struggling on to Latium, so that they too never saw their Promised
Land.[1]

And now the sudden tumult dies away as swiftly as it came.

> Then, when those shades so far from us had passed
>   That nothing could be seen of them, there rose
>   New fancies in my mind, whence thick and fast
>
> Came others, countless, various; and from those
>   To these I drifted, down so long a stream
>   Of rambling thought, my eyes began to close,
>
> And meditation melted into dream.

"*E il pensamento in sogno trasmutai*"—the canto sighs itself out on
the light, soft, double-vowelled rhyme. Dante's descriptions of falling
asleep and waking are always extraordinarily convincing. His dreams,
too, are very much more like real dreams than the usual neat symbolic
demonstrations vouchsafed to the talented dreamers of edifying literature. Even as a child, I remember thinking that Pharaoh's dream of the
kine and ears of corn was a trifle too symmetrical to be convincing; and
think to-day that the historian must have edited it slightly. But the
dream of the Siren, which opens the next canto, has a queer dream-
logic which sounds, somehow, authentic. It is, indeed, the most profound and subtle of the three dreams of the *Purgatorio*, and has
kept the commentators busy finding explanations that will go on
all-fours.

It is ushered in by one of Dante's astronomical time-indications:

> What hour the heat of day can warm no longer
>   The chill moon's influence, because the cold
>   Of earth, or sometimes Saturn's power, is stronger;
>
> When geomancers, looking east, behold
>   Their Greater Fortune rising, through a reach
>   Of sky that darkness cannot long enfold—

In plain English, it was getting on for 4 a.m., about two hours before
dawn. The group of stars called by geomancers "Fortuna Major" lies
partly in Aquarius and partly in Pisces; Pisces, therefore, was rising,
and the sun, which as we know was in the next sign, Aries, would
follow it up two hours later. This is the third time that Dante has
had to mention the rising of this sign. In *Inf.* xi, he said simply,

---

[1] *Aen.* v. 604 seq.   [2] *Loc. cit.*, 113.

"Horizon-high the twinkling Fishes swim";[2] in *Purg.* i, he varied this by an allusion to Venus:

> The lovely planet, love's own quickener,
>   Now lit to laughter all the eastern sky,
>   Veiling the Fishes that attended her.[1]

Nothing could have been more charming, or more suitable to that glad moment of release from the stink and squalor of Hell. Now he is faced yet again with this recurrent kettle of Fish; the skilled craftsman in him looks about for yet a third variant, and the Fortuna Major presents itself. I do not know that we need search very much further for deep significations here. It does not do to underestimate the amount of plain, honest workmanship that goes into the building of a long narrative poem. One avoids, if possible, repeating one's effects. But what we can say is this: that the effect chosen is always appropriate to the context. The contempt for fortune-telling which lodges geomancers and their like in the ludicrous humiliations of the Fourth Bolgia makes the mention of them as unthinkable in Canto i as it is admirably suitable here, where the mention of "love's own planet" would have been correspondingly out of place. For the dream thus ushered in at the dawn-hour, the hour when dreams come true, is a dream of "that ancient witch who has beguiled so many"; and witches and fortune-tellers have a natural affinity. There is here a touch of mystery, and of a not very pleasant or creditable mystery.

The air is cold; vitality is at its lowest ebb; the twisted things that slumber in the subconscious creep over the threshold into the undefended no-man's-land of dream. And this is what Dante saw:

> In dream a woman sought me, halt of speech,
>   Squint-eyed, on maimed feet lurching as she stept,
>   With crippled hands and skin of sallowy bleach.
>
> I gazed; and as to cold limbs that have crept
>   Heavy with night, the sun gives life anew,
>   Even so my look unloosed the string that kept
>
> Her utterance captive, and right quickly drew
>   Upright her form that all misshapen hung,
>   And stained her withered cheek to love's own hue.

---

[1] *Loc. cit.*, 19–21.

Then she began to sing, when thus her tongue
 Was freed—and such a spell she held me by
 As had been hard to break; and so she sung:—

"Lo, the sweet Siren; yea, 'tis I, 'tis I
 Who lead the mariners in mid-sea astray,
 Such pleasures in my melting measures lie.

I turned Ulysses from his wandering way
 With music; few, I trow, to me who grow
 Know how to go, longing I so allay."

Her lips yet moved to that melodious flow
 When hard at hand a lady I espied,
 Holy, alert, her guiles to overthrow.

"O Virgil, Virgil, who is this?" she cried
 Indignant; and he came, with heedful eyes
 On that discreet one, and on naught beside.

The first he seized, and, rending her disguise
 In front, showed me her belly, which released
 So foul a stench, I woke with that surprise.

I looked about for my good lord: "At least
 Three times", said he, "I've called thee; rise and come;
 Let's find the breach whereby thou enterest."

Before we go any further, look at the curious rightness of the dream-psychology. Virgil has called Dante three times; his voice, heard but not registered, brings him into the sleeper's consciousness as a character in the dream, and at the same time breaks the dream and wakes the sleeper, leaving that momentary confusion of mind between vision and reality which persuades us that here is a genuine dream.

The signification is, on the surface, simple; but it is not so simple as it seems, and slips and shifts under examination as dream-logic so often does when we examine it with the waking mind. We know, from what Virgil says later, that the Siren is "that ancient witch because of whom, alone, those above us weep". We know also that those on the upper cornices of the mountain are purging excessive love for the "secondary goods". The "secondary goods" are those things which, though good in themselves, must be loved only in proper measure, and not with that exclusive devotion due to God, the "Prime Good", which can never be misplaced or excessive.

"mentre ch'egli è ne primi ben diretto,
e ne'secondi se stesso misura
esser non può cagion di mal diletto."[1]

Thus Virgil, in the seventeenth Canto; and though Virgil may some-times be inadequate, he is never dead wrong. The conscious desire (*amore d'ánimo*) for the "secondary goods" (the good things of this world) is therefore right up to a certain point and if directed to right objects. We must not fall into the trap of saying that the Siren re-presents the secondary goods themselves, and that Dante is preaching a Manichean and heretical doctrine that all material things are *ipso facto* evil, or even that he advocates what people are pleased to call a "monkish asceticism" and complete repudiation of the world. That would involve complete contradiction of the whole trend of the poem. It is true that, later on, when Beatrice asks Dante how he came to be unfaithful to that desire of her which had led him to love "the Good beyond which there is nothing left to aspire to", he falters out: "*Le presenti cose Col falso lor piacer volser miei passi, Tosto che il vostro viso si nascose.*"[2] Whereupon she bids him to be henceforth of stouter heart when hearing the Sirens. But this tells us only, what we knew already, that the Siren has to do with the "false pleasure of present things". What is the "false pleasure", which Beatrice also calls "false images (*imagini*) of good?" and how does the false image differ from the true?

It is here that there lies the whole peril of the Affirmative Way—a peril so acute that it has driven many to the Way of Negation and repudiation of all images—though the Negative Way, too, has dangers of its own. The attitude of the Catholic Christian to "present things" and "secondary goods" must always be ambivalent; for if they are not seen and loved for the sake of the Prime Good which they image, they easily become idols—"*imagini false*"—which image something quite different, and are the means, not to Heaven but to Hell.

When at long last Dante is confronted with Beatrice, he sees her

---

[1] When to the great prime goods it makes full claim,
        Or to the lesser goods in measure due,
        No sin can come of its delight in them.
                            Purg. xvii. 97–99.

[2] "Things transitory, with their false delight",
        Weeping I answered, "turned my steps aside,
        Soon as your face was hidden from my sight."
                            Purg. xxxi. 34–36.

exalted upon the Car that is drawn by the Griffin whose double nature signifies the two Natures united in Christ—the human and the divine. He has heard her saluted by the hymn, *Benedictus qui venis*,[1] which is sung before the Holy Host, the sacrament of the two Substances, the earthly bread and wine and the heavenly Body and Blood. And she speaks to him—she, the Florentine girl whom in her fleshly body he recognised as the vehicle of the Divine Glory:

> "*Guardaci ben; ben sem, ben sem Beatrice.*"[2]

Is it a coincidence that the song of the Siren opens with something very like this:

> "*Io son*", *cantava*, "*io son dolce sirena*"?

With a poet like Dante, that sort of thing is no coincidence. His intention is written large in such parallels, and is heard in the very movement of the verse. The Siren is the false Beatrice, the lie which is so like the truth that it may deceive the very elect; the "ape of God"— *diabolus simius Dei.*

Her first appearance is harmless and helpless—alien and rather repellent than otherwise. The avarice, intemperance and lust of the adult world are incomprehensible to uncorrupted childhood. Traherne has described how the first, Beatrician, image was driven from his mind by the example of his parents and companions, and "the evil influence of a bad education":

It was a difficult matter to persuade me that the tinselled ware upon a hobby-horse was a fine thing. They did impose upon me, and obtrude their gifts that made me believe a ribbon or a feather curious. I could not see where was the curiousness or fineness. And to teach me that a purse of gold was of any value seemed impossible, the art by which it becomes so, and the reasons for which it is accounted so, were so deep and hidden to my inexperience. . . .

My soul was only apt and disposed to great things; but souls to souls are like apples to apples, one being rotten rots the other. When I began to speak and go, nothing began to be present to me, but what was present to me in [my companions'] thoughts. Nor was anything present to me any other way than it was so to them. *The glass of imagination was the only mirror, wherein anything was represented or appeared to me*. . . . So I began among my

---

[1] Blessed art thou that comest.

[2] Look on us well, we are indeed, we are
    Beatrice.
                              Purg. xxx. 73.

playfellows to prize a drum, a fine coat, a penny, a gilded book, etc., who before never dreamed of any such wealth.[1]

"The glass of imagination"—the gaze of the soul, fixed upon the sin, sees it transformed and beautified in the mirror of the imagination. And that false image drives out the first. "As for the Heavens and the Sun and Stars they disappeared, and were no more unto me than the bare walls; So that the strange riches of man's invention quite overcame the riches of Nature, being learned more laboriously and in the second place." [2]

Thus Traherne, to whom God had given a beautiful and childlike soul, and to whom, in due time, the First Image returned, as it did also, after many days, to Dante.

But there are other souls, less innocent, to whom the Siren appears, not in the mirror of other men's minds, but in their own, at a far deeper and more deadly level, and for whom there may well be no return. To such men, the warmer kind of sin at first offers no attraction; it seems but a blind and feeble groping after things of no importance, because they are so wrapped up in their own pride and egotism that the whole outer world is to them as a thing dead and indifferent. But if that inner core of integrity, whatever it is, which is for them the First Image, should become corrupted and lost, then the Ego seeks compensation by projecting a monstrous image of itself upon the outer world.[3] This it contemplates, hypnotised by itself; and since it has no real communication with any creature but itself, it feeds upon its own imagination, until at length it passes under the domination of the image it has evoked, and ends in obsession and madness. This image is the Siren, the "ancient witch" whom Rabbinical tradition calls "Lilith", the first wife of Adam—not a true other, made of his flesh, like Eve, but spun from his own imagination, his own desire answering to his own desire; and in magical lore she is also called the Succubus.

Those who have read Charles Williams's novel, *Descent into Hell*,[4]

---

[1] Thomas Traherne: *Centuries of Meditations* (Dobell, 1934), *Cent.* iii. 9, 10 (*italics mine*).

[2] *Ibid., loc. cit.*

[3] cf. Fr. Gerald Vann: "If you exalt the objects of your love until your picture is a false one; if you idealise them; *if you project upon them your own ideal picture of your own ideal self;* then you are loving not a real person but a dream . . . and real love is still as remote from your heart as ever." (*italics mine*)—*The Seven Swords* (Collins, 1950), p. 41.

[4] Charles Williams: *Descent into Hell* (February, 1937); the refs. are to the 1949 edn.

will recognise his imaginative and terrifying treatment of this theme of
the Succubus. It is, I think, largely based on this passage of Dante, and
is an illuminating comment on it. It illuminates particularly the mysterious figure of the "*donna*" who comes to defeat the Siren, and over
whose identity so many exegetical battles have been waged. Some
have thought she was meant for Lucia; others, for Matelda; and others
again, for Beatrice herself. She cannot, certainly, be Beatrice—even in
a nightmare, Dante would not have failed to recognise *her*. And I do
not think she is anybody to whom a definite name could be put. One
must not try to treat poems as though they were actual history; there
is nothing in a poem except what the writer chooses to put there; and
if Dante has not given a name to the Lady, it is that he wished her to
be nameless. The dream is presented to us *as* a dream, with an un-
identified Lady in it; the most we are entitled to ask is, what *sort* of
heavenly interference does this Lady represent? The only things we
are told about her are that she is "holy and alert", and that she is much
quicker off the mark than Virgil, whom she indignantly summons to
come and expose the pretensions of the Siren. She is, therefore, not
Reason: she is something that acts more swiftly than Reason, but she
cannot of herself make the dreamer see the illusion into which he has
fallen—only Reason can do that. The Lady is something that acts, we
may say, irrationally and almost automatically. She shows the red light
before our wits can get to work. She is an immediate reaction to the
Siren-song in the heart. I should be inclined to say that she is something in the nature of a conditioned reflex in our moral make-up; or
simply an ingrained good habit.

In *Descent into Hell*, if I am not mistaken, the Lady puts in two
major appearances, one before and one after the actual appearance of
the Succubus, and a reference to the book may make this point a little
clearer.

The man to whom all these things happen is called Wentworth. He
is a military historian, and when the book opens, he is beginning to
lose his integrity as a scholar. He is publicly engaged in argument over
a minor point with an aged historian called Aston Moffatt: "a pure
scholar, a holy and beautiful soul who would have sacrificed reputation, income, and life, if necessary, for the discovery of one fact. . . .
Wentworth was younger, and at a more critical point, at that moment
when a man's real concern begins to separate itself from his pretended,
and almost to become independent of himself. He raged secretly as he
wrote his letters and drew up his evidence; he identified scholarship

with himself, and asserted himself under the disguise of a defence of scholarship." [1] The First Image then, in so far as he ever knew it, is lost; he no longer sees Divine Truth shining through the truth of the scholar. "He was beginning to twist the intention of the sentences in his authorities, preferring strange meanings and awkward constructions, adjusting evidence, manipulating words." [1] (This, incidentally, is a sin into which it is very easy for commentators to fall—commentators on Dante not least. I can only hope that I am not going Wentworth's way. I cannot answer for it.) "He was", the book goes on, "still innocent enough to be irritated . . . and he was intensely awake to any other slights from any quarter." [1]

While Wentworth is in this state of mind, he begins to bolster up his self-confidence by a compensatory desire to possess and dominate a young woman called Adela. He transfers to her the lust for victory which has substituted itself in him for the image of truth. He is a man who "had never had a friend or a lover; he had never, in any possible sense of the word, been 'in love' ". The "secondary good" which is the love of one's neighbour had, that is, always been to him a thing "stammering, squint and maimed", without attraction; but he now begins to gaze at it, and under his gaze it becomes a thing desirable.

Then he discovers that the influence he always thought he had had over Adela never existed at all; she is attached to a young man of her own age and type. He suspects that the two have conspired (as indeed they have) to slight him, and make a fool of him. He goes out to spy upon them, filled with a poisonous rage and a morbid desire to create a Hell of hurt pride for himself; and his suspicions are confirmed. He is thrown back upon himself to eat his own heart out among his own imaginations.

A little later than this, the first attempt at interference is made by the powers who have him in charge. He sees in a newspaper that a knighthood has been given to the rival historian, Moffat:

There was presented to him at once and clearly an opportunity for joy—casual, accidental joy, but joy. If he could not manage joy, at least he might have managed the intention of joy, or (if that also were too much) an effort towards the intention of joy. The infinity of grace could have been contented and invoked by a mere mental refusal of anything but such an effort. He knew his duty—he was no fool—he knew that the fantastic recognition would please and amuse the innocent soul of Sir Aston, not so much for himself,

---

[1] *Op. cit.*, pp. 38–39.

as in some unselfish way for the honour of history. . . . Wentworth knew he could share that pleasure. He could enjoy; at least could refuse not to enjoy. He could refuse and reject damnation.

With a perfectly clear, if instantaneous, knowledge of what he did, he rejected joy instead. He instantaneously invoked anger, and at once it came; he invoked envy, and it obliged him.[1]

This is, I think, the first appearance of "the Lady"—the summons to perform a simple, almost instinctive, duty—to make the proper and customary reaction. Instead, he gives deliberate way to rage. And immediately there offers itself to him the horrible image of his own desires, the succubus fashioned in the shape of the girl Adela, but in fact a mere projection of his own ego. And from then onwards, he withdraws more and more into a hideous solitude with this illusory being whose response to his lust is always perfect because it is only his own response to himself:

The shape of Lawrence Wentworth's desire had emerged from the power of his body. He had assented to that making . . . he had assented to the company of the shape which could not be except by his will and was imperceptibly to possess his will. . . . Adela walked by him and cajoled him —in the prettiest way—to love her. He was approached, appeased, flattered, entreated. There flowed from the creature by his side the sensation of his absolute power to satisfy her. It was what he had vehemently and in secret desired—to have his own way under the pretext of giving her hers.[2]

That is the Siren. She is made by the Ego gazing upon itself, and it responds, seeming to woo and promising perpetual peace, perpetual satisfaction, until the will that summoned it up is wholly subject to the thing it has summoned and all touch with reason and reality are lost:

> "*Io son*", *cantava*, "*io son dolce sirena*
> *che i marinari in mezzo mar dismago,*
> *tanto son di piacere a sentir piena.*
>
> *Io volsi Ulisse del suo cammin vago*
> *col canto mio; e qual meco si ausa*
> *rado sen parte, sì tutto l'appago.*"[3]

The song, with its exaggerated alliteration and emphasised play of long vowels, is meretricious, and meant to be so, in every sense of the word. The last lines are a lingering and luscious menace:

> *qual meco si ausa—*

---

[1] *Ibid.,* p. 80. [2] *Ibid.,* p. 127. [3] For translation see p. 137 above.

he who dwells with me, grows to me, makes a habit of me—

rado sen parte, sì tutto l'appago.

Seldom, indeed, can he get loose from that suffocating embrace. In *Descent into Hell*, "the Lady" makes one more effort to free Wentworth. It is made in the simplest possible way. Some private theatricals are in progress, and he is appealed to, as the historian who has designed the soldiers' costumes, to say whether they have been correctly carried out. He sees they are wrong. There is a trifling error in the shoulder-knots which he could put right in no time.

> He looked at them, for the first moment, almost with the pure satisfaction of the specialist. . . . He looked . . . and he swung . . . as if at a point of decision. . . . The shoulder knots could be altered easily enough. . . . They could be defended, then and there with half a dozen reasons . . . but he was something of a purist; he did not like them. . . . He could do what the honour of his scholarship commanded . . . it meant only his being busy with them that one evening, and concerning himself with something different from his closed garden. He smelt the garden.
>
> Mrs. Parry's voice said: "Is the Guard correct?" He said: "Yes." It was over, he could go.[1]

So he goes—to damnation. But the appeal to ingrained habit—the automatic reaction to something wrong in what was his own special subject, had very nearly succeeded, that time, in breaking the spell and rousing Virgil.

I have referred—perhaps at too great length—to this novel by a modern Master of the Affirmative Way, partly for the light it throws on the *meaning* (as distinguished from the possible identification) of the Lady; and partly because it provides the test which distinguishes the right measure of love for the "secondary goods" from the "love excessive". When such a love is rightly ordered (in St. Francis's phrase) it makes known the good things of this world as vehicles and sacraments of the Glory and, being directed through them to the Prime Good, leads to the Beatific Vision. When it is pursued disorderly and with a greedy excess, it makes of those goods only a series of mirrors reflecting the image of the Self, and leads to the "Miserific Vision" of that which grinds its impotent teeth in the ice of Giudecca. All love of transient things is, essentially, of the one kind or the other, and tends, by little or much, in one of those two directions.

[1] *Op. cit.*, p. 144.

My third reason for quoting the book is that it is well, from time to time, to bring the *Commedia* into touch with the mystical experience which lies at the roots of all religious knowledge. Dante has suffered somewhat from being interpreted too exclusively in terms of political theory and moral platitude. Both these things are wholesome, but a little dry; and explanations along these lines are apt to be presented with a pigeon-holing neatness suggestive of packeted food. It is a good thing sometimes to return to the well-springs of wonder and imagination and splash about there, among the live fish and growing grass, even though the results may be a little untidy.

The dream troubles Dante. And as the poets, released from enforced inertia by the daylight that now fills every ledge of the mountain, proceed upon their way, Dante (who has taken himself with unwonted seriousness throughout the last two cantos) relapses into self-mockery, and enlivens the description of his distress by one of his usual grotesque similes:

> So, following on along the circle's edge,
>> With bended brow, like one who, bowed in thought,
>> Makes of himself the half-arch of a bridge,
>
> I heard: "Come, here's the pass", in accents fraught
>> With so benign a tenderness of tone
>> As never ear in mortal precinct caught.
>
> He who thus spake, wide-winged as 'twere a swan,
>> Signed our steps upward to our destination
>> Between the two unyielding walls of stone;
>
> Then fluttering, fanned us with his wings' vibration,
>> And told us, blessed should *qui lugent* be,
>> Having their souls made queens of consolation.

This is the angel of Zeal, and the wide sweep of the wings with which he erases the P of Sloth from Dante's brow expresses the speed with which he hastens to execute his service. The beatitude: "Blessed are they that mourn" has, I think, a twofold application. Sloth is, in general, the sin of not-caring, and the grief of the spirits who have at last learned to care in desperate earnest about their short-comings is now abundantly blessed. But more particularly there is included in the sin of Accidie the depression that sits down and wrings its hands instead of reacting vigorously to trouble and difficulties; and it is this

passive grief, now turned into an active repentance, which will have
its sorrow turned into joy, so that they who once despaired will have
"*di consolar l'anime donne*". The word "*donne*" implies lordship; once
they succumbed to circumstance; now they will not only receive but
possess the power of consolation.

Despite this reassurance, Dante remains troubled, for the lure of the
Siren extends over the three cornices that are yet to be traversed. Virgil
rallies him: "*Che hai, che pur inver la terra guati?*" [1] So Dante confesses
that he has been frightened by a disturbing dream which he cannot get
out of his mind. He is rewarded by one of the most astonishing pieces
of imagery that have ever entered a poet's mind:

> "Saw'st thou that ancient witch for whose sole snare
>   The mount above us weeps? and how one deals
>   With her", he answered, "and is rid of her?
>
> Suffice it thee! Spurn earth beneath thy heels;
>   Look only to the lure the eternal King
>   Whirls yonder with the great celestial wheels."

Of all the images of Deity with which religious literature has supplied us, I know nothing, not even among the Metaphysicals at their
most extravagant, which can compare for boldness, for gaiety, and for
sheer, breathtaking excitement, with this picture of God the Falconer,
riding out, hawking for souls, whirling the whole glitter of the immeasurable heavens about His head like a lure. Its vigour and audacity
are so dramatic that one feels like waving one's hat and shouting. The
verse itself is a shout of delight:

> *Bastati, e batti a terra le calcagne;*
>   *Gli occhi rivolgi al logoro che gira*
>   *Lo Rege etterno con le rote magne.*

No wonder it puts heart into Dante. And see how the image of the
falcon is picked up in the following stanza. (Dante is always good on
falconry, it must have been his favourite sport):

> Like to a hawk, that sits with folded wing,
>   Eyeing its feet, and at the call turns swift,
>   Eager for food, wings spread to soar and swing,

---

[1] "Still gazing on the ground? what aileth thee?"
Purg. xix. 52.

Such I became; and so, right through the rift
    One climbs by, up to where the shelf runs round
    Once more, did I my cheerful flight uplift.

And there, on that cheerful note, we will leave him.

(Summer School of Italian Studies
1950)

DANTE AND MILTON

SETTING aside both that sense of awe, and also that invitation to rhapsody, which the contemplation of these *etterni Gemelli* might naturally arouse in a commentator, I will begin this study with a modest entry from a popular encyclopaedia of literature. I apologise beforehand for its style, which is that of its humble species.

"The author of the great poem of the Divine Way was born into an epoch of violent political faction and civil war, marked by savage disputes about the derivation of secular authority and the respective functions in the commonwealth of Church and State. It was this external situation which, provoking a sharp personal crisis in his own life, deflected for a time what appeared to be the natural development of his genius, and eventually determined the shape and character of that master work with which his name is associated for all time.

"Descended from good native stock, gentle though not noble, the young man received the best education that his age afforded, and gave early proof of an intellectual and literary ability which was recognised by all his contemporaries. Endowed with a sensuous and highly sensitive temperament, his mind steeped in the Scriptures as well as in the romantic and classical poetry which formed the cultural background of his time, he struck a new lyrical note, instinct with freshness of feeling, and combining a vivid awareness of earthly beauty with an acute religious sensibility. To this period belongs the composition of a body of love-poetry and a number of very noble odes which would in themselves suffice to crown him with fame. Though deeply devoted to learning, and filled with a solemn sense of his poetic vocation, he delighted in art and music, and in the gay company of cultivated men and women, as well as in the sports and manly exercises which contribute to the making of a whole and many-sided life.

"At the moment, however, when all the omens pointed to a peaceful and prosperous development of his natural gifts, the ship of his fortunes was struck by a political tornado. With the same passionate energy which he had devoted to the service of the good and beautiful, he now threw his whole soul into the task of partisan apologetics, producing among other things a treatise on the theory of government and a number of pamphlets characterised on the one hand by a savage and abusive eloquence and, on the other, by outbursts of prophetic rhapsody which reflect the intense religious fervour with which he and his looked forward to the advent of a political millennium. Greatly as one must admire the powerful sense of duty and the patriotism which prompted these efforts, one cannot but recognise that the rough-and-tumble of controversy is not the most favourable forcing-ground for the poetic temperament. The touchiness, the self-defensive egotism under attack, the inevitable coarsening of the spiritual fibre, and the over-ingenuity of special pleading which form the stock-in-trade of the politician work their harm more intensively in the finer material, and the prose works of this period, full as they are of passages of a noble eloquence, display our poet in perhaps his least admirable, and certainly in his least amiable aspect.

"The high hopes were doomed to perish; the reign of the saints was postponed. The bitter reproaches addressed to those countrymen of his who had betrayed the cause gave poignant proof of the poet's outraged feelings. Impoverished, disappointed, and in considerable political peril, he returned to his true calling, and poured into a great sacred poem—at once a parable of human destiny and a *summa* of the writer's religious and political faith—all the ardour, the passion, and the experience of his frustrated life. The experience had, after all, not been wasted; deepened and fortified by suffering, his power discharged itself with multiplied energy through the proper and natural channel to which it had thus returned. Discarding the Latin of which he had from time to time shown himself master, and using the beloved vernacular in which he could appeal most intimately to the hearts of his compatriots, the poet forged for himself a new poetic form and a new poetic diction which were to leave their impress upon the native style for centuries to come. He was 56 years old when he completed the stupendous task which had occupied him, under conditions of more than ordinary difficulty, for many laborious years.

"He stands upon the threshold of two epochs, rather summing up the age which was past than ushering in that which was to come. To-day, looking back to him across an alien and intervening development, we are perhaps in a better position to appreciate the full scope and meaning of his achievement than were the critics of the centuries immediately succeeding him.

"Of his private life, apart from one overwhelming emotional shock which set its stamp upon his sexual experience and had important aesthetic results in his work, the details do not greatly concern the purely literary critic. His marriage would seem, on the whole, not to have been very happy. He had four children, one of whom (a boy named John) died at an early age; the other three survived him. The effigies, somewhat grim and forbidding, which are usually prefixed to his collected works probably do less than justice to one who, if he made some enemies, was deeply loved by those who knew him best; they need to be looked at in the light of the one youthful portrait which remains to us, showing the cheeks unfurrowed by care, and the mutinous, sensual mouth. Even in later life, though reserved and autocratic in manner and somewhat given to sarcasm, he was found excellent company by those to whom he could open his heart freely. And while his popular legend rests chiefly upon his reputation as a poet of Hell, yet to judicious minds the tenderer passages of his Divine poem display no less genius than the rest, with perhaps a superior subtlety of feeling and rhythmical invention—in especial the exquisitely human and moving scenes which take place in the Terrestrial Paradise.

"Among his less-read works may be mentioned an ambitious prose treatise of a philosophical and theological character, and an unfinished philological essay."

To this hypothetical entry, it is necessary to add only a couple of dates and a name—John Milton, or Dante Alighieri; it is all one.

The surprisingly close parallelism between their careers makes a comparison between the two great poets of Western Christendom easier and more fruitful than that between some other pairs of writers whom critical convention habitually links together—often for no better reason than mere contemporaneity or a superficial resemblance of form or subject-matter: Tennyson and Browning, for instance; Dickens and Thackeray; Corneille and Racine; Goethe and Schiller; Shelley and Keats; Tasso and Ariosto; Balzac and Flaubert; Homer and Virgil. Dickens and Thackeray lived in the same reign and both wrote very long novels, but their characters and circumstances were totally different, and their worlds scarcely touch. Virgil modelled his epic style upon Homer, but their aims and outlook were so little akin that com-

parison between them has darkened rather than enlightened counsel
and induced more critical irrelevancies and miscarriages of justice than
one could enumerate in a month of Sundays. But Dante and Milton,
endowed with temperaments curiously alike and intellects evenly
matched, did, at three centuries' distance from one another, encounter
much the same vital problems, endure similar vicissitudes, tread the
same path foot for foot, produce a body of work which is comparable
not only in general but in detail, and build each his enduring monu-
ment with a poem which is the statement and justification of his faith.
Where the resemblance runs so deep, we may be sure that comparison
will be genuinely relevant, and that any contrasts which emerge will
be significant. Indeed the contrast between them is as striking as the
likeness; and it is not accidental.

The sin which besets all makers of critical comparisons is, of course,
the sin of partiality. It is only too easy to institute a kind of competition: to claim for this poet or that a superiority in suffering, to set-off
the pathos of exile against the pathos of blindness, to allot conduct-
marks, and draw up a profit-and-loss account ending in a nasty little
subtraction sum purporting to show the measurable amount of
"greatness" by which the one exceeds the other. I shall not be exempt
from this failing. Due discount must be made for the fact that I can be
at home in the universe of Dante's mind as I cannot be in Milton's,
because Dante and I share the same faith; on that side, therefore, my
sympathy is likely to overweigh my judgement. On the other hand,
my judgement tells me this: that if (as the world on the whole seems
to think) Dante's achievement is more satisfying, intellectually and
aesthetically, than Milton's it is largely because Dante's whole nature
was integral with, and fully expressed in, his faith, as Milton's was not.

The other great factor that operated to nourish Dante's poetic
development and to stunt or distort Milton's was the factor of sexual
experience. The reader will have noticed that my "encyclopaedia
entry" went very gingerly over this point, for here the two men stand
at opposite poles. Religion, the temper of the times, and the personal
equation all had their share in this—and, in addition, the sheer luck
of the draw: bad luck for the one; for the other, that Holy Luck whose
divinity he celebrated.

To put the thing shortly: Milton was a Dante deprived of Beatrice—
of Beatrice, that is, in the whole range of her significance, literal and
allegorical.

About Milton's education we know more plain facts than we do about Dante's. He began under a tutor at his home in Cheapside; at or before the age of twelve he went to St. Paul's School. In 1625, when he was seventeen, he matriculated at Christ's College, Cambridge, taking his B.A. in 1629 and his M.A. in 1632.

For Dante, we have only his own vague reference to the educative influence of Brunetto Latini, and we get the impression that his schooling was, on the whole, less regular. But it is fairly clear from internal evidence that by the time he wrote the *Vita Nuova* he was pretty thoroughly grounded in the mediaeval *trivium* (Grammar, Dialectic and Rhetoric) and knew at any rate something of the four parts of the *quadrivium* (Music, Astronomy, Arithmetic and Geometry). Subsequently, we know that he devoted himself to the pursuit of Philosophy; and at some time or other he attended the Schools in Bologna and in Paris. We cannot anywhere pin him down, like Milton, to a regular University career, and it would seem as though the course of his studies was largely self-directed. The educational advantage here might appear to lie with Milton, but in some ways Dante was the luckier. He came too late for the great twelfth-century heyday of Scholasticism, but its life was still vigorous. He fed eagerly and throve upon the "bread of angels", and the Heaven of the Sun bears witness to his lifelong enthusiasm and reverence for the mighty doctors whose memory was still fresh in men's minds. By Milton's time the mediaeval scholastic system, still clamped down upon the Universities, had declined into a mechanical sophistry, whose rigidity was splitting everywhere like the outworn shell of a lobster, under the pressure of Renaissance learning. Milton reacted violently against it. He despised the training in formal logic and disputation no less than the "quibbles" (as he calls them) of the scholastic philosophers, and advocated a radical reform of education in the direction of a more liberal and humane curriculum: history, geography, and natural philosophy based on experimental knowledge. Not that Milton gained nothing from his training. His debt to it is obvious, particularly in the disputation between Satan and Abdiel in the Fifth Book of *Paradise Lost*, where both parties are, as C. S. Lewis points out, "sound Aristotelians", and evidently learnt dialectic under the same master. But the Baconian era was setting in. Milton not only felt these dissatisfactions, but voiced them loudly and rudely in his *Prolusions* and elsewhere, with the not unnatural result that he got into trouble with the dons and made himself at first very unpopular with the undergraduates, for the general level of whose intellects he felt and expressed the utmost contempt.

"It looks", says Doctor Tillyard,[1] "as if he had suffered something of a shock when he came up. Prone, as he later showed himself, to expect too much from normal humanity, he doubtless expected to find himself in company with other Miltons under the tuition of men more remarkable for piety and learning even than Young [his old tutor] and the Gills [headmaster and usher at St. Paul's]." Doubtless he did. Milton was always like that; he quite simply and innocently expected perfection of everybody—of humanity, of women, of Englishmen, of the Presbyterians, of the Cromwellian government—and his whole life was in consequence a series of shocks and disillusionments. Dante, no less arrogant about his own intellectual superiority, was, probably from the beginning and certainly in the end, much more of a man of the world. Milton, though he lived through a civil war and many violent political changes, led on the whole a sheltered life: he was never knocked about in the rough school of experience—exiled, humiliated, beaten from pillar to post, fending for himself, threatened with death by burning. Other troubles he had, but not those. To the end he retained an engaging simplicity: the wickedness of the world continually took him by surprise. He was always vulnerable. Dante learned not to be vulnerable. The harshness and bitterness of the great Florentine are his protective casing; beneath them the deep springs of joy and tenderness well up clear and untroubled; but when Milton is hurt the hurt is vital—the iron entering the soul and the spring poisoned at the source. We have run rather ahead of our subject, but it is perhaps well to get this difference between the two men clear at the start. For we are coming to that region of the emotions where all poets, and indeed all men, are most vulnerable, and where the nature of any shock, and one's reactions to it, are liable to leave a mark for life.

At the age of eighteen, Dante Alighieri fell violently, and notoriously, in love. He says himself that he had received the first shock of that experience nine years earlier, and that even then it had powerfully affected him, head, heart and reins. We need not, perhaps, attach too great an importance to that statement, except in so far as it shows that he was by nature susceptible and had from an early age gone about seeking love. But at eighteen the real thing happened:

It came to pass that this wondrous lady appeared to me, dressed all in pure white, between two gentlewomen of riper years: and as she passed me in the street she turned her eyes toward the place where I stood trembling,

---

[1] E. M. W. Tillyard: *Milton* (Chatto & Windus, 1946), p. 17.

and of her unspeakable courtesy, which now has its reward in the better world, she bestowed on me a salutation of such virtue that I felt myself then and there transported to the uttermost bounds of bliss (*mi parve allora vedere tutti i termini della beatitudine*). . . . And inasmuch as that was the first time that her words had set forth to come to my ears, so sweet a delight (*tanta dolcezza*) overwhelmed me that I became as it were drunken, and fled from everybody and shut myself up alone in my room to think upon this marvel of courtesy.[1]

It was then that he beheld the vision of Love as a "Lord of terrible aspect", who seemed "to have such joy within himself as was a thing marvellous; and he spoke many things whereof I understood but few, and among them I understood this: *Ego dominus tuus*".[2] Then he tells how he saw Beatrice lying naked in Love's arm, and how Love gave her a burning heart to eat, saying to him, *Vide cor tuum*.[3] And a little after he saw Love's joy changed to bitter weeping, "and thus weeping he gathered this lady up in his arms and it seemed he went away with her into Heaven".[4]

How much of this vision is true reporting and how much of it was imagined, as it was recorded, after the death of Beatrice, is matter for speculation;[5] in any case it bears witness to this: that for Dante love was from beginning to end associated with worship, fear, beatitude, sorrow, wonder, and loss. It was a mystical experience, touching the heights and the depths, and having no connection either with the violent possessiveness of passion or the mutual comfort of marriage.

In this, he was of his day. Courtly love, *Frauendienst*, had always reckoned itself a thing apart, cut off on either side from the commonplace of sexual experience, and the *dolce stil nuovo* which Guido Guinicelli and his followers had grafted upon the romantic love-theme of the Provençal poets enhanced the spiritual and mystical implications of the cult. If young poets of Dante's time fell in love, they expected it to be like that, and since that was what they expected, that was what they got. Lust was a different matter; they knew all about that; and

---

[1] *Vita Nuova*, iii.   [2] I am thy lord.
[3] Behold thy heart.   [4] *Vita Nuova*, iii.

[5] The dream itself was, of course, recorded at the time, in a sonnet which Dante circulated among his friends, with a request for comment and elucidation. (Dante da Maiano put it down, rather unkindly, to indigestion.) But the mysterious speech of Love, and the declaration *Ego dominus tuus*, together with the words "into heaven" are found only in the prose commentary, written at a later date, and may have been added in the light of later events. The "terror" of Love's aspect is, however, already stressed in the sonnet: *cui essenza membrar mi dà orror.*

although in practice courtly love might decline into lust only too often, in theory lust was reprobated as an outrage upon love. Marriage, too, was a different matter: it was a social contract, arranged for one by one's parents, very often when both parties were in the cradle, and its objects were the security of inheritance, the smooth ordering of households, and the perpetuation of the family. It was an honourable estate, calling for sobriety of behaviour without enthusiasm. The Church, hovering always between the opposing conceptions of sexuality as a sin and marriage as a sacrament,[1] deprecated violent and irrational passion, whether in marriage or out of it. With the phenomenon of courtly love she coped slowly, reluctantly, and unimaginatively, seeing its dangers rather than its possibilities. It was the poets who seized upon it to make that unstable yet ecstatic synthesis between religion and love whose psychology has haunted the Western consciousness ever since the twelfth century. It is an inflammable and dangerous mixture, but the greatest of all driving powers for certain temperaments as, among others, the names of Dante and of Donne bear witness.

Now, however odd or extravagant the doctrine of courtly love may appear to us, it is well to bear in mind that the mediaeval attitude to sexuality was, like everything else in that age, governed fundamentally by a quite ruthless rationality and realism. The men of that period distinguished three types of relationship between the sexes: passion, married love (the *debito amore*) and *Frauendienst* and, while awaiting a synthesis, they kept them distinct, with a firmness which looks at times like cynicism. But three hundred years later the whole situation had given place to Platonic idealism. The poets had worked out their synthesis and imposed it upon society. You may follow the details of this process in C. S. Lewis's *The Allegory of Love*; but for the present purpose it is perhaps enough to say that between Dante and Milton there lies Spenser. The spiritual ecstasies of *Frauendienst*, together with the physical ecstasies of passion, had been as it were carried over into the married state, which was now expected to accommodate and provide fulfilment for all three types of sexual relationship. This was a resounding triumph for Christian ethics, carried through in the teeth of the Church who, though she was forced in a sense to accept and even bless it, was always, and remains still, alive to its perils. For it is obvious that it set the standard of marriage impossibly high, and put upon it a tension that was liable to strain it to the breaking-point. We

[1] The opinions of the Doctors on the sinful element in (fallen) sexuality may be found conveniently epitomised in C. S. Lewis's *The Allegory of Love*, pp. 13 *seq.*

are in fact experiencing to-day the breakdown of the late-mediaeval synthesis; and the marvel perhaps is that it has lasted so long. For it demanded that every marriage should be an ideal marriage; and to that lofty conception our popular sentimental literature still bears witness. So, after another manner, do the divorce-courts. We have by now come to think that a marriage is no marriage if it does not provide us with life-long glamour and life-long passion. The Church was, and is, much less idealistic and much less naïve.

At the age of nineteen, John Milton fell in love. It was then, as before and since his time, expected of young poets that they should fall in love, and he duly did so and wrote a Latin poem about it.[1] It seems to have been a quite healthy and quite passing affair. He was walking out one day, saw a young lady of surpassing beauty, and felt his heart burning with an unwonted flame. He lost sight of the girl, and apparently never set eyes on her again. Later, he was ashamed of the episode and apppended to the poem a tail-piece explaining how learning had taught him to throw off the servile yoke of love:

> Then on a sudden, the fierce flame supprest,
>   A frost continual settled on my breast,
>   Whence Cupid fears his flame extinct to see,
>   And Venus dreads a Diomede in me.[2]

So far, so good. But if anything is evident from the early poems of Milton it is that his temperament could never be satisfied by learning and asceticism. He was, and indeed remained all his life, passionate, sensuous, quiveringly sensitive to beauty, and an idealist in love as in everything else. In these respects he is Dante's blood-brother. But he was not so lucky. His idealism was his undoing and his very virtues betrayed him. We see him, a delicate, fastidious, beautiful young man, greatly endowed, a poet to his finger-tips, deeply and sincerely religious, consciously preparing himself through many years for his divine vocation and with the utmost seriousness and simplicity dedicating himself to the Muse and to chastity. We cannot but admire him —but for a man of his nature it was a perilous undertaking. No sensitive person reading *Comus* can avoid, I think, feeling a certain uneasiness; the tension between the matter and the manner of the poem is too great. The praise of chastity, so voluptuously sung, makes us feel

---

[1] There are also, of course, his Italian love-sonnets; it is difficult to say what, if any, personal experience underlies them.

[2] *Elegia Septima* (Cowper's translation).

that we are walking on thin glass over a furnace. We are accustomed to think of Milton as a Puritan, but he was never by temperament a Puritan in the popular sense of the term—only in the sense that he set an almost exaggerated value upon purity. Any man with that temperament and those values will be well advised to marry early, or, failing that, to marry a woman of experience. Milton did neither. In the summer of 1642,[1] he went away on a month's visit and returned home with a wife.

The bridegroom was a male virgin of thirty-three; the bride a totally inexperienced girl of seventeen. We hear of no difficulty on the physical side, though it is likely enough that the inexperienced husband may have been clumsy, exacting, and inconsiderate through no fault of his own. Mutual love and affinity of mind could easily have got over that; or, on the other hand, a deep and mutual physical delight might have smoothed the way to love and understanding. But on Milton's side there was a strong and religiously rooted conviction of the natural inferiority of woman combined (perhaps inconsistently) with very high expectations of companionship in marriage. Courtly love might have saved him—but courtly love had gone, its place being taken by the synthesis. Moreover, poor Mary Powell had come from a large and merry cavalier family, and now found herself called upon to provide mental companionship for a scholar of retired and solitary habits, twice her age. Disaster was only to be expected, and it came quickly. After only a few weeks of marriage, the bride—lonely, bored, and terrified—ran away home and refused to come back, leaving her husband to thunder in pamphlet after pamphlet against the divorce laws which took no account of anything but the crude fleshly tie, and left a man humiliatingly bound for ever to one with whom he could never fulfil the nobler ends of marriage.

The shock to Milton was appalling, and he never recovered from it. Neither the subsequent return of Mary Powell, nor his too-brief second marriage to her to whom he called his "late espoused saint" could avail to give him that balance in the matter of women which his education had failed to supply. What is of great interest to us is the mention which he makes of Dante in *The Apology for Smectymnuus*, where he is (ironically enough) defending himself against a pamphleteer who had accused him—of all things!—of having persistently frequented brothels.

[1] This date, suggested by Burns Martin, seems more reasonable than 1643, as given by Phillips.

He says that in his youth he was delighted by "the smooth elegiac poets" (of Greece and Rome), and had resolved to imitate, though "with more love of virtue", their praise of woman's "high perfections".

Nor blame it, readers, in those years to propose to themselves such a reward, as the noblest dispositions above other things in this life have sometimes preferred: whereof not to be sensible when good and fair in one person meet argues both a gross and shallow judgment, and withal an ungentle and swainish heart. For by the firm settling of these persuasions, I became, to my best memory, so much a proficient, that if I found those authors anywhere speaking unworthy things of themselves, or unchaste of those names which before they had extolled, this effect it wrought with me, from that time forth their art I still applauded, but the men I deplored; and above them all, preferred the two famous renowners of Beatrice and Laura, who never write but honour of them to whom they devote their verse, displaying sublime and pure thoughts, without transgression.

Apart from a reference to Casella in the sonnet to Henry Lawes, and the use of a few stanzas from the *Comedy* as missiles to hurl at the Papacy, this is, I think, Milton's only overt reference to Dante in his published works,[1] and it is rather unexpected. One sees, of course, how the tone of Dante's "most chaste love" for Beatrice chimed in with the young Milton's pre-occupation with purity—but what did the man who was to write "he for God only, she for God in him", and to insist so strongly upon the divinely-ordered subjection of woman to man as to make it the key and turning-point of the loss of Paradise— what did he make, then or later, of the exaltation of Beatrice? One would expect it to appear to him not merely unnatural but blasphemous. One wonders what parts of Dante's work he was thinking of, when he read him as a young man and when, later on, he wrote the *Apology*. Of the *Commedia*, which we know he had read? Of the *Canzoni*, some of which were probably available to him,[2] though he may not have distinguished very well between the praise of Beatrice, the Pietra Odes, and the so-called "Philosophic" Odes addressed (or not addressed) to the "Donna Gentile"? Or of the *Vita Nuova*, which was printed in 1576, and certainly available? If it was the *Vita*, was he at that time, before his disastrous marriage, ready to understand or accept the "lord of terrible aspect"? or to receive that saying, "*Ego dominus tuus*"?

[1] In his common-place Book, he cites the *Commedia* several times, and shows that he knew of the *De Monarchia*, though it does not appear that he had read it.

[2] The 14 "Convivio" Odes were printed in Sermartelli's edition of the *Vita Nuova*, 1576.

or to meditate upon those six gifts of love: worship, fear, beatitude, wonder, sorrow and loss? There is nothing in all his works to suggest that he could ever have embraced salvation on those terms. Throughout the Divorce Tracts there is the persistent demand that the woman should be a "help meet" for the man, but it is always she who must conform to him, not he to her. That Milton could feel the other impulse, which moves toward mutuality and the exchange of hierarchy, is proved by Adam's famous speech to Raphael:

> when I approach
> Her loveliness, so absolute she seems
> And in herself compleat, so well to know
> Her own, that what she wills to do or say
> Seems wisest, virtuousest, discreetest, best;
> All higher knowledge in her presence falls
> Degraded, Wisdom in discourse with her
> Looses discount'nanc't, and like folly shewes;
> Authority and reason on her wait. . . . [1]

And so on. But this is heard by the angel "with contracted brow", and proves the very root of Adam's offending. And indeed it outruns Dante, who would never in his wildest moments have dreamed of saying that the higher knowledge fell degraded in Beatrice's presence, or that her discourse discountenanced wisdom. On the contrary.

Yet when we read of the unfallen nuptials of Adam and Eve, or of the tender and moving reconciliation that follows the Fall, we are so persuaded and carried away that criticism "loses discountenanced"; and it is difficult to see what is lacking—until we remember "*Ego dominus tuus*", and that stranger saying: "*Ego tanquam centrum circuli, cui simili modo se habent circumferentiae partes; tu autem non sic*", [2] whose riddle is never solved until the last stanza of the *Paradiso*:

> *ma già volgeva il mio disio e il velle,*
> *si come rota ch'egualmente è mossa,*
> *l'amor che move il sol e l'altre stelle.* [3]

---

[1] *Paradise Lost*, viii. 546 seq.

[2] I am as the centre of the circle to which all parts of the circumference bear a like relation; but with thee it is not so.

V.N. xii.

[3] Yet, as a wheel turns smoothly, free from jars,
Already my will and desire were wheeled by love,
The Love that moves the sun and the other stars.
Para. xxxiii. 143–145.

What is lacking is the sacramental mystery, and the taking up of all love into the one Love.

This unearthly quality of Dante's love has, of course, brought him into contempt with the modern humanists. Let us quote George Santayana, who has brought the misunderstanding of Dante to a fine art. He observes:

Love, as he feels and renders it, is not normal or healthy love. It was doubtless real enough, but too much restrained and expressed too much in fancy; so that when it is extended Platonically and identified so easily with the grace of God and with revealed wisdom, we feel the suspicion that if the love in question had been natural and manly, it would have offered more resistance to so mystical a transformation. The poet who wishes to pass convincingly from love to philosophy should accordingly be a hearty and complete lover—a lover like Goethe and his Faust—rather than like Plato and Dante.[1]

Well, if we want that hearty kind of love, we can find it in Dante, though not in connection with Beatrice. His love spread over more than one object—which, incidentally, is also true of Goethe. If we believe what he says (and there is no reason, except sentimentality, to disbelieve him) he had no particular obsession about purity; he sinned and repented. His contemporaries, including his own son, say that in his youth he was much given to sensuality, which amounts to the same thing. He was, in any case, married—probably (though sentimentality again protests) before the death of Beatrice—to Gemma Donati, to whom he had been contracted at the age of twelve.[2] Of one poem we can say with certainty that it was written by a man of considerable

[1] George Santayana: *Three Philosophical Poets* (Harvard University, 1910), p. 129.

[2] Manetto Donati executed a settlement of Gemma's dowry in 1277. Alighieri *père* died not later than 1283, and Umberto Cosmo thinks that his son's marriage must have taken place within a year or so of his death (*Handbook to Dante Studies*, Eng. trans. Blackwell, 1950, p. 23). Étienne Gilson, on the other hand, thinks that in 1295, after a period devoted to debauchery and (possibly) unnatural vice with Forese Donati, Dante—now repentant and preparing to write the *Commedia*—'had to readjust his moral life by marrying the patient Gemma" who "had spent a long time waiting for him" (*Dante the Philosopher*, Eng. trans. Sheed & Ward, 1948, pp. 66, 61). You pay your money, and you take your choice. Personally, I am ready to accept the early marriage, or the period of debauchery, and could make out an excellent case, on paper, for the unnatural vice (though my instincts are against it). But as to the date of the marriage there can be no real certainty unless and until somebody unearths either the actual *instrumentum dotis*, or the birth-date of the first child born in wedlock.

experience, and that is the notorious *Aspro parlar*, which is one of the
rare poems which deal with sheer animal passion, and with nothing
else. It is an outcry of rage and torment against the denying of the
flesh, and it ends (this is the point) by describing in some detail what
he would do to the girl if she were burning for him as he for her. It
recognises therefore (and that is important, for it is rarer than one
might suppose) that bodily desire is, and should be, mutual—there
is no attempt to extract pleasure out of the woman's coyness or
subjection—even out of that "sweet, reluctant, amorous delay" which
delights Milton's pre-lapsarian Adam. And it goes on (which is rarer
still) to recognise that it is the man's duty to bestow pleasure and to
content desire—not exclusively the other way round. It is a ferocious,
fleshly, only-too-aphrodisiac poem, but it is full of a kind of plangent
beauty and a blazing generosity.

> *S'io avessi le belle treccie prese*
> *Che fatte son per me scudiscio e ferza*
> *Pigliandole anzi terza*
> *Con esse passerei vespro e le squille:*
> *E non sarei pietoso nè cortese,*
> *Anzi farei com'orso quando scherza;*
> *E se Amor me ne sferza,*
> *Io mi vendicherei di più di mille*— [1]

This to be sure, is the very rough-and-tumble of passion; but when he
says he will "take a thousand revenges" he certainly does *not* mean that
he will beat her, still less that, as Papini disgustingly suggests, he will
tear her hair out by the roots.[2] He will indeed punish her by a little
delay for the delay she has imposed on him, and then:

> *Poscia le renderei con amor pace.*[3]

---

[1] Once let me grasp the golden braids entwined
    To be my scourge and lash, those locks of hers,
    I'd cling them close from terce
  Till vesper bell and evening bell had tolled;
  Clement I would not be, nor courteous-kind,
    But like a bear at play; and though Love's fierce
    Hand lay his whips on worse
  I'd be revenged for all a thousandfold.   *Canz. Così nel mio parlar.*

[2] The matter of "love's revenge" may be further studied in Giacomino Pugliese's
poem *Ispendiente stella d'albore*, where the significance of the *vengianza* is not
far to seek.

[3] And then with love would yield her peace thereafter.
                              Canz. Così nel mio parlar.

The man who wrote that knew all about it and had no doubts of himself. Whether or not he and Gemma got along comfortably or otherwise, we may believe him to have been a satisfactory bed-fellow. The legend that his marriage was unhappy rests on Boccaccio's splenetic outburst against wives in general, and the statement that Gemma and he never came together again after his exile. If that is true, there may have been other reasons for it. Two things are certain: one, that he understood, as few men do, the kind of humorous tenderness and despair with which a woman contemplates the childish absurdity of the man she loves. He transfers this to Beatrice, but it is a thing learned chiefly in marriage, and, as the late Charles Williams used to say, there is probably more of Gemma in Beatrice than Dante himself ever knew. The second is that nowhere in Dante do we find the smallest vestige of contempt for, or resentment against, Woman in general. I know no great religious book, except the Gospels and *The Pilgrim's Progress*, which is so totally free from these accustomed railings. Taking the thing all round, Dante gives one the impression of being sexually balanced as very few men have been. He is never peevish, and he is never vulgar. He is quite incapable of Milton's terrible archness:

> from his lip
> Not words alone pleased her— [1]

a picture which suggests not so much Eve in Paradise as the first Mrs. Copperfield perched on her Doady's knee while he wrestles with the household accounts. But Dante was sexually centralised, as Milton and Dickens were not. His state was the more gracious. He was ready to give much, and whatever was granted him in return he accepted as a gift and not as a right, so that he never knew satiety or disillusionment. And Holy Luck was with him.

Whether Holy Luck was with him in his political troubles is perhaps more open to doubt. In this context neither he nor Milton can be said to have earned the blessing of the meek. The shock of his ruin and exile is comparable to the shock of Milton's marriage-disaster, in that the blow was unexpected and by him unsought. He felt that his misfortunes were undeserved, and he never ceased to resent them; the wound was permanent. The promising course of Milton's career was likewise diverted by the outbreak of political upheavals, but in his case by his own act. He was in the middle of a delightful tour in Italy and was just preparing to go on to Greece when he heard that a storm

[1] *P.L.* viii. 56–57.

was blowing up at home, and he at once cut short his journey and returned to England, because, as he said: "I thought it disgraceful, while my fellow-citizens fought for liberty at home, to be travelling for pleasure abroad." That was nice of him; in the same spirit, many of his fellow-countrymen hastened homeward in 1939, to endure bombs, rationing and other discomforts along with the rest of us. He threw up all his prospects, and chose deliberately the arduous service of his country. The choice must have been a hard one. Yet it was to his own country that he came; he never had to learn:

> How salt the taste of alien bread, how hard
> The going up and down another's stairs.[1]

Dante was flung out of Florence against his will, and the ignominy of that rejection remained with him. He could never forget it, never keep off the subject; it is burned into stanza after stanza of the *Comedy*. One may wonder whether most to admire Milton for his voluntary, or to pity Dante for his involuntary sufferings; whether in trying circumstances a man is better sustained by knowing the heroism of his own choice or by stiffening his pride against the spurns that patient merit of the unworthy takes. There is at any rate little doubt which situation is the more humiliating:

Through well-nigh every region in which this tongue is spoken have I traipsed, a wanderer, all but a beggar, displaying against my will the wound of fortune, which is often unjustly cast in the teeth of him that is wounded. Truly I have been a ship without sail and without rudder, drifted upon divers harbours and straits and beaches by the dry wind that blows from miserable poverty. And I have been made to look cheap in the eyes of many who, because of some certain reputation, had perhaps expected something very different; and not only has my person been cheapened, but also all my work. . . .[2]

The lot of the shabby-genteel is hard to bear. They are apt to be touchy and hypersensitive under criticism; and we must not blame Dante too much if he took refuge in some very tricky shuffling about the Lady of the Window. Later on, when he had, by God knows what shifts, got himself to Paris, he likewise, hearing the sound of the trumpet, threw up his studies and hastened back to Italy to welcome in the Emperor. For that, he too may be given credit.

Whether it was a shock to John Milton, whose fastidious delicacy

---

[1] *Para.* xvii. 58–59. [2] *Convivio,* I. iii. 4–5.

had formerly earned him the title of "the Lady of Christ's", to find himself in the open arena, standing up to be shot at with all the scurrility which his uninhibited age deemed indispensable to political and religious controversy, we do not know. If so, he soon recovered himself, and plunged with zest into the slanging-match, returning dirt for dirt, and brickbat for brickbat, with interest. Not, however, without indignation and outrage. The blows stung, even—or especially—when (as in the charge of frequenting brothels) they were aimed at random. Dante's abuse of the Florentines is mild and dignified compared with Milton's abuse of More. Detailed comparison would not be very profitable. Milton's output is by far the more voluminous; but he held a Government appointment, whereas Dante was self-appointed to his task. Nor need we pause to weigh the merits and importance of the *De Monarchia* against for example the *Areopagitica*; or to ask which conditions were the more unfavourable to work and contemplation—wandering up and down the country, living on casual patronage and odd jobs, and borrowing books when and where one could, or struggling with the daily demands of a secretaryship, and coping at home with the distractions of children, schoolboys, and a horde of one's wife's impecunious cavalier relations, who, when the royal cause came to grief, descended upon Milton like a swarm of locusts. These things would fill a book. It is another curious little bit of parallelism that both men, during their "prose period", suffered from eye-strain. Milton, knowing what he did, wrote himself into total blindness in producing the *Defensio pro Populo Anglicano*; Dante, with more common-sense, or less patriotism—or simply better luck—cured himself with rest and cold water.

Critics have not failed to notice in both men about this period a fervour of exaltation issuing in a heady prophetical rhetoric, and amounting almost to megalomania. Here is Dante, calling upon Italy to welcome "the glory of thy people, the most clement Henry, Divus, and Augustus, and Caesar":

Nor do I exhort you only to arise, but to stand dumb before his presence. Ye who drink his streams and sail upon his seas; who tread upon the sands of the shores and the summits of the mountains which are his; who possess whatsoever public rights you enjoy, and all things you hold in private, by the bond of his law and not otherwise; deceive not yourselves in ignorance, nor dream in your hearts, saying: "We have no lord"; for all that heaven circles is his orchard and his lake. For "the sea is God's and He made it, and His hands established the dry land"; and that being so it is clear, from miraculous events, that God chose the Roman prince before, and the church declares that by the word of the Word he confirmed him after.[1]

Henry is God's vicegerent on earth, and Dante is his prophet. And here is Milton, preparing to hymn the reign of the saints:

Then, amidst the hymns and hallelujahs of saints, some one may perhaps be heard offering at high strains in new and lofty measures to sing and celebrate thy divine mercies and marvellous judgements in this land throughout all ages; whereby this great and warlike nation, instructed and inured to the fervent and continual practice of truth and righteousness, and casting far from her the rags of her old vices, may press on hard to that high and happy emulation to be found the soberest, wisest, and most Christian people at that day, when Thou, the eternal and shortly expected King, shalt open the clouds to judge the several kingdoms of the world, and distributing national honours, and rewards to religious and just commonwealths, shalt put an end to all earthly tyrannies, proclaiming Thy universal and mild monarchy through heaven and earth. . . . [2]

England is the chosen people, and Milton her David and Isaiah. And in either case one is moved to exclaim that this is the very madness of political enthusiasm. Both writers were "fey" and inviting the doom of *hubris*.

For Dante the doom fell with a merciful swiftness. Henry's expedition failed, and he was left lamenting—but not as one without hope; for his remedy for the world's ills had not been tried and found wanting; it had never been tried. But Milton had the devastating experience of seeing his remedy fail. The reign of the saints turned out to be but another tyranny; new presbyter was but old priest writ large; his chosen people turned renegade; the Restoration rolled in over the New Jerusalem and swept it away as though it had never been. He himself was treated with extraordinary clemency. Although he had advocated regicide and written the *Eikonoclastes*, no measures were taken against him; he was left unmolested to remake his work and his life. Dante, who had urged the destruction of Florence, though he himself refused to take active part in it, was also offered clemency, but upon terms that he indignantly rejected; the edicts were renewed against his life and the life of his sons, and he remained in exile. Nevertheless, I think that Holy Luck was with him. At the time of the extinction of hope Dante was forty-seven, and Milton fifty-two; and

[1] Epistle to the Kings and Princes of Italy (*Ecce nunc tempus acceptabile*).
[2] *Reformation in England*.

both the great poems whose business it now became to examine into the causes of this world's present discontents and propose the remedy were already under way.[1]

Milton, according to himself, set out "to justify the ways of God to man". Dante apparently did not think that God's ways needed justification; he set out, also according to himself, to show man the way to God. The difference is characteristic. And I hope and think I shall not be gravely wronging Milton if I point out that in starting, as both poets needs must, by asking what the root of the trouble is, Milton replies: "Man's first disobedience"; but Dante, "*I* went astray".

They both, of course, mean the same thing: the trouble is man's sin. But Dante is ready to identify himself with erring humanity, to accept the blame and guilt, to say (like Milton's Messiah, though after a different manner), "on me let Thine anger fall, Account me man". With all his arrogance, with all his resentments, he was content to show himself weeping and trembling at the judgement seat, humiliated before angels and men. It is well to remember that from the beginning of the *Vita Nuova* to the end of the *Paradiso* humility is Dante's theme-song, and he sings it all the more passionately and sincerely because he found it a very difficult virtue to acquire.

It is obviously impossible, at the end of a paper, or in any one paper, or in a series of papers, to make an exhaustive comparison between the *Comedy* and *Paradise Lost*. I have looked in vain for any trace of the direct influence of the one on the other.[2] There may be a line or two here and there—for instance, Milton's

> underneath, a bright sea flowed
> Of Jasper or of liquid Pearle, whereon
> Who after came from Earth, sayling arriv'd,
> Wafted by angels

is faintly reminiscent of the ship of souls in the second canto of *Purgatory*. But even here, Milton expunges the resemblance by adding:

> or flew o're the lake
> Rapt in a chariot drawn by fiery steeds;

just as, when saying that after the Fall the Earthly Paradise became an island, as it is in Dante, he hastens to make it a very different sort of place—no "holy hill" or "sacred forest", but

[1] See Note A at end of this paper.

[2] A list of possible parallels is given in Paget Toynbee's *Dante in English Literature* (Methuen, 1909), Vol. I, pp. 127–128.

> an Iland salt and bare,
> The haunt of Seales and Orcs, and Sea-mews clang;
> To teach thee that God attributes to place
> No sanctity, if none be thither brought
> By men who there frequent or therein dwell.[1]

Indeed, I get the impression—it is no more than an impression—that whenever Milton feels Dante's influence he deliberately goes out of his way to repudiate it. Witness his contemptuous equating of Limbo with Ariosto's Paradise of Fools, his care not to place Hell at the centre of the earth, his Empyrean "undetermined round or square" (bringing down, as it were, with right and left barrels both Dante's mystic rose and his true Empyrean "which hath no *where* but in the mind of God"), not to mention subtler things, such as his curious imitation and distortion of Dante's use of the Proserpine image as applied to Eve.[2] Indeed, it was impossible that Milton should not repudiate Dante, who stood for so many things alien or detested: Catholicism, Scholasticism, Monarchism, Woman-worship. Dante might be invoked against Popes, but not against Rome; he was sound (except as regards Woman) on the natural hierarchy, but unfortunately he believed in a social and ecclesiastical hierarchy also; he too had striven passionately for liberty, but what Dante called liberty Milton called tyranny; and great poet as Dante was, his style was no pattern for Milton's. The Reformation and the Renaissance lay between them.

Yet it is very easy to exaggerate the Protestant elements in Milton. As he was not by temperament a Puritan, so neither was he in doctrine a Calvinist. Calvinism has four certain marks: hatred of the flesh, contempt of the natural law, distrust of human reason, and the doctrine of total depravity. Milton has none of them. The last, which is the origin of the others, he expressly refutes; when he makes Samson say, "Down, reason, down", he quickly adds, "at least, vain reasonings down"; in various places he rests his arguments on the natural law, and sometimes seems inclined even to place it above the law of Christ; and his insistence, in *Paradise Lost*, upon the purity and holiness of the flesh is so passionate and reiterated that it sometimes makes us uneasy, like his insistence upon chastity in *Comus*, and for a similar reason. In all these four respects he stands, in fact, on the Catholic side, and in isolation from many of his fellow-Protestants. One might almost say that—with one very important exception—he is by temperament what his grandfather actually was: a lapsed Catholic, with all the

---

[1] *P.L.* xi. 830–834.   [2] See Note B at end of this paper.

violence of reaction and the suppressed nostalgia characteristic of the lapsed. His real heresies, I think, are quite different. He was in his heart of hearts, a Pelagian, like so many Englishmen and like most Renaissance Humanists: he felt that men's nature was sufficient in itself to achieve perfection in this world and salvation in the next. This unacknowledged instinct was always obscurely at war with the Protestant doctrine of Grace, and it was at the root of his deadly disappointment over the failure of Cromwell's régime. It is this which accounts for the depression of spirits which overtook him in his later life, and which spreads that coldness and blight which every critic and reader has noticed over the concluding books of *Paradise Lost*. But the major heresy which hits his great poem at its aesthetic centre is one which he knew about and expressly defended in the *De Doctrinâ Christianâ*: he was an Arian. He did not believe in the full divinity of Christ.

Now it is quite true that he did not openly introduce this heresy into *Paradise Lost*—he skated very carefully round it. But it is quite useless to affirm, as so many writers have done, that it made no difference to his poetry, as poetry. It made all the difference. Just where there should have been a warm focus of love and hope, there is a frozen void, so that the whole structural balance of the poem is upset. Adam is the dramatic centre of the action, but he cannot, in the nature of the story itself, be its hero—Pelagianism or no Pelagianism. Adam is the bone over which the Hounds of Hell and the Hound of Heaven are fighting; dramatic peripeteia demands that our sympathies, after being at first seduced by the specious heroism of Satan, should be swung over to the true heroism of the Son of God. That *is* Milton's intention, as outlined in the first five lines of the poem:

> Of Mans first Disobedience, and the Fruit
> Of that Forbidden Tree, whose mortal tast
> Brought Death into the world, and all our woe,
> With loss of Eden, *till one greater Man*
> *Restore us, and regain the blissful seat*—

The story should have ended in triumph; Milton makes all the necessary formal dispositions to that end and keeps on assuring us that the triumph has been achieved. But aesthetically, poetically, emotionally, it has not. Why? Because (we are frequently assured) the task was impossible. Everybody can feel sympathy with rebellion; nobody can feel sympathy—not *sympathy*—with Omnipotence. Consequently, though Satan's stature is duly reduced as the poem goes on, the stature of Messiah is not raised correspondingly. How could it be? they say.

But of course it could be. Messiah has been and is the world's great fairy-tale hero—the God who puts off His Godhead and subjects Himself to humiliation, suffering and death for His people's sake. But two things are necessary: that the suffering, death, and humiliation should be real, and that the Godhead should be really God. Milton knows this —that is why he has tried to keep his Arian opinions out of the way of the story. But they were too much for him all the same—they kept him from feeling in his heart the height and depth of the great paradox; and what a poet does not feel, he cannot communicate. Let us look at Messiah's famous speech, in which the Atonement doctrine is stated, perfectly accurately, in its simplest and crudest form, and with a genuine power and tenderness:

> Father, thy word is past, man shall find grace;
> And shall not grace find means, that finds her way,
> The speediest of thy winged messengers,
> To visit all thy creatures, and to all
> Comes unprevented, unimplor'd, unsought,
> Happie for man so coming; he her aide
> Can never seek, once dead in sins and lost;
> Attonement for himself, or offering meet,
> Indebted and undon, hath non to bring:
> Behold mee then, mee for him, life for life
> I offer, on mee let thine anger fall;
> Account mee man; I for his sake will leave
> Thy bosom, and this glorie next to thee
> Freely put off, and for him lastly die
> Well pleas'd, on me let Death wreck all his rage;
> Under his gloomie power I shall not long
> Lie vanquisht; thou hast giv'n me to possess
> Life in myself for ever— [1]

and so on, to the end in which joy and triumph are nobly and beautifully expressed; after which:

> His words here ended, but his meek aspect
> Silent yet spake, and breath'd immortal love
> To mortal man, above which only shon
> Filial obedience; as a sacrifice

[1] *P.L.* iii. 227–244.

> Glad to be offer'd he attends the will
> Of his great Father. Admiration seis'd
> All Heav'n, what this might mean, and whither tend
> Wond'ring.[1]

What is wrong with this? One feels ashamed to suggest that there could be anything wrong. Yet something, surely, is lacking—the horror of the unspotted holiness at being, in St. Paul's terrible phrase, "made sin for us"; the agony of exultant spirit, undergoing the blood and dust of crucifixion; the enormous humiliation of immortal Godhead being thrust through the gates of Death and Hell. The phrase "*Account mee man*" is unfortunate: it suggests that the Manhood will be not a true incarnation but a legal fiction. The turn:

> on me let Death wreck all his rage;
> Under his gloomie power I shall not long
> Lie vanquish't—

is too quick. It is almost jaunty. It is *almost* as though there were a "because" understood—as though Messiah had said: "Let death do his worst; he can't hurt me." The Father's comment:

> So Heavenly love shall outdo Hellish hate,
> Giving to death, and dying to redeeme,
> So dearly to redeem what Hellish hate
> So easily destroy'd— [2]

is equally, as it were hasty; and although the word "humiliation" does occur, it is only in passing—it is mentioned only to be dismissed:

> because in thee
> Love hath abounded more than Glory abounds,
> Therefore thy Humiliation shall exalt
> With thee thy Manhood also to this throne.[3]

And the angels, in their subsequent hymn of praise seem also to take the matter—as one might say—lightly.[4]

---

[1] *P.L.* iii. 266–273.   [2] *Ibid.* 298–301.   [3] *P.L.* iii. 311–314.

[4] "The failure lies not in the depiction of Satan but in that of the heavenly values which should subdue him. Those values are only imperfectly realised. . . . Milton's God is what his Satan never is, a collection of abstract properties, or, in his greatest moments, a treatise on free-will. The Son moves us more deeply, particularly in the quiet, firm monosyllables in which he announces his sacrifice. But the spare precision of the language Milton gives him is lit only seldom by the ardour which should inform it."–B. Rajan: *Paradise Lost and the Seventeenth Century Reader* (Chatto & Windus, 1947), p. 106. See also the passage (too long to quote) in the same work, pp. 127–128.

Put beside this, not for the moment Dante, not even any of the great Trinitarian poets who have extolled the Cross, but something very modest, very simple—two verses from Dean Milman's unpretentious little Palm Sunday hymn:

> Ride on, ride on in majesty;
> The angel armies of the sky
> Look down with sad and wondering eyes
> To see the approaching sacrifice.

> Ride on, ride on in majesty;
> The last and fiercest strife is nigh;
> The Father on His sapphire throne
> Awaits His own anointed Son.

That is not great poetry—scarcely perhaps poetry at all—but it has what the other has not: the pathos of the "lowly pomp"; the sadness in the angelic wonder; the "fierceness" of the struggle; the sense of longing and expectancy; the "anointing" of the king, of the priest, of the dying.

Now let us take Dante, in his very different manner. He does not, of course, represent the thing dramatically or make God speak. His narrative was not of that kind—and perhaps he had too much prudence. Beatrice is the speaker; she is quite as theological as Milton in her statement of Atonement doctrine, and more subtle. She first explains the double nature of Christ, and how the sentence executed upon Him, though wholly unjust in so far as he was God, was wholly just in so far as He had taken upon Himself the guilty nature of man. Having thus asserted the great paradox at its most startlingly paradoxical, she points out that God might have dealt with Man in either of two ways: He might have arbitrarily abolished the results of the Fall, thus reducing man to the state of an automaton, whose actions have no real consequences; or He might have demanded the full penalty—which Man of himself could never pay because "he could not descend so deeply by humility"—mark the keyword—"as by obedience he had sought to raise himself" (that is, to become "as God"). But since neither way alone would have been satisfactory, God chose both.

> And since the doer's actions ever show
> More gracious as the style of them makes plain
> The goodness of the heart from which they flow,

That most high Goodness which is God was fain—
  Even God, whose impress heaven and earth display—
  By all His ways to lift you up again;

Nor, between final night and primal day,
  Was e'er proceeding so magnifical
  And high, nor shall not be, by either way;

For God's self-giving, which made possible
  That man should raise himself, showed more largesse
  Than if by naked power He'd cancelled all;

And every other means would have been less
  Than justice, if it had not pleased God's Son
  To be humiliate into fleshliness.[1]

That, in its spare doctrinal austerity, stands as far from our Palm
Sunday hymn on the one side as Milton stands on the other; but it
conveys an extraordinary kind of cerebral emotion, working upon
what Wordsworth called "the feeling intellect"; and the effect is
enhanced by the movement of the verse in the last three stanzas:

> nè, tra l'ultima notte e il primo die,
>   si alto e sì magnifico processo,
>   o per l'una o per l'altra fu o fie:
>
> che più largo fu Dio a dar se stesso,
>   a far l'uom sufficiente a rilevarsi,
>   che s'egli avesse sol da sè dimesso;
>
> e tutti gli altri modi erano scarsi
>   alla giustizia, se il Figliuol di Dio
>   non fosse umiliato ad incarnarsi.

There is a wonderful "dying fall" for you: *non fosse umiliato ad
incarnarsi!* Notice, too, how enormously the force of the great
doctrinal paradox is increased by simply calling Christ "God"
unqualified until the precise moment of His humiliation.

My own judgement is that Dante succeeds here in carrying aesthetic
conviction as Milton does not: I mean by that, that the form of
his verse does communicate his own conviction together with the
appropriate emotions—I am not talking about any other kind of
conviction. Milton expounds the orthodox doctrine quite correctly—
it is only from outside sources that we know he was not orthodox—
but just where there should be an emotional crisis there is only an

[1] *Para.* vii. 106–120.

emotional blank, which every critical reader feels as an aesthetic failure, whether or not he can account for it intellectually. The reason is that Milton's emotion was not there because the belief was not there. Milton falls between two stools: a Catholic belief in the true Divinity would have saved the balance of his poem; but so would a thorough-going Evangelical or Calvinistic fervour of gratitude to the Being who (whether very theologically perceived or not) had died to save His elect from the condemnation due to total depravity. But Milton was torn in three directions—by his Catholic temperament, by the political temper of his time, which was Protestant, and by his stubborn native independence of mind, which would not allow him to surrender himself wholly to either position.

I have taken Milton at his weakest. This, you will say, is not just. Let us take him instead at his most magical—a very short extract from his description of the Earthly Paradise, where, after mentioning the fountain which feeds the paradisal river, he goes on to tell:

> How from that Saphire Fount the crisped brooks,
> Rowling on Orient Pearl and sands of Gold,
> With mazie error under pendant shades
> Ran Nectar, visiting each plant, and fed
> Flours worthy of Paradise, which not nice Art
> In Beds and curious Knots, but Nature boon
> Powrd forth profuse on Hill and Dale and Plaine,
> Both where the morning Sun first warmly smote
> The open field, and where the unpierc't shade
> Imbrownd the noontide Bowrs: Thus was this place,
> A happy rural seat of various view:
> Groves whose rich Trees wept odorous Gumms and Balme,
> Others whose fruit burnisht with Golden Rinde
> Hung amiable, *Hesperian* fables true,
> If true, here only, and of delicious taste:
> Betwixt them Lawns, or level Downs, and Flocks
> Grasing the tender herb, were interpos'd,
> Or palmy hilloc, or the flourie lap
> Of som irriguous Valley spread her store,
> Flours of all hue, and without Thorn the Rose:
> Another side, umbrageous Grots and Caves
> Of coole recess, o're which the mantling Vine
> Layes forth her purple Grape, and gently creeps
> Luxuriant; mean while murmuring waters fall
> Down the slope hills, disperst, or in a Lake,

That to the fringed Bank with Myrtle crownd,
Her chrystall mirror holds, unite thir streams.
The Birds thir quire apply; aires, vernal aires,
Breathing the smell of field and grove, attune
The trembling leaves, while Universal *Pan*
Knit with the *Graces* and the *Hours* in dance
Led on th'Eternal Spring.[1]

That hardly needs comment. As C. S. Lewis says, "We always knew it would be like that"—and there it unbelievably *is*. The verse meanders like the river, leisurely coiling and uncoiling among the scents and colours and contours of that exotic, yet in some ways curiously English landscape. This, Milton has felt, imagined, seen with his eyes (though now grown blind), and for its music he has pulled out all the sweetest stops on his great Renaissance organ. By comparison, Dante's "lonely flute" sounds thin and reedy, hardly more than a "scrannel pipe". I think, by the way, that this may be a passage where Milton had Dante definitely in mind: the Italianate "inbrowned" for "darkened"; the close association of the quiring birds with the "trembling leaves" which the scented airs "attune", the trees weeping "odorous gums and balm" and recalling the "amomum and tears of incense" of the phoenix-passage in *Inf.* xxvii, the reference to "Hesperian fables true, if true here only", which reminds us of Matelda's words to Dante about the Golden Age, and the Proserpine-image which immediately follows the lines I have quoted, as it does in Dante—separately, these are poetic commonplaces, but their presence here all together suggests that at this point Milton remembered his great predecessor and perhaps deliberately set out to surpass him. Here, at any rate, is Dante:

> *Vago già di cercar dentro e dintorno*
> *la divina foresta spessa e viva,*
> *ch'agli occhi temperava il novo giorno,*
>
> *senza piu aspettar, lasciai la riva,*
> *prendendo la campagna lento lento*
> *su per lo suol che d'ogni parte oliva.*
>
> *Un aura dolce, sanza mutamento*
> *avere in sè, mi feria per la fronte*
> *non di più colpo che soave vento;*

[1] *P.L.* iv. 237–268.

per cui le fronde, tremolando, pronte
tutte quante piegavano alla parte
u' la prim'ombra gitta il santo monte;

non però dal loro esser dritto sparte
tanto, che li augelletti per le cime
lasciasse d'operare ogni lor arte;

ma con piena letizia l'ore prime
cantando, ricevìeno intra le foglie,
che tenevan bordone alle sue rime,

tal qual di ramo in ramo si raccoglie
per la pineta in su'l lito di Chiassi,
quand' Eolo Scirocco fuor discioglie.

Già m'avean trasportato i lenti passi
dentro alla selva antica tanto ch'io
non potea rivedere ond'io m'intrassi

ed ecco il più andar mi tolse un rio,
che 'nver sinistra con sue picciole onde
piegava l'erba che'n sua ripa uscio.

Tutte l'acque che son di qua più monde,
parrìeno avere in sè mistura alcuna,
verso di quella, che nulla nasconde,

avvegna che si mova bruna bruna
sotto l'ombra perpetua, che mai
raggiar non lascia sole ivi nè luna.[1]

---

[1] Eager to search in and throughout its ways
　　The sacred wood, whose thick and leafy tent,
　　Spread in my sight, tempered the new sun's rays,

I made no pause, but left the cliff and went
　　With lingering steps across the level leas
　　Where all the soil breathed out a fragrant scent.

A delicate air, that no inconstancies
　　Knows in its motion, on my forehead played,
　　With force no greater than a gentle breeze,

And quivering at its touch the branches swayed,
　　All toward that quarter where the holy hill
　　With the first daylight stretches out its shade;

The rivulet—it is but three paces wide—"with its ripples small bending the grasses at the edge of it", compared with Milton's "river large", and the "crispèd brooks rowling on orient pearl and sands of gold" is like a Fra Angelico hung beside a Titian. If Dante has the advantage anywhere it is in his birds—but Dante was always a great man for birds—and, perhaps, in his imaginative apprehension of a place of *innocence*; for that is what the Earthly Paradise primarily is. And his magic—for he has a magic of his own—is of a different kind. Milton's Paradise is enchanted; Dante's is haunted.

One would like to make a thousand more comparisons; the grandeur of Milton's Hell with the squalor of Dante's; or the human drama between the fallen Adam and Eve, with the human drama of Dante's meeting with Beatrice; where both poets are at the top of their form. It is only when we lay the last books of *Paradise Lost* side by side with the *Paradiso* that we begin really to see what life had done to Milton. Where there should have been the triumph of redemption, there is only a muted stoicism, a resigned acquiescence, a stubborn courage to endure all things, a firm holding to the hope of salvation

> Yet ne'er swayed from the upright so, but still
> The little birds the topmost twigs among
> Spared not to practise all their tiny skill;
>
> Rather they welcomed with rejoicing song
> The dawn-wind to the leaves, which constantly
> To their sweet chant the burden bore along.
>
> So, in Chiassi's pinewood by the sea,
> From bough to bough the gathering murmurs swell
> When Aeolus has set Scirocco free.
>
> Now, when my footsteps, slowly as they fell,
> So far within the ancient wood were set
> That where I'd first come in I could not tell,
>
> Lo! they were halted by a rivulet
> Which ran from right to left, its ripples small
> Bending the grasses on the edge of it;
>
> And whatso waters over here we call
> Clearest, were cloudy by comparison
> With this, which hides not anything at all,
>
> Though darkly, darkly it goes flowing on
> Beneath the everlasting shade, which never
> Lets any ray strike there of sun or moon.
>   *Purg.* xxviii. 1–33.

but without ecstasy, a turning-in of the soul upon itself to find "a Paradise within thee, happier farr". He recognises at last that the world is very evil, and he has almost ceased to be angry about it.[1] The verse itself, except for the magnificent last twenty lines or so, seems cramped, cold and dispirited. This has been said so often that it seems unkind to say it again. But with Dante, the strong flight into felicity is maintained to the very end, with increasing vigour and certainty. As in his own great simile of the lark ascending, the higher he goes, the sweeter and louder he sings; his adoration is drunken with delight. Nor is the edge of his wrath ever blunted—it bites against Boniface as sharply in the Eighth Heaven as it did in the Third Bolgia; and where there is anger against men there is always hope for humanity. Dr. Tillyard speaks of Milton's "mature, one may say middle-aged, philosophy of life". Dante was never middle-aged—not even at forty-six when he was writing the *Convivio*; at fifty-six he is as young as he was at eighteen, only more mature. He is completely untamed: if you hate him, you will hate him even more at the end than at the beginning, and for the same things; if you love him, you will love him more. For he does not fundamentally change, he only expands; he turns not inward but outward; his exultation is not in the past nor in the world to come, but here and now, and he feels it as he writes, and that very exultation is to him the assurance of beatitude:

> *credo ch'io vidi, perchè più di largo,*
> *dicendo questo, mi sento ch'io godo.*[2]

After finishing *Paradise Lost*, Milton lived to write *Paradise Regained* and *Samson Agonistes*. He died of the gout, at sixty-five, in his home near Bunhill Fields, where in his last years "he used to sit in a grey coarse cloth coat . . . in warm, sunny weather, to enjoy the fresh air". Dante, as soon as he had completed the *Commedia*, went back into his old political harness, being sent by Guido Novello on a fruit-less embassy to Venice. On his way back along the swampy and

---

[1] " He [Michael, in Bk. xii] talks dejectedly of spiritual armour, wearily opposes ceremonies to conscience, and refers to wolves and hirelings in the church in words which have no hint of the white-hot anger of *Lycidas*."—B. Rajan: *Paradise Lost and the Seventeenth Century Reader* (Chatto & Windus, 1947), p. 84.

[2] Yea, of this complex I believe mine eyes
Beheld the universal form—I feel,
Even as I speak, such springs of rapture rise.
Para. xxxiii. 92–94.

pestilential coast road, he was seized by malignant malaria, and reached Ravenna only in time to die there. No mosquito ever brought down a more towering quarry. He was fifty-six years old. Public affairs, which robbed Milton of his eyesight, robbed Dante of his life; we are tempted to feel that never was a great life so uselessly sacrificed. But he had finished his work; he was not suffered to set hand to anything less than his greatest, and it may be that in this, too, Holy Luck was with him.

(Summer School of Italian Studies
1952)

NOTE A

The Poet as Politician. The question whether it is ever right or wise for a poet to abandon the exercise of his "proper virtue" in order to make direct political statements, wherein his competence is no greater than that of any other amateur critic, is examined by Stephen Spender, speaking out of his own experience, in *Life and the Poet* (Secker & Warburg, 1942). His conclusion is that the poet will achieve more efficiency with less falsehood by working in his own medium; thus, in this sphere also, the "autonomy of techniques" should be respected. Consequently, the return from apologetics to poetry ought not to be looked upon either as "escapism", or as being in itself a confession that the poet has lost all faith in political action. I mention this because there is a tendency with some writers to assume that Dante ended by transferring the possibility of the "good life" from this world to the next. To conclude so is to fall into a double confusion, (*a*) of the literal and allegorical levels of interpretation; (*b*) of political with poetic technique.

NOTE B

The Proserpine Image in Dante and Milton. It is often felt, by those accustomed to the more luxuriant treatment of the poetic image in the Renaissance writers, that Dante's handling of it is stark almost to desiccation. "Austere Dante" is not altogether true in the sense in which it is commonly used; but it is true of his method with the image. There is a development here which needs fuller investigation. For Dante the image exists in its own right, but never for its own sake.

In later hands, as the image comes to be less and less an image *per essentiam* and more and more so *per accidens*—moving from the status of image to that of illustration—it comes to be cultivated more and more for its own sake. In Dante, the image, being an image in virtue of what it essentially *is*, needs as it were only to be mentioned in order to perform its function as imagery; and since, with him, the function is not for the sake of the image, but the image for the sake of its function, he does not elaborate or sophisticate it.

Compare the Proserpine passages in *Purgatorio* and *Paradise Lost*. Here is Dante:

> *Tu mi fai rimembrar dove e qual era*
> *Proserpina nel tempo che perdette*
> *la madre lei, ed ella primavera.*[1]

That is beautiful in itself, but it is beauty unadorned and could scarcely be briefer or more concise. It recalls the facts of the Proserpine story, but makes no attempt to extract from them any beauty or any emotion which is not inherent in the facts themselves, and in the mere melody of the words. The lines are, of course, the more pithy and pregnant in that the Italian word *primavera* means *both* "spring" and "spring flowers" (cf. *Paradiso*, xxx. 63), so that the picture of the flowers falling from Proserpine's lap is integrated with the loss of the "eternal spring" itself. But the image is only stated and not exploited.

And here is Milton:

> Not that fair field
> Of Enna, where Proserpin gathering flowers,
> Herself a fairer flower, by gloomy Dis
> Was gathered, which cost Ceres all that pain
> To seek her through the world; nor that sweet grove
> Of Daphne, etc.[2]

That, in its richer style of beauty, is incomparable. It is a matter of personal responsiveness whether one finds it more or less moving than the Dante lines, or both equally so. All the things which are, in Dante, left implicit in the bare facts are here made explicit: "fair field of Enna",

---

[1] O thou dost put me to remembering
  Of who and what were lost, that day her mother
  Lost Proserpine, and she the flowers of spring.
          Purg. xxviii. 49–51.

[2] *P.L.* iv. 265–272.

"herself a fairer flower", "gloomy Dis", "all that pain to seek her through the world".

When, however, it comes to *function*, it seems that Dante's lines perform the more important and the more intellectually complex function—or else, if Milton had the same function in mind, then the Dante passage is ín every word more closely related to that function; and its placing in the poem is also eminently functional.

Shelley, coming after both Dante and Milton, translates Dante's lines and, in the pursuit of beauty, contrives to miss the function almost altogether:

> like Proserpine, in Enna's glen,[1]
> Thou seemest to my fancy, singing here
> And gathering flowers, as that fair maiden, when
> She lost the spring, and Ceres her, more dear.

That, in itself, is pretty enough, except for the feeble "more dear" tagged on for the rhyme; but he hasn't seen what it is all *about*. It's not "about" singing and gathering flowers (Dante has done all that part of it in the thing imaged—Matelda—and except for *primavera* does not waste words describing it all over again in the image). It is *about* "who" and "where" and "motherhood" and "loss"; the key-words are *dove, qual, madre, perdette*—and Shelley has left out three of them. "*Riguarda qual son io*";[2] Proserpine is the daughter of the Great Mother, and the "where" is the land of eternal spring, the Earthly Paradise in which Dante and Matelda are at the moment standing. The first Mother (Ceres/Eve) loses her daughter (Proserpine/Humanity) —or perhaps, in a tacit conflation as bold as Milton's, "the fairest of her daughters, Eve"—and the place lost is the Land of Spring/Earthly Paradise. The image is picked up again and resolved in xxx. 52: "*nè quantunque perdeo l'antica matre*".[3]

At this point, Shelley's "more dear" is seen to be not merely feeble, but actually naughty, because it distracts the mind from the real point of the allegory, the loss of Paradise, and intrudes an unmeaning distinction between the two losses which Dante is at pains to integrate.

---

[1] Clearly influenced by Milton—"Enna", "gathering flowers", "Ceres" are not in Dante.

[2] Look at me, see what I am.
Para. xxiii. 46.

[3] Nor yet for all that our First Mother lost.
Purg. xxx. 52.

(Incidentally, how *could* Shelley weaken "*tu mi fai rimembrar*" into "thou seemest to my fancy"? It is memory, not fancy, that is awakened: "you make me mindful of the thing I had always known, but had forgotten—you are bringing back the old memories". And the moment is coming when *all* the past, *all* the buried memories are going to be conjured up from the very bottom of Dante's mind—the "*antica fiamma*": the old love, and the old vision and the old loss. All Dante's emotion, like all his imagery, is sinewy with intellect. Everything is knitted into the poem—structure, literal and allegorical, simultaneously. Perhaps it is not fair to criticise Shelley—the translation is only an unfinished fragment—but he does seem to have put up his scaffolding wrong.)

In Milton, the Proserpine image (iv. 268) appears, from the context, to be used only to illustrate the beauty of the Garden of the "eternal spring". "Appears"—because Milton may well have had the further *significacio* in mind (indeed, the preceding phrase about the "eternal spring" suggests that he had, and perhaps had the Dante passage consciously in his mind also). But, if so, he has diluted it by making the image only the first of a long series of highly-elaborated groves and isles, not particularly associated with loss; and also by placing it at an enormous distance from the loss of Paradise itself.

On the other hand, he recalls the Ceres/Proserpine image when Eve is going out to encounter Satan (ix. 395), which is where Dante would have put it; but strangely enough he here *expressly dissociates Ceres from Proserpine*, and so from the substantial part of the image—the triumph of Dis and the eating of the Underworld Fruit.

> Ceres in her prime
> Yet virgin of Proserpina from Jove.

This looks as though he had not so much missed as deliberately rejected the *significacio*. This is a little puzzling. If he had picked up and emphasised the *significacio* here, then the placing of the earlier *Proserpine* passage would have been a wonderful piece of big-scale architectonics. Here again the Ceres/Proserpine image comes as one item (this time the last) of a series of similes—none connected with loss—into which Ceres seems to be rather awkwardly dragged. It is as though Milton felt that the Ceres-image "belonged" to the imagery of the Fall, but had for some reason determined to ignore it and substitute a new one. The new association seems to be that of fertility; and one sees, of course, the relevance of Mother Ceres before the birth of Proserpina to Mother Eve before the birth of mankind. But the peculiar force of this is rather weakened by the previous mention of Artemis, who is in no way associated with motherhood, though she is in some respects a goddess of flocks and herds and pastoral fertility, and of Pomona and Pales, who preside respectively over vegetable and animal fertility—to say nothing of the Oreads and Dryads. Nor was Eve a virgin at the time (as Milton has been careful to insist); though, in view of the emphasis he places on the sexual results of the Fall, one sees in a way what he is getting at by this juxtaposition of the images of virginity and fertility.

In any case, the contrast of method in the two poems as regards the handling and placing of the Ceres/Proserpine image is interesting.

THE POETRY OF THE IMAGE IN DANTE
AND CHARLES WILLIAMS

THE title of this paper demands perhaps a little explanation. In one sense every poet, even the prosiest and most analytical, is a "poet of the image"—indeed, every writer of whatever kind, and every living man who is able to speak may be called so, because his communication is by means of living language, that is to say, it is a communication of imagery.

This has been said a thousand times; but it is perhaps desirable to say it again and to keep on saying it, because in an age like the present, which remains enamoured of the science of quantitative measurement, there is a tendency, not so much to forget this fact about language, as to resent it and try to abolish it. To demand, as certain schools of modern philosophy do demand, that the same word should bear the same meaning in every context, or (on the other hand) that a set of words should be exactly definable in terms of other words, is to demand, literally, miracles—that is to say a continual reversal of the order of nature.

Every word is a unique event: there is nothing exactly like it in the universe. Every word is an encounter in history: a meeting-place of images, each of which comes—like those Kings of Orient, who are shown assembling at the birthplace of the Word—bearing gifts, and attended by a long and glittering train of associates. Every word sits, like the city of Venice in her prime, at the meeting-place of east and west, land and sea, past and present, taking in and sending forth rich ladings, and functioning in the market-place of exchange. We can never permanently empty a word of all meanings save one: we can at most choose to restrict ourselves temporarily to a particular meaning in the context of a particular argument. We can never define one word or sentence in terms of another: we can at most find analogies between one unique event and another. For as a word is a unique event, so a sentence is a unique series of such events, and a work of art is a unique universe whose history bears no relation, except by analogy, to that of another. That is why it is impossible, in commenting or "explaining" any work of art, to substitute the explanation for the work. We may remember the poet, Peter Stanhope, in Charles Williams's novel, *Descent into Hell*:

There was a story, invented by himself, that *The Times* had once sent a representative to ask for explanations about a new play, and that Stanhope, in his efforts to explain it, had found after four hours that he had only succeeded in reading it completely through aloud. "Which", he maintained, "*was* the only way of explaining it." [1]

That is perfectly true, as every writer knows. Analysis of the complex image which every poem is can do little of itself to explain or interpret it; and unless the analysis is done with great delicacy and care it will only disintegrate the image. The best that the interpreter can do is to contemplate the image with an open and a humble mind in the hope that it may communicate to him something of the reality which it images. In the course of this contemplation, other images may arise in his mind which appear to him to illustrate in a different, though analogous way, the relation between the original image and its reality, and by means of these he may cautiously try to convey to others the meaning which the poet's image has for him. His meaning will never be *exactly* the same as the poet's meaning; it will be as a rule less balanced, laying emphasis on one aspect of the image to the neglect of the others. Nevertheless, since a great and pregnant image will bear all the interpretations that can reasonably and congruously be put upon it, every fresh interpretative image will bring an added significance to the original; so that a great poem like Dante's *Divine Comedy* comes to us now enriched not only with all those events and associations of the past out of which the poet fashioned his image, but also with the accreted events and associations of the six hundred years of his future and our past which lie between us and him. To him all the poets who have ever drawn sustenance from him return, bearing their sheaves with them, because he is in a manner the creator of their work as well as of his own. His glory goes out, and the reflected splendour returns to him, so that he himself is seen as an analogue and image of the Absolute Creator, concerning whom he said:

> The glory of Him who moves all things soe'er
> Impenetrates the universe, and bright
> The splendour burns, more here and lesser there.[2]

When I say "he", I mean his work, as when we say "you will find this

---

[1] *Op. cit.*, chap. i.   [2] *Para.* i. 1–3.

in Dante", or "in Shakespeare", meaning by that "in the works of those poets". For the poet and his work are not the same; they are separate images, separate unique events, and they cannot be substituted one for the other. You can never fully understand the poet by analysing his work, neither can you fully understand the work by analysing the poet; it is the great corrupting heresy of contemporary literary criticism to believe that you can. The image made by the poet includes an image of himself, though he himself transcends that image. It also includes an image of exterior reality, though not of the whole of reality. It is something more complex than either: an image of the relation between the poet and the exterior reality (that is, between the self and its true other); and it must not be identified with either in separation.

I have said all this by way of preamble, before coming to an explanation of my title. The phrase "Poetry of the Image" is here intended to designate the work of those poets who belong to a particular philosophical and mystical tradition: the philosophy which affirms that all images of reality are valid (so far as they go) for the apprehension of reality; the theological doctrine which affirms that the sole ultimate Reality which is God can be truly (though only partially) apprehended by means of the Creation in which it is imaged. I emphasise "as far as they go" and "partially" in order to warn us all off the error of trying to substitute the image for the reality—an error which in philosophy produces various unsatisfactory and mutually contradictory schools of thought such as materialism, logical positivism and solipsism, and when applied to the knowledge of God tends to issue in what theology calls pantheism and religion calls idolatry.

The tradition of Affirmation runs back a very long way, both in the philosophical and in the poetical line. Side by side with it runs also the other great way—the way of Negation, or Rejection of the Images. This way is not my present concern, so I will say only two things about it. The first is that while (rather naturally) it has comparatively few poets, it is particularly strong on the mystical side—so much so that when mystics or mysticism are mentioned, most people take it for granted that the Negative Way is meant. The second is that in the mystical approach to reality the followers of the two ways are not nearly so sharply and antagonistically divided as the philosophers. Nearly all of them tend, at some point in this journey, to use the language belonging to the other way—sometimes using both simultaneously with a strong effect of paradox, as in that phrase which Charles Williams thought he quoted, but perhaps invented: "This also is Thou; neither is this Thou." Others imply rather that the two Ways are successive stages on the same Way. The great Masters of the Negations, who have mapped their Way on the whole more exactly than the Masters of the Affirmations, usually say that one must begin by meditation on, and the contemplation of, the images, before rising to that stage in which all the images are naughted and lost in the darkness of negation. Thus, for example, the pseudo-Dionysius, who, though he too uses the language of paradox: "God must be both nameless and yet possess the names of all things", yet concludes that in the highest and closest state of union with Absolute Reality all the images are transcended and lost. The Masters of the Affirmations, on the other hand, tend to say with Charles Williams: "After the affirmations we may have to discover the rejections, but we must still believe that after the rejections the greater affirmations are to return."[1] Dante himself, the greatest of all the poets of the Affirmative Way, and perhaps its only systematic doctor, keeps a firm hold of the images throughout the ascent and even into the Beatific Vision itself—with three moments of exception, whose significance has never, I think, been properly explored. When he passes from the last Heaven of the Active Life, the Heaven of Jupiter, to the first Heaven of the Contemplative Life, that of Saturn—the smile of Beatrice is extinguished. Now, he says in the *Convivio* [2] that "the *eyes* of wisdom are her demonstrations, whereby the truth is seen most certainly, and her *smile* is her persuasions, whereby the inner light of wisdom is revealed behind a certain veil". At this point, therefore, he may mean that persuasion—the argument of the discursive intellect, is quenched. At the same time, the great songs of the Blessed fall silent. In the next Heaven, that of the Fixed Stars, he is so blinded with excess of light that he can see nothing at all, not even Beatrice; and it is, significantly perhaps, out of this total absence of every kind of image that he is called upon to speak to the love that is in him. In the third Heaven of Contemplation—the Primum Mobile—he first sees God as a point upon which "Heaven and all nature hang"; then this image vanishes and he is left in an empty Heaven, alone with Beatrice—the most permanent and intimately-experienced of all his "God-bearing images". In the Tenth, or true Heaven—the Empyrean—all the images return, complete in bodily form and substance. Quite what is meant by this interesting succession of symbols I do not know; but I think it is clear that he means to describe how, in one stage of his progress the mystic of the Affirmative

---

[1] *The Figure of Beatrice*, p. 10.   [2] *Com.* III. xv.

Way has to pass through a period of the negation or rejection of images, and how, "after the rejections, the greater affirmations are to return".

The sanction of the Affirmative Way lies in three great Christian doctrines: the first, which is inherited from Jewry, is the doctrine of a true creation. The visible universe is not an illusion, nor a mere aspect of Divinity, nor identical with God (as in Pantheism), still less a "fall into matter" and an evil delusion (as in the various Gnostic or Manichee cults). It is *made* by God, as an artist makes a work of art, and given a genuine, though contingent, real existence of its own, so that it can stand over against Him and know Him as its real Other. Every creature in it possesses a true self which, however much perfected or (in Dante's words) "in-godded", is never swallowed up or lost in God. Therefore, all God's creatures are images of Him in the same way, and to the same limited extent, as a work of art is an image of its maker—his, yet in a manner distinct from him.

The second doctrine is that of the Incarnation, whereby God Himself became manifest in mortal flesh. In that flesh His glory dwelt, and was seen so dwelling by Peter and James and John at the Transfiguration, when their eyes were opened to behold it. It was always there—it was not really He that was changed, but their sight. From the Incarnation springs the whole doctrine of sacraments—the indwelling of the mortal by the immortal, of the material by the spiritual, the phenomenal by the real. After an analogous manner, we all bear about with us not only the immortal soul but also the glorified body in which we shall be known at the Resurrection, though now it is known only to God, or to those to whom love may reveal it. It is this that lies at the bottom of Dante's whole Beatrician Vision: because he loved the mortal Florentine girl, it was given to him to behold her, as it were, walking the earth in her body of glory.[1] And this is why, in the *Commedia*, a stress so disconcerting to the minds of those who like their religion to be very "spiritual" is laid continually upon her bodily beauty. A sure mark of Catholic Christianity is the honouring of the "holy and glorious flesh",[2] and indeed of all material things, because they are sacraments and symbols of the Divine glory.

The third doctrine is the doctrine of the Trinity, which affirms that the Image actually exists within the very mystery of the Godhead

---

[1] *Vita Nuova*, xix: *Donne ch'avete intelletto d'amore*, and Williams: *Figure of Beatrice*, p. 27.

[2] *Paradiso*, xiv. 43.

Itself. Behind the Incarnation and the fleshly Image stands that ultimate mystery of the Divine Image, who is called also the Son and the Word. The unfathomable and unimaginable Being of the Father is known to Itself in the Son, whom the writer to the Epistle to the Hebrews calls: "the brightness of the glory and the express *image* of His Person".[1] It is because of this eternal presence of the Image within the Godhead that it is possible to pursue the Way of Affirmation to the very confrontation of the soul with the immediate presence of God. We may reject all other images, but *that* Image we never can reject, because it subsists in the inmost mystery of the Divine Substance.

It might therefore be claimed that the Way of Affirmation is the more Christian of the two. In view of the experience of so many great Christian mystics I would hesitate to say this. But one might say, I think, that it is the more *characteristically* Christian. The Way of Negation is common to many religions, including those which deny the true selfhood of the creature and the holiness of matter. The Way of Affirmation—creative, incarnational, and sacramental—asserting the relative validity of *all* the images, from the lowest and simplest up to the highest and so to the one and only perfect and eternal Image— proclaims and depends upon its Christian sanctions at every stage of the journey.

The image in which Dante thus beheld the Eternal Love transfigured was, as everybody knows, the image of a woman. It need not always be so. The theology of Romantic Love is only one of the theologies of the Image. In the earlier Middle Ages the allegiance to the glory tended to direct itself upon the male friend or the feudal over-lord. In the nineteenth century it is in Nature that Wordsworth beheld that

> Wisdom and spirit of the universe

which gives

> to forms and images a breath
> And everlasting motion.[2]

For Traherne in the seventeenth century, the entire creation of things and people is from the start transfigured:

The corn was orient and immortal wheat, which never should be reaped nor was ever sown. I thought it had stood from everlasting to everlasting. The dust and stones of the street were precious as gold. . . . The green trees when I saw them first through one of the gates transported and ravished me, their sweetness and unusual beauty made my heart leap, and almost mad

---

[1] *Heb.* i. 3.   [2] *Prelude*, 401–403.

with ecstasy. . . . The Men! . . . immortal Cherubims! And young men glittering and sparkling angels, and maids strange seraphic pieces of life and beauty. Boys and girls tumbling in the street and playing, were moving jewels. I knew not that they were born or should die; But all things abided eternally as they were in their proper places. Eternity was manifest in the light of the day, and something infinite behind everything appeared: which talked with my expectation and moved my desire.[1]

But Dante came at the close of that century which, speaking loudly and clearly through the lips of the Provençal poets, had discovered the image of the Lady. The originality of a great poet is seldom shown by the invention of new images, but rather by infusing into the dominant image of his day an electric current of personal experience and intellectual power which attracts into, and concentrates upon, that image a universal significance. The image of the Lady was already charged with the values of honour and courtesy and gentlehood, obedience and faith, solace and joy and devotion, when Dante, walking along a street in Florence and receiving the salutation of Beatrice, felt himself consumed with such a flame of charity that he forgave all who had ever injured him, and "if at that moment I had been questioned of anything whatsoever, I should have answered simply Love, with a countenance clothed in humility".[2] Upon that image, which this vivid personal experience thus rendered an irresistible field of force, every other image of love came at length to swarm and cluster as bees cluster about their queen. Or one may say in another metaphor, that this image became the conduit through which every stream of love discharged itself, until the time came for the particular type to be taken up into its eternal archetype, "the Love that moves the sun and the other stars".

It is this image which in Dante is seminal to all the other poets of Romantic Love who have followed him, finding in themselves an experience corresponding to his. It was seminal, in particular, to Charles Williams, who in The Figure of Beatrice expounded its theology, and in his novels and poems conceived and brought forth new and in their turn fruitful images, in which the implications of that theology are explored in fresh directions and charged with the accrued experience of the intervening centuries. Further in the same direction, indeed, no poet could go. But there is in the images of every poet of preëminent stature a wealth of latent potentiality from which other poets of original mind can draw their driving power. For, as André Malraux

[1] Centuries of Meditations. Cent. iii. 3.   [2] Vita Nuova, xi.

and others have of late pointed out, art draws its chief sustenance from the art of the past, and not (as people often like to imagine) directly from life. Life is its material basis, but its informing soul is inherited art. No one has yet discovered the trick of making art and poetry from raw life, any more than of making robots from raw matter. Art, like humanity itself, must be begotten in the first place, before it can maintain itself by feeding. The poets are each other's heirs; and Charles Williams in his later work inherited so much from Dante that not only is Williams the most illuminating commentator of Dante, but Dante is the most illuminating commentator of Williams—with one exception in each case. It is true of either man that his work is so clearly integrated about certain images and affirmations that no one part of it can be thoroughly assimilated without the help of the rest; so that Dante on Dante and Williams on Williams are their own best interpreters; but, after this, then each other's.

In order to show the gathering of all images into the basic image which characterises this kind of poetry, I will put forward an image from Dante: not one of the most obvious and well known, but an image so subtle, so daring, and so idiosyncratic that but few commentators, and those late-comers, have interpreted or even noticed it—or (it may be true to say) have ventured to notice or interpret it. We have already seen that the whole doctrine of Affirmation is sacramental through and through. Since the *Divine Comedy* is not only a great Christian poem but also a poem containing (explicitly and implicitly) a complete *summa* of Catholic theology, one would expect to find in it a central place given to the central Christian sacrament of the Eucharist. Yet, although the sacrament of Baptism is mentioned over and over again, and although the sacrament of Penance forms the entire theme of the *Purgatorio*, the one overt reference[1] to the Eucharist is so fleeting and casual that many people have said that the Eucharist has no place in the *Comedy*, and some have gone on to draw strange conclusions about Dante—as that he was a Protestant before his time, a Manichean heretic, or even an atheist. The truth is quite the contrary: the Eucharist is there, and its position is indeed central; but it is writ so large and veiled so intimately within the master-image, that it is literally too big to be seen.

When, after scaling the height of Mount Purgatory, Dante enters the Earthly Paradise, he sees a great procession coming towards him through the Sacred Forest.[2] First come Angels bearing the seven candles

[1] *Para.* xviii. 129.   [2] *Purg.* xxix, xxx.

"which are the seven spirits of God"; then follows a train of four-and-twenty Elders, crowned with white lilies, representing the books of the Old Testament; behind these come four Living Creatures, in appearance like those which Ezekiel saw coming in whirlwind and fire, but winged like those in the Apocalypse—the Four Evangelists, certainly, but also an image of the meeting of the Old and New Testaments; and after these, other figures crowned with red roses, representing the books of the New Testament. In the midst of the four Living Creatures there goes a triumphal car, with the three Christian Graces dancing by the right wheel and the four Cardinal Virtues dancing by the left. And the car is drawn by a Gryphon—the beast in whom (it is insisted on over and over again) two natures unite. "Golden was he as far as he was bird" (that is his heavenly part); "the rest all dappled red-and-white was he" (that is his lion-part, his earthly part). Why is he dappled red-and-white? The Old and New Testaments again? Possibly. Faith and Charity? Possibly, also. But surely, far more obviously, the colours of the Sacrifice: the Bread and the Wine, the Flesh and the Blood. The car is empty; and now all the angelic creatures begin to sing and cry: "Come, spouse of Lebanon!" and again—strangely, the masculine adjective unaltered from the rite of the Mass: "*Benedictus qui venis!*"

What comes next? Surely, if our minds were not by this time pre-occupied with Dante's personal feelings and the looked-for end of his love-quest, we should recognise in this the symbolic pageant of a Corpus Christi procession, with the seven lights borne before it; the meeting of prophecy and revelation in the Incarnate Sacrifice; the image of the Hypostatic Union drawing the car which (for reasons connected with another part of Dante's symbolism) here replaces altar or canopy; the introit of the Mass. Surely, that which is to descend from Heaven upon the waiting car amid the songs of the Church Militant must be, cannot be anything else but, the Holy Host Itself.

But what in fact do we get, when, like the sun rising through a mist, the Heaven-descended glory is revealed?

> So, even so, through cloud on cloud of flowers
>   Flung from angelic hands and falling down
>   Over the car and all around in showers,
>
> In a white veil beneath an olive crown
>   Appeared to me a lady, cloaked in green,
>   And living flame the colour of her gown;

> And instantly, for all the years between
>> Since her mere presence, with a kind of fright
>> Could awe me and make my spirit faint within,
>
> There came on me, needing no further sight,
>> Just by that strange, outflowing power of hers,
>> The old, old love, with all its mastering might.[1]

It is in fact what all our poetic instinct had led us to expect; it is, it is indeed Beatrice.

What are we to make of all this? Most people, not noticing the special Eucharistic implication, have said simply that Beatrice here "represents" the Church, or Theology, and leave it at that. Others, bluntly accusing the poet of blasphemy, have said that he was simply making the Florentine girl into a goddess. The late J. D. Sinclair,[2] of all the commentators I have read, has alone plainly faced the facts. He says, and he is manifestly right, that Beatrice *is* the Host; or rather she is the Image of the Host. Indeed, since the poem is an allegory, we could not here have the Host Itself, for that would be to replace the figure by the thing that is figured. Beatrice is the particular type and image of that whole sacramental principle of which the Host itself is the greater Image. The Eucharist is displayed nowhere else in the poem because it is displayed here. In the literal sense, what Dante looks upon is Beatrice; but on the three allegorical levels at which (Dante says) the poem is to be interpreted, she is Sacrament. Morally (i.e. as regards the way of the individual soul) she is, to Dante and to each one of us, the manifestation of the Divine glory in whatsoever beloved thing becomes to every man his own particular sacramental experience. Historically (i.e. in the world of human society) she is the Sacrament of the Altar. And those who say that in this passage Beatrice represents the Church are not wrong; for I think that Dante is here reflecting that older, Apostolic conception of the Eucharist, still surviving in Aquinas, which looks upon it, not exclusively as the commemoration of a single act in time, but as the presentation in Christ to God of Christ's true Body the Church (the *verum corpus*), which is made in the offertory of the bread and wine, so that, as St. Augustine says: "being joined to His Body and made His members, we may *be* what we *receive*". Thirdly, on the mystical level, Beatrice is here the whole doctrine of the Way

---

[1] *Purg.* xxx. 28–40.
[2] J. D. Sinclair: *The Divine Comedy with Translation and Comment:* Vol. II (John Lane, 1939), comment on *Purg.* xxx and xxxi.

of Affirmation—the union of the soul with God in and through all the images.

By meditating upon this august image, we may see how the Poets of the Image work. There is not—or at any rate there need not be—any overt, rationalised *statement* about the reality which the image is put there to convey. There is simply the showing of a picture, or the telling of a story, in which the truth is shown in action, and the universal structure of reality is laid bare. Because it is an image, and not an argument, it speaks directly to the senses and the intuition of those to whom it is shown; and because it springs out of personal—if you like, out of existential—experience, it appeals to the personal and historical experience of men, and gathers into itself all the experience which they themselves are able to bring to it. And because it is rooted in the fleshly and the visible, it remains an expression of the *whole* of human experience: it does not encourage what is so often (rather tiresomely and unchristianly) called "a more spiritual attitude to life", but rather, one might say, calls for a much more living attitude to the spiritual.

Returning to Dante's central experience of the "theology of Romantic Love", let us now see how patiently and gladly it accepts enriching additions and interpretations from the experience of another, and later, poet of the Image, in whose mind it has seeded and brought forth new flower and fruit. To Dante, living in an age of fixed hierarchies and penetrated by the doctrines of courtly love—which is the one-sided devotion of a man to a woman—the communication of the glory is always from above downward. Throughout the great ladder of creation, each rank draws up the one below it by the cords of love; every being looks up in love (*eros*) to the one above it and downward in charity (*agape*) to the one below it, so that, as Dante says of the heavenly hierarchy, "*tutti tirati sono e tutti tirano*—all are drawn and draw".[1] To this noble conception, Charles Williams, living in an age which calls itself (for want of a better word) democratic, and one in which the relations between men and women are somewhat differently conceived, brings the further conception of the exchange of hierarchies. He thus resolves the difficulty which always lurked at the heart of the mediaeval theory of *amour courtois*—the fact that the romantic adoration of a woman ran counter alike to theological theory and to social practice, both of which subordinated the woman to the man. Between Dante and Williams lie six centuries of human experience, during

[1] *Para.* xxviii. 129.

which—and largely through the influence of the courtly poets themselves—the possibility of exchanged love within the bonds of a more
equal notion of matrimony had been persistently explored; six
centuries, also, in which the idea of social hierarchy had been largely
replaced by the idea of social equality. Not wholly abandoning the
conception of hierarchy, not wholly accepting an absolutism of
equality (a thing difficult enough socially and impossible when it is a
question of an equality of gifts) the later poet sees a humanity in which
the relation of higher to lower is fluid. I am superior to you, it may be,
in certain respects—very good: for that "you do me honour, and therein do well"; in other respects, you are superior to me—that too is right
and good, and for that "I do you honour and therein do well".[1] We
draw one another up by a continual exchange, passing one another, as
it were, by turns upon the ladder of ascent, the higher always giving
a hand to whoever is at the moment the lower.

Thus, in the hierarchy of man as such and woman as such, we may
at one moment feel that Williams stands for what we may call the
ecclesiastical (as opposed to the Dantean) view, namely, that the man
is the superior. We think of Peter Stanhope in *Descent into Hell*, who
is light and guide to Pauline Anstruther; of Anthony Durrant, in *The
Place of the Lion*, exhibiting the authority of Adam over the created
powers and over the rebellious self-assertion of Eve in the person of
Damaris Tighe; of the King's Poet, Taliessin, in the Arthurian poems,
exercising spiritual lordship over his household. We observe, however, that in two of these cases, the authority is that of poetry rather
than of sex. And we find other types: the aged Margaret Anstruther,
lesser than Peter Stanhope in art, greater than he in mystical experience.
We think of Lester Furnival, the dead wife in *All Hallows' Eve*: in life
she has been, in some ways, rather less developed in understanding
than her husband Richard; but the experience of death sets her ahead
of him on the Way. And there is a pair of pregnant passages in which
Richard looks back on his past conduct to his wife. In the first, he
remembers how on one occasion she had demanded that they should
go into the town on some rather unnecessary errand:

She had insisted, and because he always wished to consider her and be as
unselfish as possible, they had gone. He was surprised . . . to remember how
much he had considered Lester. A score of examples rushed vividly through

---

[1] *Fannomi onore, e di ciò fanno bene: Inf.* iv. 93.

his mind, and each of those he remembered was actual and true. He really had considered her; he had been, in that sense, a very good husband.[1]

But later, when other events have intervened to open his eye to himself, he looks back on this episode with distaste:

> What did distress him, as it crept back into his mind, was a memory of . . . his indulgent self. He had . . . been kind to his wife. She (whatever her faults) had never been like that to him: she had never been dispassionately considerate. But he—he undoubtedly had. . . . He all but threw his hairbrush at his face in the mirror, as he thought of it. But his new energy compelled him to refrain, and to confront the face, which, as he looked at it, seemed to bear the impress of love behaving itself very unseemly. Her love had never borne that mark. Rash, violent, angry as she might have been, egotistic in her nature as he, yet her love had been sealed always to another and not to herself. . . . When she had served him—how often!—she had not done it from kindness or unselfishness; it had been because she wished what he wished and was his servant to what he desired. Kindness, patience, forbearance, were not enough: he had had them, but she had had love.[2]

In these two characters, therefore, the balance swings; he may not condescend to her from his superior poise and judgement, for in the hierarchy of the understanding of love she is above him.

With Peter Stanhope and Pauline Anstruther, we are shown another kind of exchange of hierarchy. Pauline looks upon Stanhope with, we infer, the kind of devotion with which Dante looks upon Beatrice: he is to her the vision of the glory incarnate. But in the story, it is she who visibly possesses a glorified "other self", which she herself actually sees, and of whose unearthliness she goes in dread. In the mystery of exchange—the vicarious bearing of burdens—Stanhope lifts this dread from her and carries it for her. And she finds that in fact this mysterious terror that has haunted her all her life is not really hers: it is the terror of an ancestor of hers, who was burned at the stake in the Marian persecutions. In a vision of two worlds, in which time turns backwards, she sees this ancestor, torn with fear, and terrified that he may recant for dread of the burning. Her old terror comes over her again, but as she looks down the centuries at the terror of the persecuted man, she hears him cry out:

> The cry freed her from fear and delirium, as if it took over its own from her. . . . The trap, if there had been a trap, had opened, and she had come out beyond it. But there was another trap, and this man was in it. He cried

---

[1] *Op. cit.*, chap. v   [2] *Op. cit.*, chap. ix.

again: "Lord God!" . . . She said in a voice breathless only from haste: "Can I help you?" . . . He said: "Lord God, I cannot bear the fear of the fire." She was here. She had been taught what to do. She had her offer to make now, and it would not be refused. She herself was offered, in a most certain fact, her place at the table of exchange. . . .

But she felt, as she stood, that she could no more do it than he. She could never bear that fear. . . . She opened her mouth and could not speak. . . . In front of her, alone in his foul Marian prison . . . her ancestor stood centuries off in his spiritual desolation. . . . He could not see beyond the years the child of his house who strove with herself behind and before him. . . . Pauline could not see the prison, but she saw him. She tried to choose and to speak.

Behind her, her own voice said: "Give it to me, John Struther." He heard it, in his cell and chains, as the first dawn of the day of his martyrdom broke beyond the prison. . . . He stretched out his arms again: he called: "Lord, Lord!" It was a devotion and an adoration; it accepted and thanked. Pauline heard it, trembling, for she knew what stood behind her and spoke. It said again: "Give." He fell on his knees, and in a great roar of triumph he called out: "I have seen the salvation of my God."

Pauline sighed deeply with her joy. . . . This other . . . had done what she had desired, and yet not the other, but she, for it was she who had all her life carried a fear which was not her fear but another's, until in the end it had become for her in turn not hers but another's. . . .

Pauline turned. . . . She whirled on the thing she had so long avoided, and the glorious creature looked past her at the shouting martyr beyond. . . . She opened her eyes . . . there—as a thousand times in her looking-glass— there! The ruffled brown hair, the long nose, the firm compressed mouth, the tall body, the long arms, her dress, her gesture. It wore no supernatural splendour of aureole, but its rich nature burned and glowed before her, bright as if mortal flesh had indeed become what all lovers know it to be.[1]

In this elaborate exchange of hierarchies, moving from man to woman, and from woman back to man, and from the present into the past and back again, we see what one original poetic mind can do with the image implanted in it by another. Dante sees Beatrice's body transfigured; Charles Williams's Pauline sees her own. The concept of the vicarious endurance of suffering, derived from the archetype of Christ's Passion, is not in Dante's poem very explicit, except in its Archetype. It is found in the great seventh canto of the *Paradiso*, which is perhaps the finest poetic exposition of Atonement theology ever written. Here, Williams blends it with Dante's own imagery, in a new apprehension of the exchanged hierarchies.

[1] *Descent into Hell*, chap. ix.

Finally, as regards the exchange between man and woman, there is the perfect equipoise of relationship in *Many Dimensions* between the Chief Justice, Lord Arglay, and Chloe Burnett, his secretary, where he excels in wisdom and prudence, and she in spiritual power, each gravely doing worship to the other.

"You love her?" the Hajji said, half in statement, half in interrogation.

"Why, I do not very well know what love may be," said Lord Arglay, "but so far as is possible to men I think that there is Justice between her and me."[1]

And if we ask what is here meant by "Justice", we shall do well to turn again to Dante, for whom the Heaven of Justice is the highest of the six Heavens of the Active Life. Here the flames which are the blessed souls of the Just form themselves into the image of an Eagle. He says "I saw and heard the beak [of the image] talk and utter with its voice *I* and *mine* when its meaning was *we* and *ours*." And he adds: "As a single glow is felt from many brands, so from that image came forth a single sound of many loves."[2] Wherever that is, there is unity and community, and the realisation of the other in the self. There is Justice, and the equivalence of balanced powers.

Briefly and sketchily as I have perforce treated these few examples, they may yet serve to show how pregnant the images of a great poet are, and how another, inheriting his tradition, may (like the householder in the parable) bring out of his treasure things new and old. For though in a sense the later poet, bringing fresh thought and fresh experience to his task, adds fresh lustre to the original image, which thereafter shines with all the light he has thrown back upon it, yet in another sense the new images were always latent in the old; so that it is possible to say that there is nothing in Williams which was not potentially in Dante, and, *a fortiori*, that there is nothing in Dante which is not, actually, in Christ. To that Image, all the images return, as, in *Many Dimensions*, all the types of the Stone return to the Stone. This is not, of course, a complete interpretation of the imagery of that remarkable book; but it is one interpretation, and one, I think, which Williams himself would have approved.

There is no room in this paper to examine the astonishing process of interpretation to which, in *Descent into Hell*, Williams has submitted Dante's Dream of the Siren, in the nineteenth canto of the *Purgatorio*.[3]

---

[1] *Op. cit.*, chap. xiii.   [2] *Para.* xix. 10–12; 19–21.
[3] I have examined it in detail in *The Cornice of Sloth*, pp. 136 *seq* above.

This image, which is very compact and concentrated, has frequently puzzled commentators, who have fround it either dry and formal, or else incoherent and contradictory. But if we read it carefully, relating it to Virgil's great discourse on Love, which occupies the greater part of the two preceding cantos, and particularly to the lines which say, without emphasis, that love must always be directed to "something actually existing outside the self"—that is to a true other; and if we then read *Descent into Hell* with its terrible myth of the self-centred man who falls under the domination of a horrible projection of his desires—then we shall realise how greatly and imaginatively Williams interprets Dante, and also how greatly and—shall I say *solidly*—Dante interprets Williams. It is a matter of temperament which of the two things one finds the more puzzling: the rock-like classicism and epigrammatic brevity of Dante, or the highly-coloured romanticism and rhapsodical fervour of Charles Williams; but by the time that one has set the two images side by side and really studied them one with the other, little cause for perplexity will remain in either of them.

If we now pass on to look at the *kind* of imagery used by these two poets, we are struck immediately by one great and obvious resemblance. Both build their fabric of the inherence of the metaphysical in the physical upon the experience of very ordinary people in very ordinary circumstances. Dante begins with a young man seeing the girl with whom he is in love walking along the streets of Florence, or at a wedding-party, or in distress about the death of her father. Dante himself was not, it is true, altogether an ordinary young man, but lovers as such are ordinary enough, and there is nothing in what happened to him that might not happen to anyone. Neither is there anything which leads us to suppose that Beatrice was a miracle of nature, except in the sense that any beloved object is miraculous in a lover's eyes. There is a little contemporary evidence to show that she was in fact a beautiful and a gracious young woman—but gracious and beautiful young women are not, fortunately, so rare as all that; and we are well enough accustomed to seeing young men struck all of a heap by young women who, to eyes not illumined, appear at most pleasant and personable. Neither, although Dante in the *Vita Nuova* represents Beatrice as being pious and good and as having a great devotion to Our Lady, and although he himself mingles the language of religion with the language of human love in a manner which in our ears may easily sound either blasphemous or affected, is there anything in his account of the matter which makes us feel that the central experience—or, indeed, its great later development into the mystical experience of the *Comedy*—is anything that is by its nature confined to persons of especially religious temperament, or distinguished by peculiar mystical gifts. It is the story of Everyman's pilgrimage; it happened to a poet and a banker's wife in Florence; it might just as well happen to-day to a clerk and a typist in Manchester.

With even more emphasis does Charles Williams stress the commonplace of circumstance, the casual distribution of grace. Where Dante, in nearly all his images, makes use of actual historical persons, Williams invents his characters; and though here and there we éncounter a Lord Chief Justice, an Archdeacon, a poet of national importance, we have for the most part to do with ordinary middle-class people, living in London or its suburbs—people often with small religious experience and less dogmatic knowledge. Housewives and secretaries and young men in minor government departments find themselves unexpectedly handling the reins of supernatural authority; the archetypal powers manifest themselves in a small town in Hertfordshire; thirty miles from London, the graves are opened and the vials of the Apocalypse discharge themselves; the house of Simon Magus stands in a Holborn side-street, the dead walk upon Westminster Bridge, and greet each other by Leicester Square Tube Station; the figure of a London policeman takes on the majestic semblance of embodied Empire. "The Coningsbys usually went to Eastbourne for Christmas" is the phrase which opens a chapter in *The Greater Trumps*: it is upon a family of these sedate and unimaginative habits that the ends of the world are come. The Glory manifests itself with an almost shocking impartiality; the powers, whether of Heaven or of Goetia, use, it would seem, such instruments as come most readily to hand.

There is here, in these poets of the Affirmation, a strong resistance to all that conception of the metaphysical which we conveniently call Gnosticism—the idea that the supreme supernatural experiences are confined to peculiar persons, secret cliques, groups of initiates, addicts of hidden mysteries. Characters in the novels of Williams who separate and seclude themselves from the common experience of all men—such as Simon the Priest in *All Hallows' Eve*, or Wentworth in *Descent into Hell*—are marked by that very withdrawal as the servants of him whom Dante secluded and bound fast in the bottom of Hell; they are doomed to the Circle of the Sorcerers, if to nothing worse. The mystery of Good is an open secret, available to all, yet manifesting itself with an inscrutable singularity to persons chosen, it would seem, almost at random. If we ask, "Why this person, or why that? Why Hampstead Garden Suburb rather than Chelsea or Wimbledon?" we shall get no answer but that which Peter Damian gives when he is asked why he, out of all the thousands of rejoicing spirits in the Heaven of Saturn, should be chosen to salute and welcome Dante:

"That soul in Heaven which is most illumined, that seraph whose eye is most fixed upon God, will not satisfy thy questioning; for what thou askest is so utterly remote in the abyss of the eternal statute that it is cut off from all created vision." [1]

The singular choice, that is—for in a finite universe choice must be singular, despite the outraged feelings of those who like to think in terms of general tendencies and emergent evolution—the singular choice may light at any moment, in any place, on any person who is ready to receive it; and the readiness is all.

Thus far we have considered the likeness and derivation between the two Poets of the Image; and there is much more that might be said along those lines. But in conclusion, we may profitably glance at one rather striking difference. To put it as briefly as possible, Dante is pre-occupied by the inherence of the metaphysical in the physical; Williams—in his novels especially—by the irruption of the metaphysical into the physical. Dante knew well enough the appalling abyss of potential and actual evil that opens up within the soul, and how thin is the crust that separates our daily life from Hell; but his chief concern is not with spiritual wickedness in high places, but with common human sin. He knew also, and perhaps had personally experienced, the possibilities of union and communion with thrones, dominations, authorities and powers of Heaven, but he knew them only as friendly, and as ordering the ways of the visible world in accordance with Eternal Law. But Williams is haunted always by the vision of trespass upon the borders of two worlds—the breaking-up of the crust, the calling down of naked and impersonal powers out of the realm of spirit into the realm of time and space. All the Williams novels are concerned in one way or another with magic: with the unlawful attempt to seize and possess the metaphysical powers and make use of them. In *War in Heaven* the object about which the struggle rages is the Holy Cup of the Grail Mystery; in *Many Dimensions*, it is the magical Stone of Solomon; in *The Greater Trumps* it is the Tarot pack and the Golden

[1] *Para.* xxi. 91–96.

Dancers; in *All Hallows' Eve*, it is the soul of Betty Wallingford, which the magician wants to use as his emissary in the world beyond death; in *Descent into Hell*, the witch, Mrs. Sammile, sets her trap for souls, and lures Wentworth to destruction with the magical body of the succubus; in *The Place of the Lion* the Platonic Ideas, or Universals, are released into the world by a group of people who are, or some of whom at least suppose themselves to be, actuated by a vague hankering for "uplift" and spiritual knowledge, but of whom one who knows them says: "They wanted to get as far as they could, all right, but I doubt if it was really to contemplate the principles of life. It was much more likely unconsciously to be in order to use the principles of life." [1] And the fact that such people are for the most part undistinguished nobodies of very limited intelligence does not save them; for spite and malice and the lust to tyrannise—even over a paid companion or a business associate—makes them as ready tools for evil as though they were world-dictators.

It is the task of the "good" characters always to stand in the breach of the worlds and to dismiss the invoked powers to their own place. These men and women—whether knowing what they do, or simply following their own decent instincts, but in any case obedient to the good they know—submit their own wills to the Unity behind the powers, and so make a path for the return of the powers into the Unity. In *The Place of the Lion* we have, side by side with Anthony Durrant, who thus dismisses the powers and restores the images, the figure of Richardson who, following the Way of Negation, offers himself to the Unity and returns to it along with the powers.

In Dante, there is little of all this. His struggle is almost exclusively moral, and his mysticism purely religious. He is content with a simple repudiation of "black" magic; the "white" magic of his Virgil bears rule only among the lost; so far as his poem is concerned, Heaven and Hell with all their powers remain in their appointed places. His angels and devils do their work in the world, and are exhibited in the world, through the actions of men, never by means of naked and unscreened assaults. The result of this difference between the two writers is that, from one point of view, Dante appears as an august, classical, intellectual, and ethical poet, by contrast with an obscurantist fabricator of sensational, and sometimes rather nasty, "spiritual thrillers"; or from another point of view, as a smug dogmatic moralist, living in a safe, neat, mechanical universe, by contrast with a poet of great imaginative

[1] *Op. cit.*, chap. 8.

originality, to whom the unknown potentialities of a complex and mysterious universe are present as a menace of very real terror.

Neither of these views is altogether just in what it condemns, though it may be to some extent justified. It must always be remembered that Dante lived at the close, and summed up the experience, of the great Age of Reason; whereas Williams lived in the age which experienced the Flight from Reason. For the men of the twelfth to fourteenth centuries, Reason reigned supreme, inherent in the Godhead, active in the Intelligences which ruled the course of Nature, expressed in Theology, consonant with Revelation, authoritative in the Will and Judgement of Man, sublimely ordering all things. The vital task, whether of Philosophy, Ethics, Sociology, or Psychology, was the establishment of rational order in human affairs, to conform with the rational order—the Divine Law—by which the universe was controlled. Conceptions of the just war, the just price, the just code, the just stewardship of natural resources, the justice of Empire, just judgement in the things of the intellect, a just scale of values in the things of the heart, were all bound up together in the master-conception of the Divine Reason. "Set love in order, thou that lovest Me", said the Divine Love by the mouth of St. Francis, His most romantic follower. We must not be misled by phrases. The progression from the so-called Ages of Faith to the so-called Age of Reason saw, in fact, the progressive *exclusion* of Reason from all spheres but one—the sphere of quantitative and measurable science. This development has had manifold consequences, one of them being the emergence into human society of sanctions for uncontrolled power, of which Magic is the means and archetype. The Middle Ages were not, as is sometimes supposed, the heyday of the magician; that came later. There is a sinister parallelism between the aims of magic and the aims of what nowadays we are accustomed to call "science". Both aim at the possession and use of power—whether physical or metaphysical—for human ends unrelated to any conception of a transcendent order. To-day, even scientists themselves are beginning to believe that the justification of their work is not knowledge, but the fact that "knowledge is power", and still more is the common man persuaded that the powers of Nature exist to be exploited for greed and gain. Most sinister of all, the rise of a psychology of the irrational has made it possible for the few masters to exploit the many by propaganda or by the process hideously known as "conditioning", and to be approved for doing it. And, politically, my own generation has lived to witness the change from the last lingering memory of the rule of Law, to the open worship of crude power. Between the aims of the exploiters of power to-day and the aims of the magician there is no difference; the only difference is one of method.

Of the licence given to unreason and the exploitation of power, the magical element in Charles Williams's work stands as the image and symbol. For he is a poet of the Image, working always by means of images. Dante himself knew well what was the end of the irresponsible pursuit of power—his Hell is full of these practitioners: the tyrants in the boiling river; the usurers, exploiters of man's labour and natural resources, on the burning and sterile sand of their dust-bowls; the flatterers, exploiters of the power of words, plunged in liquid filth; the sorcerers, exploiters of men's passionate credulity, twisted for ever and walking for ever backwards; the falsifiers, who corrupt all means of human exchange, corrupted for ever by disease. He knew also the end of the irresponsible pursuit of knowledge, and has fixed it in the great image of Ulysses, voyaging into the forbidden seas and sucked down by the whirlpool, to abide in Hell for ever in blindness and burning. But he did not see the issue of these things; he only foresaw it. His pupil lived to see it.

It is the mark of the Way of Affirmation that it asserts the ingrained reasonableness of the universe. It proclaims that what our senses show to us is not wholly delusion; that what our reason tells us is truth so far as it goes; that all Art is valid, so long as it is true to its own standards; that the whole man, flesh and mind and spirit, is by his nature *capax Dei*—capable of God. It will not allow the total submergence of the reasonable creature even in the Divine, much less in any other power or powers. And it lays down with no uncertain voice that for those who live in matter and space and time, the right way, and the only safe way, to approach the Powers is by means of the images. It distrusts, in every context, the "flight of the alone to the Alone", for it is not good for Man to be alone; his way lies through the streets of the City, through Florence or through London, through the Republic or through the Empire, to that one City of which we are all citizens, "the Rome", says Dante, "where Christ is a Roman".[1] And there, having with an ordered love adored all the types, we shall be permitted to look upon the Archetype,—the Image within the Godhead, which by the taking up of the images into itself is also—again in Dante's words—"dyed with our image". It is only right to say again, before leaving the

---

[1] *Purg.* xxxii. 102.

subject, that if the danger of the Way of Rejection is a solitary madness, the danger of the Way of Affirmation is precisely the worship of the images themselves—that is, idolatry. Without the doctrine, neither Way is safe; with the doctrine, both lead to the same place. So Taliessin speaks, riding with the Lady Dindrane, who is leaving Camelot to take the veil at Almesbury:

> the king's poet kissed Dindrane's hand.
> He said: "Blessed one, what shall I wish you now
> but a safe passage through all the impersonalities?"
> And she: "Most blessed lord, what shall I wish
> but the return of the personalities, beyond
> the bond and blessing of the departure of personalities?"
> And he: "I will reject all that I should—
> yes, and affirm; the term of Camelot, my adored,
> lies at the term of Almesbury. The Grace be with you;
> which, as your face made visible, let your soul sustain." [1]

(Chelmsford Arts Association
1952)

[1] *The Region of the Summer Stars: The Departure of Dindrane.*

INDEX